The Roaring Twenties
Biographies

The Roaring Twenties
Biographies

Kelly King Howes
Julie L. Carnagie

U·X·L
An imprint of Thomson Gale,
a part of The Thomson Corporation

THOMSON
™
GALE

Detroit • New York • San Francisco • San Diego • New Haven, Conn. • Waterville, Maine • London • Munich

THOMSON
★
™
GALE

The Roaring Twenties: Biographies
Kelly King Howes

Project Editor
Julie L. Carnagie

Rights Acquisitions and Management
Kim Smilay, Margaret Abendroth

Imaging and Multimedia
Robyn Young, Lezlie Light, Dan Newell

Product Design
Jennifer Wahi

Composition and Electronic Prepress
Evi Seoud

Manufacturing
Rita Wimberley

For permission to use material from this product, submit your request via Web at http://www.gale-edit.com/permissions, or you may download our Permissions Request form and submit your request by fax or mail to:

Rights Acquisition and Management Department
Thomson Gale
27500 Drake Rd.
Farmington Hills, MI 48331-3535
Permissions Hotline:
248-699-8006 or 800-877-4253, ext. 8006
Fax: 248-699-8074 or 800-762-4058

Cover photographs reproduced by permission of AP/Wide World Photos, Inc. (portrait of Al Capone), Hulton Archive/Getty Images (portrait of Babe Ruth and portrait of Louis Armstrong), and The Library of Congress (portrait of Edna St. Vincent Millay).

While every effort has been made to ensure the reliability of the information presented in this publication, Thomson Gale does not guarantee the accuracy of the data contained herein. Thomson Gale accepts no payment for listing; and inclusion in the publication of any organization, agency, institution, publication, service, or individual does not imply endorsement by the editors or publisher. Errors brought to the attention of the publisher and verified to the satisfaction of the publisher will be corrected in future editions.

LIBRARY OF CONGRESS CATALOGING-IN-PUBLICATION DATA

Howes, Kelly King.
The roaring twenties biographies / Kelly King Howes.
p. cm. – (The roaring twenties reference library)
Includes bibliographical references and index.
ISBN 1-4144-0211-2 (hardcover : alk. paper)
1. United States–History–1919-1933–Biography–Juvenile literature.
2. Nineteen twenties–Juvenile literature.
I. Title.
E784.H695 2006
920.073'09'042–dc22
2005010815

This title is also available as an e-book.
ISBN 1-4144-0609-6
Contact your Gale sales representative for ordering information.

Printed in the United States of America
10 9 8 7 6 5 4 3 2 1

Contents

Reader's Guide

The Roaring Twenties is one of the most colorful eras in U.S. history. Bordered on one side by the end of World War I (1914–18) and on the other side by the Great Depression (the severe economic downturn that began in 1929 and lasted until the early 1940s), this short period would later be remembered by historians largely as a time of excitement and fun. It was the decade, after all, when daring young women called flappers danced the Charleston, and Charles "Lucky Lindy" Lindbergh crossed the Atlantic Ocean in a tiny airplane. It was a time when the economy was strong, and many had extra money in their pockets. Yet this was also a period of changes. Some of these changes, such as advances in technology and medical care and new freedoms for women, were welcomed by many people. There were others, however, who found some of the changes— such as the new reliance on science over religion, or the large number of immigrants living in the nation's cities, or the fact that not everyone shared in the economic prosperity of the Twenties—more troubling.

The Roaring Twenties: Biographies presents the life stories of twenty-five notable personalities of the 1920s drawn from the worlds of politics and government, literature, music, sports, aviation, religion, art, anthropology, and crime. Included are baseball great Babe Ruth, anthropologist Margaret Mead, artist Georgia O'Keeffe, author Zora Neale Hurston, composer George Gershwin, and gangster Al Capone. Profiles are also provided for lesser-known though no less interesting figures, including evangelist Aimee Semple McPherson, writer H.L. Mencken, and boxer Jack Dempsey.

Features

The entries in *The Roaring Twenties: Biographies* contain numerous sidebar boxes that highlight people and events of special interest, and each biographical profile offers a list of additional sources students can go to for more information. More than fifty black-and-white photographs help illustrate the material. The volume begins with a timeline of important events in the history of the 1920s and a "Words to Know" section that introduces students to difficult or unfamiliar terms. The volume concludes with a general bibliography and a subject index so students can easily find the people, places, and events discussed throughout *The Roaring Twenties: Biographies*.

The Roaring Twenties Reference Library

The Roaring Twenties: Biographies is only one component of the two-part U•X•L The Roaring Twenties Reference Library. The other title in the set is:

- *The Roaring Twenties: Almanac and Primary Sources* (one volume) presents a comprehensive overview of events and everyday life that occurred within the United States during the 1920s. The Almanac section begins with some background to the Roaring Twenties, followed by coverage of the political, economic, technological, and social events and changes that occurred during the decade. Some of the darker aspects of life in this period are explored, such as the rise of organized crime and the effects of nativism, then the focus shifts to developments in arts and entertainment and finally to the 1929 stock market crash, which launched the United States into the Great Depression, and its aftermath. The Primary Sources section tells the story of the 1920s in the words of the people who lived and shaped the decade.

Excerpted and full-text documents provide a wide range of perspectives on this period of history. Included are excerpts from political speeches; influential books of the era; and reflections by individuals who lived through the times.

Comments and Suggestions

We welcome your comments on *The Roaring Twenties: Biographies* and suggestions for other topics to consider. Please write: Editors, *The Roaring Twenties: Biographies,* U•X•L, 27500 Drake Rd. Farmington Hills, Michigan 48331-3535; call toll free: 1-800-877-4253; fax to (248) 699-8097; or send e-mail via http://www.gale.com.

Timeline of Events

1859 African American leader **W.E.B. Du Bois** illuminates black history, dreams, and concerns in *The Souls of Black Folk.*

1907 Auto manufacturer **Henry Ford** releases the Model T, fondly known as the Tin Lizzie, which will be much loved by the public for its reliability and low price tag.

1914 World War I begins in Europe. The results will be devastating, for an estimated ten million soldiers will be killed and twenty million wounded, while millions of civilians will also die from hunger and rapidly spreading diseases like influenza.

May 1915 The German navy sinks the British passenger ship *Lusitania,* killing more than one thousand passengers, including more than one hundred U.S. citizens. President Woodrow Wilson issues a warning to Germany.

April 1917 The United States enters World War I.

November 11, 1918 World War I ends.

1919 An epidemic of influenza spreads across the globe. About four hundred thousand U.S. citizens die of the disease.

January 1919 Congress passes the Eighteenth Amendment, which makes the manufacture and sale of alcoholic beverages illegal.

June 28, 1919 The Treaty of Versailles, the peace agreement that officially ends World War I, is signed. Its terms demand that Germany pay heavy reparations, or compensation, for its role in starting the conflict.

July 4, 1919 Boxer **Jack Dempsey**, known as the "Manassa Mauler," wins the heavyweight title from Jess Willard.

October 28, 1919 Congress passes the Volstead Act, which spells out the terms of the Eighteenth Amendment. Defined as "intoxicating" beverages are those containing as little as 0.5 percent of alcohol, including not just distilled liquor, but beer and wine.

1920 W.E.B. Du Bois becomes director of publications and research at the newly formed National Association for the Advancement of Colored People (NAACP), and soon founds the influential journal *Crisis*.

1920 **Sinclair Lewis**'s best-selling novel *Main Street* is published.

1920 For the first time, airplanes are used to deliver mail from New York to California.

January 3, 1920 Baseball great **George Herman "Babe" Ruth Jr.** signs with the New York Yankees. He hits fifty-four home runs his first season; in 1927, he hits a career high of sixty-two home runs and leads the Yankees to victory in the World Series.

January 16, 1920 The Eighteenth Amendment goes into effect.

March 1920 **F. Scott Fitzgerald** begins his ascent to fame with the publication of his novel *This Side of Paradise*.

May 1920 The Negro National League is formed, allowing African American baseball players more structured opportunities to play and fans additional chances to enjoy the sport.

August 18, 1920 Congress passes the Nineteenth Amendment, giving women the right to vote.

September 28, 1920 Eight players on the Chicago White Sox baseball team are charged with intentionally losing a game in exchange for money. As a result they are banned from the sport for life.

November 2, 1920 Having campaigned on the promise of a "return to normalcy," Republican candidate **Warren G. Harding** is elected president by a wide margin. For the first time, the election results are broadcast over the new technology of radio.

1921 **Margaret Sanger** founds the American Birth Control League (later named the Planned Parenthood Federation of America). Two years later, she opens the first physician-run birth control clinic in the United States.

1922 Sinclair Lewis's novel about a middle-class business-man, *Babbitt,* is published, and its title soon becomes a general term for a complacent conformist.

1922 A period of economic prosperity begins; it lasts until the U.S. stock market crash in 1929.

October 4, 1922 For the first time, play-by-play coverage of baseball's World Series is heard over the radio. The New York Giants beat the New York Yankees.

1923 The Frigidaire Company introduces the first electric refrigerator. The electric shaver is also patented.

1923 Poet **Edna St. Vincent Millay** wins the Pulitzer Prize for Literature.

1923 The New York Yankees open their new stadium, which is known as "The House That Ruth Built" because it is financed by tickets sales boosted by the stellar performance of Babe Ruth.

1923 Sales of automobiles are booming. One of every two cars sold in the United States is a Ford.

January 3, 1923 The first issue of *Time* magazine appears on newsstands.

August 2, 1923 President Harding dies unexpectedly in San Francisco, California. Vice President **Calvin Coolidge** is sworn in as president the next day.

1924 Congress passes the National Origins Act, which sets new limits on the number of immigrants allowed into the United States.

1924 The Florida land boom is underway. Many investors will lose large amounts of money on get-rich-quick land-buying schemes.

February 12, 1924 George Gershwin's jazz symphony *Rhapsody in Blue* premieres at a concert led by bandleader Paul Whiteman at New York's Aeolian Hall.

May 1924 Teenagers Nathan Leopold and Richard Loeb are convicted of murdering a fourteen-year-old Bobby Franks. Defense attorney **Clarence Darrow** argues successfully that they be spared the death penalty and sentenced to life in prison.

November 1924 President Calvin Coolidge is reelected.

1925 *The New Yorker* magazine begins publication.

1925 **Charlie Chaplin** delights moviegoers with his performance as the Little Tramp in the classic comedy film *The Gold Rush*.

1925 In a speech to newspaper editors, President Coolidge declares that "the business of America is business."

1925 F. Scott Fitzgerald's novel *The Great Gatsby,* a classic portrait of the Roaring Twenties, is published.

July 1925 In Dayton, Tennessee, high school teacher John Scopes is tried for violating the Butler Act, which prohibits the teaching of the scientific theory of evolution in public schools. **William Jennings Bryan** leads the prosecution team, while the defense is headed by Clarence Darrow.

October 8, 1925 A Ku Klux Klan parade in Washington, D.C. draws approximately forty thousand participants.

May 1926 **Aimee Semple McPherson** disappears while swimming in the Pacific Ocean and is presumed drowned. She reappears six weeks later, claiming to have been kidnapped and taken to Mexico.

July 19, 1926 A devastating hurricane ends the Florida land boom.

1927 Babe Ruth hits sixty home runs (a record that will stand for the next thirty-four years), and this season's New York Yankees are called the greatest baseball team ever.

1927 At the peak of its popularity, the *American Mercury* magazine, founded by writer **H. L. Mencken**, has a circulation of seventy-seven thousand readers.

April 4, 1927 The first scheduled passenger flight travels from Boston, Massachusetts, to New York City.

May 16, 1927 The first Academy Awards ceremony is held.

May 20, 1927 Flying in an airplane called *The Spirit of St. Louis,* **Charles Lindbergh** takes off from Long Island, New York. Thirty-three and a half hours later, he becomes the first pilot to make a solo, nonstop flight across the Atlantic Ocean when he lands in Paris, France.

October 1927 **Dorothy Parker** begins writing a weekly book review column, which she signs "Constant Reader," for the *New Yorker* magazine.

December 2, 1927 Henry Ford introduces the eagerly awaited Model A. Spectators by the thousands line up at dealerships to catch a glimpse of the new automobile.

1928 The influential book *Coming of Age in Samoa,* the result of anthropologist **Margaret Mead**'s field work among a group of adolescent girls in the Pacific Island nation of Samoa, is published.

August 27, 1928 Fifteen nations sign the Kellogg-Briand Pact, agreeing to use peaceful means to resolve conflicts and to resort to war only as a last measure. Eventually more than sixty other countries sign the agreement.

November 6, 1928 Republican candidate **Herbert Hoover** is elected president of the United States.

1929 Artist **Georgia O'Keeffe** begins spending each summer in New Mexico, creating paintings of that environment, such as *Cow's Skull: Red, White and Blue* (1931), for which she becomes well known.

1929 **Louis Armstrong** appears on Broadway in the hit show *Hot Chocolates,* singing his famous song "Ain't Misbehavin'."

February 14, 1929 In what comes to be known as the St. Valentine's Day Massacre, men from **Al Capone**'s gang enter a Chicago warehouse and kill seven members of the rival gang of George "Bugs" Moran.

March 1929 In his inaugural speech, President Hoover describes the future of the United States as "bright with hope."

September 3, 1929 Prices on the stock exchange reach record highs.

October 24, 1929 On a day known as Black Thursday, a huge and alarming sell-off of stocks occurs.

October 29, 1929 The stock market crashes on Black Tuesday, heralding the beginning of the severe economic downturn known as the Great Depression.

1930 More than one thousand banks close, and many customers lose their life savings.

1930 One in five U.S. citizens owns an automobile.

1930 Sinclair Lewis becomes the first U.S. citizen to win the Nobel Prize for Literature.

1931 More than eight hundred banks close.

1931 Al Capone, leader of a hugely profitable organized crime empire in Chicago, Illinois, is convicted of tax evasion and sent to federal prison for eleven years.

1932 At the peak of the Depression, 56 percent of black workers and 40 percent of white workers (a total of thirteen million) are unemployed, and wages are 60 percent less than what they were in 1929.

March 1932 The twenty-month-old son of Charles Lindbergh is kidnapped and ransomed for fifty thousand dollars. The child is found dead seventy-two days later, and German immigrant Bruno Hauptmann is convicted of the murder and executed.

1933 Playing for the Negro League's Pittsburgh Crawfords, pitcher **Satchel Paige** wins an astounding thirty-one out of forty-two games, including a run of twenty-one consecutive wins.

December 5, 1933 Prohibition ends as the Eighteenth Amendment is repealed.

1937 **Zora Neale Hurston**'s most acclaimed work, *Their Eyes Were Watching God,* is published.

Words to Know

A

assembly line: A factory innovation consisting of a waist-high, belt, along which parts move while workers (each performing one task over and over) gradually assemble the product.

B

Barnstormers: Pilots from the early days of aviation, who performed daring feats (such as rolling their airplanes, flying upside down, and even walking on the wings) at county fairs and other exhibitions.

birth control: The use of contraceptives, which are devices or methods to prevent pregnancy. During the Roaring Twenties, it was illegal in many states to disseminate birth control or even information about it, yet growing numbers of women were beginning to use it.

Black Thursday: October 24, 1929, when orders to sell stocks rose at an alarming rate while prices fell, leading to hysteria and panic on the streets of New York City's financial district and elsewhere.

Black Tuesday: October 29, 1929, when the stock market crashed. Banks that were suddenly forced to pay back loans ran out of cash and closed their doors. Many people lost their life savings, and the severe economic downturn known as the Great Depression began.

Bolshevik Revolution: The 1917 takeover of the Russian government by communists, which, in the United States, led to fear and distrust toward foreigners and those believed to hold radical political views.

bootlegging: The sale and distribution of alcoholic beverages made illegal by Prohibition.

C

capitalism: A political and economic system in which a country's trade and industry are controlled by private interests, for profit.

communism: A political and economic system in which all property is owned by the community and each person contributes and receives according to his or her ability and needs.

consumerism: The preoccupation with acquiring goods, which began to dominate U.S. society in the 1920s and which many feel has continued into the twenty-first century.

Coolidge Prosperity: A popular term for the revival of the U.S. economy that occurred in the 1920s, during the administration of President Calvin Coolidge.

creationists: Those who believe in the Biblical version of human creation, in which God created Earth and all its plants and animals in a week, and all people are descended from Adam and Eve, the first humans. In the 1920s, creationists were opposed to the teaching of the scientific theory of evolution in the public schools.

E

Eighteenth Amendment: Popularly known as Prohibition, this amendment to the U.S. Constitution made the manufacture, transportation, and sale of alcoholic beverages illegal.

Eugenics: A pseudo-science that not only claimed to prove the inferiority of anyone who was not of northern-European heritage but warned of the dangers of so-called "mongrelization" (the mixing of superior white blood with that of the inferior immigrants).

evangelists: Those who seek to convert others to their religious faith.

evolution theory: The idea originated in the middle of the nineteenth century by British naturalist Charles Darwin, who proposed that different animals could have descended from common ancestors; it describes changes in species over millions of years as a process called "natural selection" (also known as survival of the fittest).

F

Federal Highway Act: The 1921 legislation that provided for federal funds to states for the creation and maintenance of interstate highways.

Federal Radio Commission: The federal government agency set up in the 1920s to regulate the new technology of radio broadcasting.

flappers: Young women whose bold, carefree manner of dress and behavior signified a change in attitudes toward women's roles, and who came to symbolize for many years to come the free-wheeling spirit of the Roaring Twenties.

Florida land boom: The craze in the 1920s for buying land in Florida, with purchases often made on credit and without the buyer ever seeing or visiting the property. Many investors lost large amounts of money on these get-rich-quick land-buying schemes. The boom ended in 1926, when a hurricane devastated Miami.

Freudianism: The popular application of theories proposed by Austrian psychiatrist Sigmund Freud (1856–1939). These include the influence of childhood experiences on adult behavior, the subconscious (the part of the mind of which one is unaware) as a source of neurotic (abnormally sensitive, anxious, or obsessive) behavior and psychological problems, and the use of psychoanalysis, or talk therapy, to reveal and treat deeply buried emotional damage.

Fundamentalism: A very conservative form of Christianity that includes a literal interpretation of the Bible; that is, the Bible is considered a true account of factual events, rather than a collection of literary, mythical stories told to illustrate moral lessons.

G

Great Depression: The period of severe economic downturn and hardship when millions lost their life savings, their jobs, and the sense of security they had once known. It lasted from the stock market crash of October 1929 until about 1941, when orders for war materials and supplies for World War II (1939–45) invigorated the U.S. economy.

H

Harlem Renaissance: The period of achievement in African American culture—including literature, drama, music, visual arts, and journalism—that took place during the Roaring Twenties. Sometimes referred to as the New Negro Movement, it was centered in Harlem, the African American community in New York City.

I

influenza epidemic: An outbreak of influenza that spread across the world from late 1918 to 1919. It broke out first near Boston, Massachusetts, in September 1918, and within nine months it had killed four hundred thousand U.S. citizens (including seven hundred in one day in Philadelphia, Pennsylvania) as well as scores of others (almost twenty-two million) around the globe.

isolationism: The belief in avoiding political and economic relationships with other countries, and not getting involved in other nations' problems; a policy that dominated the United States during the Roaring Twenties.

J

jazz: A new, distinctly American form of music developed from the combined influences of European and African elements.

Jazz is said to have originated in New Orleans, Louisiana, with musicians playing on instruments discarded by Civil War-era bands. Their style incorporated offbeat rhythms and improvised solos.

Jazz Age: A term for the Roaring Twenties that originated as the title of one of F. Scott Fitzgerald's short stories and that seemed to capture perfectly the spirit of this decade of exuberance, creativity, and sometimes troubling change.

K

Kellogg-Briand Pact: An agreement intended to outlaw war between the nations of the world, justifying armed conflict only as a last resort. It was signed by fifteen nations in August 1928 and eventually by a total of sixty-two countries. The pact proved ineffective in preventing war, as World War II (1939–45) began about a decade later.

Ku Klux Klan: A white supremacist group that had carried out a brutally successful campaign against blacks during the Reconstruction Era (the period stretching roughly from the end of the American Civil War to the end of the 1870s). During the Roaring Twenties, the Klan was revived and extended its campaign of violence and harassment to include not just African Americans but also Jews, Catholics, and immigrants.

L

laissez-faire: The belief that government should loosen its control of the economy and society in general, which characterized the Roaring Twenties.

M

McNary Haugen Bill: One of few measures intended to help farmers, who were one of several groups left out of the general economic prosperity of the 1920s. President Calvin Coolidge vetoed the bill in both 1927 and 1928.

Model T: The automobile introduced by manufacturer Henry Ford (1863–1947), also known as the Tin Lizzie, which became the best-selling and most popular car in the United States for its simple design and low price tag.

Monkey Trial: The popular name for the July 1925 Scopes trial, referring to the misconception that Darwin's theory of evolution meant that human beings had descended directly from apes.

N

National Origins Act: The 1924 legislation meant to slow the flow of immigrants from southern and eastern Europe and from Asia. It capped immigration from each country at 150,000 and lowered earlier country quotas to 2 percent of foreign-born residents at the time of the 1890 U.S. census (when very few southern and eastern Europeans had been in the United States). Immigration from Asia was banned altogether.

nativism: The practice of favoring established inhabitants over new immigrants.

Nineteenth Amendment: The amendment to the U.S. Constitution that gave women the right to vote.

O

organized crime: Groups of criminals who worked together, especially in the illegal liquor trade, and often fought each other for control of particular areas or cities.

P

petting: Various forms of kissing and touching, but usually not sexual intercourse, that increasing numbers of young people were said to be engaging in during the Roaring Twenties.

Progressive Era: The period from about 1900 to about 1914, when a variety of reform groups sought to improve society through such measures as child labor laws, Prohibition, and women's right to vote.

Prohibition: The popular name for the Eighteenth Amendment to the U.S. Constitution, which banned the manufacture, transportation, and sale of alcoholic drinks.

R

Red Scare: A period when people thought to hold foreign or radical political ideas came under suspicion. In a January 1920 action known as the Palmer Raids, Attorney General A. Mitchell Palmer authorized federal agents in 33 cities to raid homes and businesses and arrest several thousand suspects. About 250 of them were eventually deported to the Soviet Union.

Roaring Twenties: The period of 1920 to 1929, when a number of factors—including a population shift from the country to the city, an influx of immigrants, advances in technology, economic prosperity, and changing attitudes and values—converged to create a decade both exciting and troubling.

S

Sacco and Vanzetti Trial: The May 1920 trial in which Italian immigrants and labor activists Nicola Sacco and Bartolomeo Vanzetti were tried, on what many considered a lack of evidence, for the robbery and murder of two employees of a shoe factory in Massachusetts. They were convicted and sentenced to death, but their execution was not carried out until 1927, due to worldwide protests.

St. Valentine's Day Massacre: A multiple murder that occurred in Chicago, Illinois, on February 14, 1929, when it was alleged that men from Al Capone's criminal organization entered a warehouse and killed seven members of the rival gang of George "Bugs" Moran. No one was ever charged for this crime.

scientific management theory: The system devised by industrial engineer Frederick Taylor for making production more efficient. It involved breaking particular tasks into separate steps and calculating the minimum amount of time needed for each step, then requiring workers to complete tasks in these scientifically determined time allotments. Managers were given increased control over workers, functions, and procedures.

Scopes Trial: A Dayton, Tennessee, court case that took place in July 1925, centering on a debate between Biblical beliefs and the scientific theory of evolution. High school teacher John Scopes was charged with violating the Butler Act, which banned the teaching of evolution. The prosecution and defense teams were led by two famous public figures: William Jennings Bryan for the prosecution and Clarence Darrow for the defense.

Sheppard-Towner Act: A 1921 law that guaranteed federal funding to states to set up and run prenatal and children's health centers.

socialism: A political and economic system in which the means of production, distribution, and exchange are owned by the community as a whole, rather than by individuals.

Spirit of St. Louis: The name of the airplane Charles Lindbergh flew in May 1927 when he became the first pilot to make a solo, nonstop flight across the Atlantic Ocean. To make room for the amount of gas needed to get Lindbergh to his destination, it carried no unnecessary gear, such as a radio or special instruments for night flying, gas gauge, or parachute.

stock market: The economic structure that allows investors to buy stocks or shares in companies with the promise of sharing in any profits the company earns. During the Roaring Twenties, more U.S. citizens were investing in the stock market than ever before, sometimes borrowing money to do so. The rapid drop in stock values contributed to the October 29 stock market crash, heralding the beginning of the Great Depression.

T

talkie: A motion picture incorporating both images and sound (initially just music, and eventually both music and voices).

Teapot Dome: The scandal that unfolded during the administration of President Warren G. Harding, in which Secretary of the Interior Albert Fall leased government oil reserves to some private oil companies in exchange for money. He was eventually convicted of bribery and sent to prison, becoming the first Cabinet member in U.S. history to serve time in jail.

trickle-down theory: The economic strategy that involves reducing taxes in order to give ordinary consumers more money to spend while also allowing the wealthy to make more investments. The benefits are expected to eventually spread down through all levels of society. This theory, popular in the Roaring Twenties, would be revived in the 1980s under President Ronald Reagan.

U

Untouchables: The nickname for the squad of special agents headed by Eliot Ness of the Justice Department's Prohibition Bureau and charged with fighting organized crime. Ness and his nine men earned this nickname through their honesty and integrity.

V

Volstead Act: Legislation passed in October 1919 that spelled out the terms of the Eighteenth Amendment (Prohibition), defining as "intoxicating beverages" not only distilled liquor, like whiskey or gin, but fermented drinks, like beer and wine, which many had assumed would not be included in the ban.

W

World War I: The bloody conflict that took place in Europe from 1914 to 1918 in which Germany, having sought to expand its territory, was pitted against the Allies: France, Great Britain, and Italy. The United States entered the war on the side of the Allies in 1917.

Louis Armstrong

Born August 4, 1901 (New Orleans, Louisiana)
Died July 6, 1971 (Long Island, New York)

Musician

Celebrated as one of the greatest jazz performers of all time, Louis Armstrong had a career spanning more than fifty years, from the 1910s to the 1960s. A supremely talented, versatile trumpet player with an unforgettable, gravelly singing voice, Armstrong was popular all over the world, especially during the last twenty-five years of his life. It was during the Roaring Twenties, though, that he played a vital role in the development of jazz, the unique new musical form that was setting the decade on fire. Armstrong's innovative approach, along with his ability to express through his music both deep sorrow and boundless joy, secured his place in history.

"No him, no me."

musician Dizzy Gillespie

An early interest in Dixieland music

Armstrong was born into poverty in New Orleans, Louisiana, on August 4, 1901 (he would later give his birth date as July 4, 1900). His parents were divorced, and for some of his childhood he lived with his grandmother and some with his father (along with his father's new family). His best years, however, were spent with his mother and younger sister

Because of his innovative approach to music, Louis Armstrong played a vital role in the development of jazz and secured his place in history. *(Hulton Archive/Getty Images. Reproduced by permission.)*

Beatrice. They lived in the run-down Storyville section of New Orleans, where bars and dance halls, popularly known as "honky-tonks," lined the streets and the air was filled with the sounds of ragtime music.

These new, popular tunes—which featured strong, syncopated melodies created when the weak beat is stressed in place of the usual strong one—represented the earliest stage of what would come to be known as jazz. New Orleans is often called the birthplace of jazz, because it was there that musicians from a rich racial mix (including African, European, and Native American) began to form Dixieland bands. Their style, played on instruments discarded by the military bands of the American Civil War era (1861–65), incorporated offbeat rhythms and improvised solos (in which individual players take off from the main melody with their own interpretations).

Armstrong was keenly interested in music from an early age. He and his friends followed behind the Dixieland bands and even formed a singing quartet, performing on street corners for coins thrown by passersby. It was not until his teenaged years, though, that Armstrong began to play an instrument. When he was thirteen he was arrested for shooting off a gun (loaded with blanks) at a holiday celebration. He was sent to the Colored Waifs Home, a reform school for boys, where he spent eighteen months.

At the reform school Armstrong learned to read music and to play instruments. He began with the drums, then moved to the bugle, and finally settled on the cornet (a brass instrument similar to a trumpet but shorter and wider). He learned quickly and was soon an accomplished player. After his release, Armstrong started hanging around nightclubs to absorb the styles and techniques of the musicians who made up the city's lively jazz scene. His own playing ability and knack for learning songs quickly became evident, and he was called upon to fill in for older players. His listeners were impressed with the joy and spontaneity that he was already able to convey through his playing.

A hot young star of jazz

Armstrong spent the years between 1917 and 1922 performing with various bands while perfecting his skills and unique style, along with his knowledge of different techniques employed by other musicians. One of these was Joe "King" Oliver (1885–1938), also a cornet player, who took a special interest in the younger musician and even gave him lessons. In 1919 Oliver left New Orleans for Chicago, Illinois, which would soon become a new hotbed for jazz. Before departing he arranged for Armstrong to play occasionally for the band headed by Kid Ory (1886–1973), for whom Oliver had previously worked. During this period Armstrong also performed on the riverboats that traveled up and down the Mississippi River.

Three years later Oliver called Armstrong to come to Chicago and join the group he had just formed, called the Creole Jazz Band. There Armstrong would continue to perfect his style, which featured a clear, broad tone; a smooth vibrato (in which the horn makes a vibrating sound); and a remarkable ability to manage high notes with ease. He played many duets with Oliver but began to be especially noted for his lively improvisations and solos. Armstrong made the first of his many recordings with the Creole Jazz Band, including "Chimes Blues" and "Dippermouth Blues" in 1923.

In early 1924 Armstrong married Lillian Hardin, a jazz pianist and arranger who strongly encouraged him to get out from under Oliver's shadow. Armstrong switched to the trumpet and, the next year, moved to New York City to join the Fletcher Henderson band, which was the featured act at the famous Roseland Ballroom. He continued to record, accompanying a number of the era's most accomplished blues singers, such as the celebrated Bessie Smith (1894–1937) on her influential song "St. Louis Blues" (1925).

Taking part in the Harlem Renaissance

Armstrong participated in the period of cultural achievement known as the Harlem Renaissance, when African American artists of all types—including writers, musicians, journalists, and painters—were exploring and expressing their rich heritage. The nightclub scene in which Armstrong thrived helped to make Harlem (New York's African American community) so special. Both black and white New Yorkers flocked there after dark to listen to the exciting jazz and blues being played not only in fancy clubs like the Roseland Ballroom or the even more famous Cotton Club, but also in speakeasies (businesses in which illegal alcohol was served) and rent parties (informal gatherings in private homes, where the fees paid by guests helped residents pay their landlords).

In 1925, convinced by his wife that he was good enough to make it on his own, Armstrong returned to Chicago. At first he

Duke Ellington: A Jazz Great

Although many of his most famous compositions were written after the Roaring Twenties had ended, Edward "Duke" Ellington, like Louis Armstrong, was a key figure among the innovative jazz musicians who dominated the decade and a star of the Harlem Renaissance.

Born in Washington, D.C., in 1899, Ellington earned the nickname "Duke" from a classmate because he was always well dressed. Although he took piano lessons as a child, Ellington did not become seriously interested in music until he was fourteen, when he heard the ragtime music (a precursor to jazz) of Philadelphia piano player Harvey Brooks. He wrote his first composition, "Soda Fountain Rag," when he was sixteen. Two years later, he formed his own band, Duke's Serenaders, and began performing at parties and other gatherings.

The group's name changed to the Washingtonians, and in 1923 Ellington and the band headed to New York City. They played at several popular clubs on the Harlem music scene, including Barron's nightclub and the Hollywood Club (later known as the Kentucky Club). By 1927 the band was performing as the Duke Ellington Orchestra and had recorded more than sixty records.

Ellington and his group attracted a steady following. In 1927 they began what would be a thirty-eight-month engagement at Harlem's premier nightspot, the legendary Cotton Club. It was here that Ellington solidified his reputation as a jazz leader. Always attired in a white tuxedo, Ellington contributed to the creation of the Big Band sound. This style featured multiple players of various instruments (for example, two trumpeters instead of one) performing carefully orchestrated compositions. The Ellington group also introduced the "jungle" sound, in which mutes (plugs placed in a horn instrument to alter its sound) imitate an animal's growl or roar.

Ellington continued to gain popularity, making hundreds of recordings and appearing on Broadway. Memorable songs Ellington wrote during this period include "Black and Tan Fantasy" (1927), "Creole Love Call" (1928), and "Mood Indigo" (1930).

In the years following the Harlem Renaissance, Ellington and his band toured the United States and Europe. Ellington wrote some of his most famous compositions during the 1930s and 1940s, including "It Don't Mean a Thing (If It Ain't Got That Swing)" (1932), "Sophisticated Lady" (1933), and "Symphony in Black" (1935). He also began collaborating with pianist Billy Strayhorn, who wrote one of the Ellington band's most famous songs, "Take the 'A' Train."

In 1943 Ellington and his band appeared at New York's Carnegie Hall, introducing a number of shorter compositions as well as longer pieces such as *Black, Brown, and Beige*. During the 1950s jazz began to move into a more modern form very different from the Big Band sound, but Ellington continued to do what he had always done, and his fans remained loyal. In the 1960s and 1970s he received many awards and much recognition for his role in the development of jazz. He kept up a rigorous schedule of performing, recording, and composing until his death in 1974.

Louis Armstrong sitting at a piano with his band, the Hot Five, in January 1925. Members of the band included, from left to right, Armstrong, Johnny St. Cry, Johnny Dodds, Kid Ory, and Lil Hardin. *(Hulton Archive/Getty Images. Reproduced by permission.)*

performed with Hardin's band, the Dreamland Syncopators, but later he formed his own group, the Stompers. Over the next several years, Armstrong made the renowned "Hot Five" and "Hot Seven" recordings with such musicians as Johnny Dodds (1892–1940) on clarinet and Ory on trombone. Armstrong had an especially fruitful and long collaboration with pianist Earl "Fatha" Hines (1903–1983). Some of the most famous tunes recorded by these gatherings of talented players (who never actually performed live together) are still considered classics that influenced the course of jazz. They include "Willy the Weaper," "Weary Blues," "Big Butter and Egg Man," and "Hotter Than That."

Armstrong took the Stompers back to New York in 1929 for an extended engagement at Connie's Inn, another famous Harlem nightclub. He also performed in the hit Broadway show *Hot Chocolates*, which featured energetic singing and dancing by an African American cast. Armstrong caused a sensation when he sang "Ain't Misbehavin'" (a tune written by the accomplished jazz pianist Thomas "Fats" Waller; 1904–1943) in a new style called scat, which features the singing of meaningless syllables, sometimes in imitation of musical instruments, that he is often credited with inventing. Over the next few years, he also made some influential recordings, such as "Body and Soul" and "Stardust," that helped to create the mellow, smooth big band sound (featuring a jazz orchestra with several musicians playing the same instruments), which would become increasingly popular during the 1930s.

Even more famous and popular in later years

Although many commentators feel that Armstrong made his most valuable contributions to jazz during the Roaring Twenties, his career continued well beyond that period. He made the first of several European tours in 1932, when he performed in Great Britain; this is where Armstrong was given the nickname "Satchmo," a short version of "Satchelmouth" (his fellow musicians, though, preferred to call him "Pops"). The next year Armstrong returned to Europe for an extended tour, but he came back to the United States in 1935 to appear in the film *Pennies from Heaven* with the popular singer Bing Crosby (1903–1977).

During the 1930s, Armstrong and Hardin divorced, and Armstrong experienced some financial problems. These were eased after he hired a new manager. He began a long string of movie, radio (he was the first African American to host a radio program), and television appearances, gradually becoming more of a popular entertainment figure than just a jazz musician. Still, during the 1940s and 1950s he performed often with his band the All-Stars, which featured Hines on piano, Jack Teagarden (1905–1964) on trombone, and Barney Bigard (1906–1980) on clarinet.

As the civil rights movement, the effort to achieve equal rights for African Americans, heated up during the late 1950s and early 1960s, some more militant black musicians began to view Armstrong with scorn. They accused him of playing up to white people's stereotypes about blacks and of using stage humor that demeaned African Americans. More recently, Armstrong has been defended as a true jazz pioneer who was, first and foremost, an entertainer. Raised in the segregated South, he adapted himself to what he felt were the expectations of his audiences.

In the last decades of his life, Armstrong traveled all over the world. He visited Europe, Africa, Japan, Australia, and South America, gaining recognition and adoration wherever he went. Fondly referred to as "Ambassador Satch," he made several tours and broadcasts that were sponsored by the U.S. State Department (the federal government agency responsible for foreign relations). In 1956, for example, he appeared before a cheering crowd of one hundred thousand fans in the newly independent African nation of Ghana.

Although health problems forced Armstrong to slow down somewhat in the 1960s, he did appear in the 1967 film *Hello, Dolly!* His recording of the song by the same title became a huge hit, even beating out the Beatles for a spot at the top of the popular music charts. Armstrong died in 1971, but he had another hit song seventeen years later, when his 1968 recording of "What a Wonderful World" was featured in the film *Good Morning, Vietnam.*

For More Information

Books

Bergreen, Laurence. *Louis Armstrong: An Extravagant Life.* New York: Broadway Books, 1997.

Brown, Sanford. *Louis Armstrong.* London: Franklin Watts, 1993.

Jones, Max, and John Chilton. *Louis: The Louis Armstrong Story.* Boston: Little, Brown, 1971.

Woog, Adam. *Louis Armstrong.* San Diego, CA: Lucent Books, 1995.

Web Sites

"Who Is Louis Armstrong?" *Satchmo.net: The Official Site of the Louis Armstrong House & Archives.* Available online at http://satchmo.net/bio/. Accessed on June 21, 2005.

William Jennings Bryan

Born March 19, 1860 (Salem, Illinois)
Died July 26, 1925 (Dayton, Ohio)

Lawyer and politician

During his long career in law and politics, including three unsuccessful bids for the presidency, William Jennings Bryan gained fame for both his speech-making skills and his passion for social reform. Nicknamed "The Great Commoner" due to his lifelong dedication to ordinary U.S. citizens, Bryan was also a religious fundamentalist (a very conservative kind of Christian who believes that the stories found in the Bible are literally true, not just illustrations or myths). In 1925 Bryan waged the final battle of his life when he took part in the famous Monkey Trial. The case involved Tennessee schoolteacher John Scopes, who had been charged with breaking a law that had prohibited the teaching of the scientific theory of evolution in public schools. As part of the team that prosecuted Scopes, Bryan stood for traditional values in a trial that pitted the ways of the past against the ideas and beliefs of the modern world.

"[It is] better to trust in the Rock of Ages [Christianity] than to learn the ages of rocks."

A strict upbringing

Born in Salem, Illinois, in 1860, Bryan was the oldest son of Silas Bryan, a prosperous Illinois farmer and judge, and his wife, Mariah. Like all of the couple's eight children,

William Jennings Bryan gained fame for both his speech-making skills and his passion for social reform during his long career in law and politics.
(Courtesy of The Library of Congress.)

Bryan was taught at home by his mother until he turned ten. During his early years he developed strong study habits and the sturdy Christianity of his parents. The elder Bryans were strict about behavior and religion, emphasizing frequent prayer and Bible reading. Young William idolized his father, who told him that a man could do the most good in the world as either a minister or a government leader.

At Illinois College Bryan studied the classics (such as works by the ancient Greek author Homer), mathematics, and U.S. history, nurturing a strong belief in democracy as the best of all possible political systems. He excelled in his studies and especially as a debater. In fact, the handsome and intelligent young man was chosen to be class orator (speech-maker) and served as vice president of his junior class. It was in college that Bryan began to form and express some of the passionate views he would continue to hold on many issues of the period. These included support for Prohibition (a proposed ban on alcoholic beverages that would become law with the 1919 passage of the Eighteenth Amendment to the U.S. Constitution) and women's suffrage (the right to vote, which would be granted with the Nineteenth Amendment in 1920).

A promising young lawyer

Bryan graduated in 1881. The year before, he had become engaged to Mary Baird of Jacksonville, Illinois. When his father died, Bryan's future seemed unclear, but his family decided that he should attend law school as planned. He entered Union College of Law in Chicago, where he spent two years. During that time he began to make political speeches. When he finished law school in 1883, Bryan went to work for the law firm of Kirby, Brown & Russell in Jacksonville. Within a year he had become successful enough to marry his fiancée. After a four-year wait, the couple wed in 1884. Over the next few years, their children Ruth and William Jr. were born.

As a young lawyer, Bryan became involved in many community activities, including playing softball with a team of attorneys, attending church and temperance meetings (the movement to get people to stop drinking alcohol), and working on local elections. Busy and absorbed in his work, Bryan paid little attention to his health and developed poor eating habits. He was eventually diagnosed with diabetes (a serious disease in which the body does not produce enough insulin, which is necessary for processing sugar, starch, and other carbohydrates).

In 1887 Bryan decided to move to Lincoln, Nebraska. He saw Nebraska, which had been a state for only twenty years, as a land of opportunity. Opening a law firm with an old friend, Bryan was soon prospering as an attorney. In three years he won all but one of his cases. He also took advantage of the chance to get involved in politics. Even though Bryan was a member of the Democratic political party and Nebraska had always been dominated by Republicans, Bryan managed in 1890 to win election to the U.S. House of Representatives. He moved his family to Washington, D.C., in 1892.

A progressive member of Congress

As a member of Congress, Bryan became a champion of the poor, farmers, the working class, and small-business owners, whose interests were often overlooked, he felt, in favor of the more privileged members of society. Bryan would become one of the leaders of the Progressive Era (which lasted from about 1900 to about 1914), during which a variety of reformers, people who believe that society needs improvement, spoke out on a number of proposed reforms. For Bryan, these included Prohibition, women's suffrage, the popular election of senators, the establishment of the Department of Labor, and consumer protection and child labor laws. Through his extraordinary ability to capture and hold listeners' attention, despite his relative youth, he earned the nickname "the Boy Orator of the Platte" (the Platte is a major river in Nebraska).

An issue that was of special importance to Bryan was that of the gold standard. The United States guaranteed its paper money with reserves of gold, but most of the other governments of the world used both gold and silver. This made trade between nations more complicated. While U.S. gold-mine owners and other business leaders fought to keep the gold standard, Bryan argued that there was not enough gold available to support all of the world's money. He felt that if the United States switched to the same combined gold and silver standard used elsewhere, trade would improve and the economy would be strengthened. One of Bryan's crowning moments came when, at the Democratic National Convention in 1896, he made his famous "cross of gold" speech, which ended on a dramatic note: "You shall not press down upon the brow of labor this crown of thorns; you shall not crucify mankind upon a cross of gold."

Presidential candidate and cabinet member

Bryan won a second term in Congress but was defeated when he ran for a third term. He then became editor of an Omaha, Nebraska, newspaper, the *World Herald.* In 1896, however, Bryan was nominated as the Democratic candidate in the presidential election. Running against the Republican nominee, William McKinley (1843–1901), Bryan campaigned vigorously. He made six hundred speeches in twenty-nine states, but the Republicans succeeded in portraying him as a radical with revolutionary ideas. Although he won 6.5 million votes out of a total of 14 million cast, Bryan lost the election. He ran for president again in 1900 and 1908 but was defeated each time.

For the next few years, Bryan remained active in Democratic Party activities, often voicing his populist (those who try to represent the views of ordinary people) opposition to special favors for the wealthy and powerful. He founded a newspaper called *The Commoner,* in which many of the concerns of the Progressive Era were highlighted. Bryan soon gained a new nickname: "The Great Commoner."

In 1913 another Progressive Era leader, Woodrow Wilson (1856–1924; served 1913–21), was elected president. The threat of war loomed in Europe, where Germany was seeking to gain territory, but Wilson vowed to keep the United States out of the conflict. Wilson appointed Bryan—who shared many of his ideals, including an antiwar stance—secretary of state, the member of the president's cabinet (made up of heads of various government departments) who is in charge of foreign relations.

Then, in April 1917, the British merchant ship *Lusitania* was struck by German missiles, killing more than one hundred U.S. citizens. Wilson felt he had to respond with protests to Germany. It gradually became clear that the United States was going to enter World War I, and Bryan wanted no part of it. He resigned his position, although he did support the U.S. war effort once the country became involved in the conflict. Bryan moved to Florida in 1920 and, though he was no longer involved in politics, remained active in the Democratic Party.

Religious and scientific beliefs clash

The year 1859 saw the publication of a controversial book that would cause a cultural divide, especially in the United States. In *On the Origin of Species,* naturalist Charles Darwin (1809–1882) proposed the scientific theory of evolution, which traced the development of human beings and other living things over millions of years. Darwin's suggestion that human beings shared some common origins with other primates (a category that includes monkeys, apes, and humans) was wrongly interpreted as meaning that people were directly descended from monkeys.

Like other scientific discoveries and theories of the late nineteenth and early twentieth centuries, Darwin's ideas were embraced by some and rejected by others. Religious fundamentalists were especially offended at the proposal of any other origin for human beings than the one described in the Bible, in which God made the world and all of its creatures in seven days, and in which Adam and Eve were the first humans. Those who believed in this story of the so-called "Divine Creation" were known as creationists, and Bryan was one of them.

In fact, Bryan was a major voice for the creationist movement, whose followers wanted to safeguard the values they believed formed the basis of U.S. civilization. They feared that the teaching of evolutionary theory in schools would cause young people to abandon the religion that had always guided the nation's people, and that society would soon fall into moral decay. Bryan became heavily involved in the effort to uphold the value of faith over science by passing laws to ban the teaching of evolution in public schools.

The teaching of evolution is outlawed in Tennessee

In 1920 Bryan published a widely distributed pamphlet titled *The Menace of Darwinism,* in which he attacked evolutionary theory as a threat to the religious foundations of U.S. society and education. Two years later he declared in a speech as quoted in L. Sprague DeCamp's *The Great Monkey Case* that it was "better to trust in the Rock of Ages

Creationism Still Attracts Believers

In the decades following the Scopes trial, the debate over evolution theory versus creationism died down somewhat. A new book published in 1961, however, created a ripple of controversy for its strict creationist account of humanity's origin. In *The Genesis Flood,* John Whitcomb and Henry Morris asserted that the Earth was just ten thousand years old and that after its formation, God had taken six days to create all plants, animals, and human beings. They claimed that humans and dinosaurs had lived on Earth at the same time, and that fossil remains may be explained as resulting from mass deaths caused by the great flood described in the Bible.

About a decade later, a small group of fundamentalists convinced the California Board of Education that creationism should be taught in public schools along with evolution theory, on the grounds that students had a right to hear alternative arguments about the subject. This victory was particularly significant in that California's school system, the largest in the nation, had a major impact on the textbook publishing industry. In 1972 the National Academy of Sciences and the American Association for the Advancement of Science, groups that had not previously considered creationism worth commenting on, issued statements denouncing it.

More recently, the theory of intelligent design has gained ground as a version of creationism adapted to the contemporary world. Proponents of this idea hold that the very complexity of the universe is proof that it must have been designed by some divine, guiding force. They continue to actively push for public schools to teach the Biblical version of creation along with the scientific one.

[Christianity] than to learn the ages of rocks." Bryan's fundamentalist fervor struck a chord with those who shared his discomfort with the new ideas and values that were transforming society.

In early 1925 the state of Tennessee passed the Butler Act, which made it illegal to teach any theory of human origin that went against the biblical story of creation. The American Civil Liberties Union (ACLU) immediately offered to assist any Tennessee teacher who wished to challenge the law. A group of citizens in Dayton, who disagreed with the law—and also wanted to bring some attention to their small town, recruited a high school biology teacher named John Scopes—who agreed to get himself arrested so that the law could be tested and perhaps overturned.

The Monkey Trial begins

In April Scopes delivered a lesson on evolution to his students and was arrested and charged with violating the Butler Act. The trial was set to begin on July 10. Now sixty-five years old, Bryan quickly offered to help prosecute Scopes, convinced that his status as a lawyer and fundamentalist crusader would help achieve a guilty verdict. Hearing of Bryan's involvement, defense attorney **Clarence Darrow** (1857–1938; see entry), himself nationally famous for his successful defense of underdog clients, offered to lead the defense team.

Darrow no doubt sensed the importance of this trial. He believed that its central issue was the constitutional guarantee of freedom of speech, which had been violated by the Tennessee law. Ironically, Darrow had previously worked on many of the same reform causes as Bryan, and he had supported Bryan in his bids for the presidency.

The case drew national attention, especially since the trial was attended by print reporters from all over the country; it was also the first court case to be broadcast on the new medium of radio. As the court date approached, Dayton was overrun by a carnival-like atmosphere, with food and drink vendors setting up stands, souvenir sellers hawking stuffed monkeys (the event had already been nicknamed the "Monkey Trial"), and street-corner preachers shouting to passersby.

Bryan added further excitement to the scene with his dramatic arrival, stepping down from his train to cheers from a crowd of several hundred admirers. For several days he was often seen wandering around town, munching on radishes (one of his favorite foods) and making speeches wherever and whenever he could. Early in the trial, Bryan delivered a seventy-minute attack on evolutionary theory that, while full of his usual passion, seemed somewhat vague and intellectually shallow to some observers. One of these was **H.L. Mencken** (1880–1956; see entry), the famously acid-tongued journalist from the Baltimore *Sun,* who was on hand to cover the trial.

Bryan called as a witness

From the beginning there was no doubt that Scopes had broken the law. Darrow's plan was to expose the law

Attorney William Jennings Bryan arguing for the prosecution during the Scopes Monkey Trial in Dayton, Tennessee, in 1925. *(Hulton Archive/Getty Images. Reproduced by permission.)*

as unconstitutional. He intended to present expert witnesses (such as scientists who were also Christians) to show that religious faith was not necessarily incompatible with a belief in the theory of evolution. Eventually, though, the judge ruled that this testimony was irrelevant, because it had nothing to with whether Scopes had violated the Butler Act.

In desperation, Darrow made a bold move: He called Bryan himself to the witness stand. Bryan's fellow prosecutors urged him to refuse, but Bryan readily agreed to take the stand. This was probably a mistake, for what followed was a confrontation that left Bryan looking foolish.

For ninety minutes, Darrow grilled Bryan on his religious beliefs. He asked whether biblical stories like that of Jonah, who was swallowed by a whale and survived in its stomach for three days, could be literally true. Bryan replied that they could, but then Darrow asked if it was true that God had made the world in only seven days. Bryan said that these may not have been twenty-four-hour days, but rather periods of time. It was this admission that proved most damaging to the fundamentalist cause, which had always centered on the belief that everything in the Bible was literally true.

The exchange ended with Bryan objecting to what he considered Darrow's slurs against the Bible. Darrow replied with his own objection, stating: "I am examining you on your fool ideas that no intelligent Christian on earth believes."

The battle ends

It seemed that Bryan had lost some ground after testifying, but he nevertheless prepared to make a grand closing statement. He intended to use his considerable powers of persuasion to dazzle his listeners and convince any doubters of the wisdom of his stance. Bryan, however, never got a chance to make his speech. The defense team had no intention of allowing Bryan such an opportunity, so they declined to make a closing statement; under Tennessee law, this prevented the prosecution from making a closing statement as well. Further, Darrow asked the jury to find Scopes guilty so that the defense could appeal the case to a higher court. The judge agreed, pronouncing Scopes guilty and fining him one hundred dollars for violating the law. The trial was over.

Despite the court decision, it was generally agreed that Darrow had won a moral victory, making a strong case for the right of educators to share new ideas with their students and exposing the fundamentalists as backward. The creationist cause, on the other hand, had been damaged by Bryan's rather befuddled testimony. The debate over the religious and scientific views of the evolution of human beings was not over, however, and in fact still continues in the twenty-first century.

Having lost the opportunity to deliver what could have been the speech of his life, Bryan spent the two days following the trial dictating his statement to his secretary, with plans to get it published. On July 25, five days after the trial had ended, Bryan attended church, had lunch with his wife, and lay down for a nap. He never awoke. His doctor said that the cause of death was diabetes, no doubt made worse by the fatigue brought on by the stress of the trial. The inscription on Bryan's tombstone characterized well the final battle of his life: "He Kept the Faith."

For More Information

Books

Anderson, David D. *William Jennings Bryan.* Boston: Twayne, 1981.

Cheney, Robert W. *A Righteous Cause: The Life of William Jennings Bryan.* Boston: Little, Brown, 1985.

Coletta, Paolo E. *William Jennings Bryan—Political Evangelist, 1860–1908.* Lincoln: University of Nebraska Press, 1964.

De Camp, L. Sprague. *The Great Monkey Trial.* Garden City, NY: Doubleday, 1968.

Dumenil, Lynn. *The Modern Temper: American Culture and Society in the 1920s.* New York: Hill and Wang, 1995.

Ginger, Ray. *Six Days or Forever: Tennessee Versus John Thomas Scopes.* Chicago, IL: Quadrangle Books, 1969.

Hanson, Erica. *The 1920s.* San Diego, CA: Lucent Books, 1999.

Larson, Edward J. *Trial and Error: The American Controversy over Creation and Evolution.* New York: Oxford University Press, 1994.

Levine, Lawrence W. *Defender of the Faith.* New York: Oxford University Press, 1965.

Miller, Nathan. *New World Coming: The 1920s and the Making of Modern America.* New York: Scribner, 2003.

Perret, Geoffrey. *America in the Twenties.* New York: Touchstone, 1982.

Tompkins, Jerry R., ed. *D-Days at Dayton: Reflections on the Scopes Trial.* Baton Rouge: Louisiana State University Press, 1965.

Web Sites

"Famous Trials in American History: Tennessee Versus John Scopes, the Monkey Trial." *Famous Trials by Doug Linder* Available online at http://www.law.umkc.edu/faculty/projects/ftrials/scopes/scopes.htm. Accessed on June 21, 2005.

Al Capone

Born January 7, 1899 (Brooklyn, New York)
Died January 25, 1947 (Palm Island, Florida)

Organized crime leader

"Everybody calls me a racketeer. I call myself a businessman."

Al Capone was one of the most notorious criminals of all time. During the Roaring Twenties, he gained fame both for the success of his criminal operation and for the violent way it was built and maintained. Capone became a symbol for the lawlessness of this decade, when Prohibition (the constitutional ban on the manufacture and sale of alcoholic beverages that was intended to improve society) seemed to lead directly to murder and corruption. With his bulky body and facial features, his slick suits and hats, his money, power, and disregard for the law, Capone remains a popular icon of the 1920s.

Growing up tough in Brooklyn

Alphonse "Al" Capone was born in the Brooklyn area of New York City in January 1899. He was the fourth of nine children born to parents who had immigrated to the United States from Italy. Capone's father was a barber and his mother a seamstress. They were a hardworking family with no apparent criminal connections or tendencies. The neighborhood, however, was tough, and Capone became involved at a very early

During the Roaring Twenties Al Capone gained fame both for the success for his criminal operation and for the violent way it was built. *(AP/Wide World Photos. Reproduced by permission.)*

age with several youth gangs, including the Brooklyn Rippers and the Forty Thieves Juniors.

When he was fourteen, Capone got into a fight with a teacher who had struck him. He dropped out of school and soon joined the Five Point Juniors, which was the youth branch of a well-known criminal organization called the Five Point Gang. Capone became a kind of apprentice to a racketeer (someone involved in illegal business activities) named Johnny

Torrio (1882–1957). He ran errands for Torrio and learned from him about using cleverness, instead of violence, to get ahead.

Despite this early involvement in the city's criminal underworld, Capone also held a number of ordinary jobs, including work as a candy-store clerk and as a paper cutter in a book-bindery. He was employed as a bartender in a saloon when he received the facial marks that earned him the nickname "Scarface." He made a remark to a young woman that her brother, who was seated next to her, found insulting. The knife-wielding brother gave Capone three slashes on the left side of his face. For the rest of his life Capone was self-conscious about the scars and tried to cover them with powder.

While he was still a teenager, Capone met the young woman who would become his wife, Mary "Mae" Coughlin, who was a department-store clerk and two years older than Capone. She became pregnant and in early December 1919 gave birth to Albert Francis "Sonny" Capone. The couple married at the end of the month. Sonny, Capone's only child, later developed a serious hearing problem that may have been the result of syphilis (a sexually transmitted disease) inherited from his father. In any case, Capone loved Sonny dearly and always provided well for him.

A young gangster gets his start

Meanwhile, Torrio had moved to Chicago, Illinois, in 1915. There he went to work for the thriving criminal operation of his uncle, James "Big Jim" Colosimo (1877–1920), who ran saloons, gambling establishments, and houses of prostitution. In 1921 Torrio invited Capone to join him in Chicago. According to some sources, Capone was fleeing responsibility for several murders when he moved his family to Chicago and joined Colosimo's organization.

Capone arrived just as Prohibition was beginning. The Eighteenth Amendment, which made Prohibition official, had gone into effect in early 1920. The ban on alcohol had been brought about by reformers who wanted to protect society from the ill effects of drinking, which they felt damaged not only people's health but also their relationships and ability to work and support their families. Although some people had opposed Prohibition from the start, especially members of immigrant communities, for whom alcohol consumption had an important cultural role, most U.S. citizens supported the ban. Even Prohibition's supporters were surprised, however, when the Volstead Act (which spelled out the terms of the amendment) defined as illegal not only distilled beverages like whiskey but also fermented ones like beer and wine, which many had assumed would not be included.

Members of criminal organizations and gangsters (the popular term for this kind of criminal) quickly realized the money-making potential of Prohibition. They knew that people still wanted to drink alcohol and that they would pay for it. Thus bootlegging (the sale and distribution of illegal liquor) became an important focus of criminal activity, though gambling and prostitution operations still continued.

Not long after Capone's arrival in Chicago, Colosimo was assassinated by some unidentified rivals; a few commentators suspected Torrio and Capone of having something to do with the murder, but this was never proved. Torrio took over his uncle's operations, with Capone as his second-in-command. Capone demonstrated a shrewd business sense and steady nerves, both qualities that would serve him well in the years to come.

A prominent public figure

During the early 1920s, Torrio and Capone expanded their activities. They formed relationships with some criminal groups, such as the Purple Gang, with headquarters in Detroit, Michigan, while engaging in bitter and often brutal rivalry with others. Their main enemies were the members of the gang run by George "Bugs" Moran (1903–1959), which operated on the north side of Chicago, while Torrio and Capone controlled the south side. In January 1925 Moran's men made an unsuccessful attempt to kill Capone, and later in the month they attacked Torrio, seriously wounding him. Spooked, Torrio retired from his life of crime and moved to Italy. That left Capone in charge of one of the most prosperous criminal organizations in history.

During the second half of the 1920s Capone ran a sprawling criminal empire that included bootlegging operations, liquor distilleries and beer breweries, speakeasies (places where illegal liquor was sold and consumed), gambling establishments, prostitution rings, racetracks, and nightclubs. At the height of his success, his income was reportedly as high as one hundred million dollars per year. He protected his businesses by bribing police officers and political leaders, and he managed to rig elections so that the right people stayed in office. One of these was the mayor of Chicago, William "Big Bill" Thompson Jr.

Capone was a well-known public figure around Chicago, admired and respected by those who considered him more a businessman than a criminal. He appeared in flashy clothes and jewelry and often demonstrated generosity toward the needy. For example, he opened one of the first soup kitchens to serve the poor during the Great Depression, the period of economic hardship that began with the stock market crash in 1929 and lasted until the beginning of World War II in 1939. Capone boasted, with some justification, that he ran Chicago. As quoted in Thomas Pegram's *Battling Demon Rum: The Struggle for a Dry America, 1800–1933,* Capone complained that "everybody calls me a racketeer. I call myself a businessman."

Capone's money, power, and glamour went hand in hand, however, with ruthlessness (showing no compassion), a hot temper, and a willingness to engage in whatever violence seemed necessary to accomplish his goals. Chicago had become a nearly lawless place, with corrupt police officers and politicians not only tolerating but even taking part in criminal activity, and gangsters frequently having shoot-outs on the streets. Capone was at the heart of the action. He was suspected of involvement in more than two hundred murders of enemies and rival gang members. Because people involved in organized crime would not talk to the police—out of fear, loyalty, or because of their own guilt—it was almost impossible to solve or prosecute these kinds of crimes.

The St. Valentine's Day Massacre

The violence continued to escalate throughout the 1920s, lending fuel to the growing public resistance to Prohibition. Finally an event occurred that sent shock waves through the nation, as Chicago became the setting for one of the most horrifying episodes of the decade. For a long time Capone had had his eye on Moran's territory. In addition, Moran had recently tried to kill "Machine Gun" Jack McGurn, one of

The S-M-C Cartage Company, the scene of the St. Valentine's Day Massacre, in which seven men who worked for mob leader Bugs Moran were killed. It is suspected that Al Capone ordered the hit. (© Bettmann/Corbis. Reproduced by permission.)

Capone's closest associates. The double motives of greed and revenge led to what came to be called the St. Valentine's Day Massacre.

Members of Moran's gang were known to use a certain garage as a drop-off point for shipments of illegal liquor. On February 14, 1929, seven gang members were at the garage when several policemen suddenly burst in; these were actually Capone's men, dressed in stolen uniforms. Assuming this was a raid on their bootlegging operation, Moran's men stood facing a wall with their hands in the air.

At this point, more members of Capone's gang ran in and used machine guns and other weapons to shoot and kill the Moran gang members, pumping almost two hundred bullets into their bodies. By a stroke of luck, Moran himself (likely the intended target of the attack) was not among them. It was probably McGurn who was responsible for the execution of this attack, but Capone is thought to have been at the heart of its planning. At the time it occurred, however, Capone was in Florida, and neither he nor anyone else was ever charged.

The Untouchables step in

News of this bloodbath shocked not only Chicago but the rest of the nation as well, including the top leaders of government. Calls for action led President **Herbert Hoover** (1874–1964; served 1929–33; see entry) to order a crackdown on organized crime, targeting Capone in particular. He was subsequently arrested on a weapons charge and jailed for a year. Capone seemed to view prison as a welcome refuge, however, since other gang leaders (especially Moran) were supposedly plotting against him.

When Capone emerged from prison, he faced more pressure from several government agencies determined to curb his illegal activities. One of these was the Justice Department, which set up a new squad of special agents headed by Eliot Ness (1902–1957), a twenty-six-year-old Chicago native who had already been working for the department's Prohibition Bureau. Ness was known for his honesty; in fact, Capone had tried unsuccessfully to bribe him and, failing that, made some attempts on his life. The young agent was authorized to choose nine other men to join him in battling bootleggers, racketeers, and corrupt police officers. Ness's hand picked agents, all of them under thirty, and each specializing in a skill such as wiretapping or weapons handling, had such spotless records that the squad was known as the Untouchables. It was understood that they would never give in to either bribery or threats of violence.

The Untouchables did much to block Capone's business operations; for example, they conducted raids that shut down thirty breweries and netted more than one hundred arrests. They did not, however, put Capone in jail. That feat was managed through a different and somewhat unusual channel. When Capone was finally sent to prison, it was not for murder or for violating Prohibition, but for tax evasion (failing to pay income tax).

Eliot Ness: Top "Untouchable"

While Al Capone was known as the most successful of the organized crime leaders who made their fortunes during the Roaring Twenties, Eliot Ness is recognized as the decade's leading lawman. As head of the squad known as the "Untouchables," Ness hindered Capone's bootlegging operation and also contributed to his eventual arrest and conviction for tax evasion.

Ness was born in Chicago, Illinois, in 1903, the son of a Norwegian immigrant. He graduated from the University of Chicago in 1925, and, two years later, he passed a civil service examination, earning a position as a special agent with the Treasury Department. He was soon transferred to the Justice Department to join the new Prohibition Bureau, an agency established to fight the recent increase in organized crime related to the illegal liquor trade, based out of Chicago.

President Herbert Hoover's particular concern over Al Capone's activities in Chicago spurred the Prohibition Bureau to establish a special group of agents to focus on shutting down Capone and his bootlegging network. Ness led the group and handpicked the agents making up the team. By October 1929 he had hired nine men respected not only for their investigative skills but for their personal honesty and integrity.

Ness took aim at Capone's sizable income (estimated at $75 million per year), which gave the gangster the power to pay the bribes and buy the special privileges that kept his business thriving. While gathering evidence to use against Capone in court, the agents also sought to destroy Capone's manufacturing facilities. Within six months, the task force had shut down nineteen distilleries (where hard liquor was made) and six breweries (were beer was brewed), costing Capone about $1 million.

After one of Capone's men offered Ness $2,000, plus weekly payments of the same amount if Ness would lay off Capone's business, Ness angrily called a press conference. He announced that Capone would never succeed in paying off either Ness or his agents. The following day, an article in the *Chicago Tribune* referred to the squad as the "Untouchables," referring to their incorruptibility.

Capone fought back, ordering the murder of one of Ness's friends and three unsuccessful attempts on Ness's life. The Untouchables continued their work, however, shutting down several more of Capone's highly profitable breweries.

In June 1931 Ness brought five thousand different Prohibition-related charges against Capone before a grand jury. By that time, however, prosecutors had already decided to charge Capone with tax evasion, a case they felt had a better chance of winning. The trial began on October 6, 1931, and lasted two weeks, with Ness present in the courtroom every day. It ended, much to Capone's surprise and Ness's delight, with the gangster's conviction; he was sentenced to eleven years in a federal prison.

From 1935 to 1941 Ness served as Safety Director for the city of Cleveland, Ohio, where he was responsible not only for investigating crimes but for implementing traffic safety and control measures. Ness was credited with significantly reducing the city's traffic fatality rate. During World War II, he was director of the Division of Social Protection, part of the Federal Security Agency. Ness later served as chairman of the board of Diebold, a company that produces safes and security systems. He died in 1957.

A criminal career finally halted

During most of the 1920s, it had been assumed that income that came from illegal activities could not be taxed. But in 1927 the Supreme Court ruled that this kind of income was indeed subject to income tax. In June 1931 Capone was indicted (formally accused) on twenty-three counts (charges) of income tax evasion. He had never filed an income tax return (a statement of earnings that must be submitted to the federal government every year), and he owned nothing in his own name. A persistent agent of the Internal Revenue Service (IRS), however, found a notebook that showed income recorded under Capone's name. Capone was charged with owing the government more than two hundred thousand dollars in unpaid taxes.

During the course of the trial, Capone tried to bribe the jury to find him innocent. The judge changed the jury at the last minute. To his surprise, Capone was convicted on four of the counts, which was enough to send him to jail for eleven years. He went first to Chicago's Cook County jail, where he could pay for privileges and comforts and even continue to conduct business from behind bars. After a year, though, he was transferred to a harsher environment at the federal penitentiary (prison) in Atlanta, Georgia. Two years later he was moved to the newly built prison on Alcatraz Island in San Francisco Bay.

Surrounded by icy, shark-infested waters, the prison was totally isolated from the outside world. During his imprisonment, Capone lost all his influence and power in the world of organized crime. Meanwhile, the syphilis he had contracted as a teenager had returned, this time in its final and worst form, leading to brain damage. By the time he was released in November 1939, Capone's mental capacity had greatly decreased. He spent his last years living quietly at his Palm Island, Florida, estate. He died in 1947, soon after his forty-eighth birthday.

For More Information

Books

Allsop, Kenneth. *The Bootleggers: The Story of Chicago's Prohibition Era.* New Rochelle, NY: Arlington House, 1968.

Altman, Linda Jacobs. *The Decade That Roared: America during Prohibition.* New York: Twenty-First Century Books, 1997.

Bergreen, Laurence. *Capone: The Man and the Era.* New York: Simon & Schuster, 1992.

Kobler, John. *Capone: The Life and World of Al Capone.* New York: Putnam, 1971.

Miller, Nathan. *New World Coming: The 1920s and the Making of Modern America.* New York: Scribner, 2003.

Ness, Eliot. *The Untouchables.* New York: Messner, 1957. Reprint, 1987.

Pegram, Thomas. *Battling Demon Rum: The Struggle for a Dry America, 1800–1933.* Chicago, IL: Ivan R. Dee, 1998.

Perret, Geoffrey. *America in the Twenties.* New York: Touchstone, 1982.

Schoenberg, Robert. *Mr. Capone: The Real—and Complete—Story of Al Capone.* New York: Morrow, 1992.

Web Sites

"Al Capone." *Chicago Historical Society.* Available online at http://www.chicagohs.org/history/capone.html. Accessed on June 22, 2005.

Comedy Kings

Charlie Chaplin
Born April 16, 1889 (London, England)
Died December 25, 1977 (Vevey, Switzerland)

Buster Keaton
Born April 4, 1895 (Piqua, Kansas)
Died February 1, 1966 (Woodland Hills, California)

Harold Lloyd
Born April 20, 1893 (Burchard, Nebraska)
Died March 3, 1971 (Hollywood, California)

Actors, film directors, filmmakers

Many people who were young during the Roaring Twenties remember with special fondness the experience of going to the movies to see the great clowns of the silent films (motion pictures did not include sound technology until the late 1920s; before that, any dialog appeared as written text on the screen). These comic actors helped to set the tone of outrageous fun that characterized the decade. In many cases, their antics not only produced smiles, but helped to express the mixed feelings that many people had about the amazing, changing, and sometimes confusing world around them. The leading comedy star was undoubtedly Charlie Chaplin, who won lasting, worldwide recognition and adoration through his Little Tramp character. Close behind was Buster Keaton, who met each hair-raising situation with a deadpan (expressionless) face, and Harold Lloyd, whose character wore trademark round glasses and a straw hat.

Charlie Chaplin

Although he earned the bulk of his fame in the United States and is commonly considered a phenomenon of U.S. culture, Chaplin was actually born in London, England, and never became a U.S. citizen. His parents both performed on the British music hall circuit in shows that combined singing, dancing, comedy, acrobatics, and pantomime. Chaplin's early life was troubled, for his alcoholic father abandoned his family. His mother, who struggled with mental illness and was sometimes institutionalized, could barely support her children. Chaplin and his older brother Sydney spent much of their youth in work houses (a last resort for the poor) and orphanages, and he received only four years of schooling.

The slapstick days

Chaplin's stage career began when he was ten years old. He went on tour with a group called the Eight Lancashire Lads, beginning a kind of apprenticeship that gave him valuable experience in character development, pantomime, and acrobatics. He would put all these skills to good use in his later film work. Eventually Chaplin got a job with Fred Karno (1866–1941), who directed several acting companies. Chaplin traveled to the United States twice to tour with a group called the Speechless Comedians. On the second trip, Chaplin attracted the attention of Mack Sennett (1880–1960), a director who made the popular Keystone Cops films. These movies were full of slapstick comedy so physical that they actually seemed noisy, despite the lack of sound.

Chaplin joined Sennett's roster of talented actors, which also included Roscoe "Fatty" Arbuckle, in 1913. During the two years he worked for Sennett, Chaplin would make nearly forty films. These were the popular short movies of the day, running on only one or two film reels and lasting less than fifteen minutes.

Charlie Chaplin was bestknown for his Little Tramp character during the 1920s silent-film era. *(AP/Wide World Photos. Reproduced by permission.)*

Chaplin's first appearance as the Little Tramp came in *Mabel's Strange Predicament* (1914). Told to get into a funny costume, the small-statured Chaplin had borrowed some very large pants from Arbuckle and put some oversized shoes on the wrong feet. He topped off his outfit with a small, round, bowler hat, a tiny mustache, and a cane. This created the look of a person who may once have been respectable but had fallen on hard times. The Tramp's funny walk came straight out of the music hall tradition, but his lovable, ever-hopeful personality was pure Chaplin.

The Little Tramp gains fame

Chaplin was eager to direct his own films, and Sennett gave him his first chance to do so in 1914 with *Twenty Minutes of Love.* The following year, Chaplin signed a new contract with Essanay Film Company, making fourteen films in which he refined his Tramp character, moving away from the pure slapstick of his earliest work and achieving a blend of romance, comedy, and sadness in such works as *The Tramp* and *The Bank.*

Chaplin's next contract was with the Mutual Film Corporation, where he made twelve films in one year. These included such memorable movies as *The Vagabond, One A.M., Easy Street,* and *The Immigrant.* Moving over to First National Films in 1918, Chaplin made *A Dog's Life* and *Shoulder Arms*; the latter expressed support for U.S. involvement in World War I (1914–1918; the United States entered the war in 1917). In 1921, he appeared in one of his most popular and acclaimed films, *The Kid.*

By now Chaplin had become one of the most recognizable and beloved figures of popular U.S. culture. In portraying the underdog who rises above his circumstances to reach his goal, which usually involved getting girl of his dreams, Chaplin seemed to embody the traditional U.S. values of optimism and hope. In real life, he was certainly living out the dream of rising from poverty to riches. By the time he was twenty-five, he had earned the then-incredible sum of $670,000.

Concerned about the tremendous growth in the movie industry and the lack of creative freedom that might signal for actors and directors, Chaplin joined with actors Douglas Fairbanks (1883–1939) and Mary Pickford (1927–1979) and director D.W. Griffith (1875–1948) to form United Artists. This company would allow each partner control over his or her own films. Chaplin's first film for United Artists was *A Woman of Paris* (1923), which was critically acclaimed but not very popular with mass audiences, probably because Chaplin himself did not appear in it.

Always a perfectionist, Chaplin now had the clout to make movies his own way, which meant taking more time (sometimes as much as two or three years per movie) and exerting total control over both the actors and the production process. The positive results of this approach were evident in *The Gold Rush* (1925), which is generally considered Chaplin's crowning achievement. This unforgettable film had the Tramp struggling with cold, hunger, loneliness, and cruelty within the setting of the Klondike (a region of Alaska) Gold Rush of 1895. In what is perhaps the most famous comic scene in movie history, the starving Tramp attempts to eat a shoe for dinner, winding the shoelaces around his fork like spaghetti and appearing to savor the nails as if they were chicken bones.

A different kind of film

During the late 1920s, technology became available to allow the use of sound in motion pictures. The first "talkie," or film with sound, was *The Jazz Singer,* starring the Broadway singer and actor Al Jolson (1886–1950). This giant leap forward was not a happy moment for many silent screen actors, though, whose voices or accents made them unsuitable for movies with sound. All of the great screen comedians, who had never needed to speak to be funny, were affected by this development, and few adapted to it well.

Chaplin met the challenge, however. In his next acclaimed film, *City Lights* (1931), Chaplin chose to use music and sound effects but no dialogue. After the film was released, he went on a world tour to promote it and was warmly applauded in every country, highlighting his status as one of the world's most beloved celebrities.

During the 1930s and 1940s, Chaplin's films reflected a general trend in U.S. culture toward more socially conscious art. In *Modern Times* (1936), Chaplin took on such issues as technology's dehumanizing effect, labor struggles, police brutality, homelessness, and hunger. *The Great Dictator* (1940) was a spoof on German dictator Adolf Hitler (1889–1945) who was then at the height of his power. The first Chaplin film to include dialogue, it was very popular with audiences, despite a long, tedious speech against tyranny at the end of the movie.

Despite the adoration he received from the public, Chaplin was plagued by personal problems and scandals throughout his career. Some of these involved taxes and politics, but many were connected with his weakness for very young women, with whom he had both affairs and marriages. He was married to actresses Mildred Taylor (1918 to 1920), Lita Grey (1924 to 1927), and Paulette Goddard (1936 to 1941). Finally, at the age of fifty-four, Chaplin achieved a longer-lasting relationship when he married eighteen-year-old Oona O'Neill, daughter of the renowned playwright **Eugene O'Neill** (1888–1953; see entry), who disapproved of the marriage so much that he disowned his daughter. The couple would have eight children, including future film actress Geraldine Chaplin, and they would remain married until Chaplin's death.

In the last three decades of his life, Chaplin made only a few movies, and they were very different from those produced during the height of the silent comedy era. *Monsieur Verdoux* (1947) centered on a man who marries and then murders women for their money, while the semi-autobiographical *Limelight* (1952), in which the central character is a music-hall performer, is set in the years just before World War I. The public proved unenthusiastic about seeing Chaplin in any role other than his familiar Little Tramp persona.

By the early 1950s, Chaplin had attracted the attention of the U.S. government through his interest in socialism (a system in which the means of production, distribution, and exchange are owned by the community as a whole) and sympathy for the Soviet Union (which had a Communist system, in which all property is owned by the community and each person contributes and receives according to his or her ability and needs). Fear and suspicion of countries and people with these ideologies had led to paranoia, resulting in the congressional hearings chaired by Senator Joseph McCarthy (1908–1957), in which many Hollywood figures were questioned about beliefs and activities suspected of being "un-American."

Soon after the release of *Limelight,* Chaplin left for Europe to promote the movie. Almost immediately, he was informed that his permission to reenter the United States had been revoked until he could prove he was a respectable, upstanding citizen. Angered by this demand, Chaplin vowed not to return to the United States at all. With his family, he moved first to England and then to Switzerland, where he lived for the rest of his life. He made two more films—*A King in New York* (1957), a satire of U.S. society, and *A Countess from Hong Kong* (1967), a romantic comedy—but neither was a critical nor popular success.

In his final decade, Chaplin wrote his autobiography as well as musical scores for several of his early films. By the early 1970s he was again recognized as a major cultural figure when he was knighted by Queen Elizabeth II (1926–) of Great Britain and honored by the Venice Film Society and the Academy Awards. (He even returned to the United States to accept the Oscar.) Chaplin died in his sleep at his Swiss home in late 1977.

Buster Keaton, American comedian of the silent-film era, who became known as "The Great Stoneface" because of his deadpan expression. *(Hulton Archive/Getty Images. Reproduced by permission.)*

Buster Keaton

Sometimes called the Great Stoneface for his expressionless demeanor, Buster Keaton was one of the most talented screen comedians of the Roaring Twenties. Like Charlie Chaplin, he was born into a performing family: his parents made their living on the vaudeville circuit, which featured entertainment combining music and comedy. Named Joseph Francis Keaton at birth, he received his nickname from magician Harry Houdini, an acquaintance of his parents, after showing very little reaction to a fall down some stairs. Houdini remarked that the tough toddler could really take a "buster" (slang for a nasty fall).

By the time he turned three, Keaton had joined his parents' act, the Three Keatons. His father developed a routine that involved Buster in some very physical, even rough comedy;

Fatty Arbuckle: A Fallen Star

During the Roaring Twenties, the making of motion pictures became a major industry centered in Hollywood, California. Although idolized by the public, movie actors and actresses were also at the center of several shocking scandals. One of the most sensational involved overweight comic actor Roscoe "Fatty" Arbuckle.

Born in Kansas in 1887, Arbuckle was a baby when his family moved to southern California. He spent his early years as a performer on the vaudeville circuit. There he perfected the acrobatic skills that he would later employ in his movies. Despite being overweight, Arbuckle was skilled at performing the crazy flips and falls that made up the very physical or "slapstick" comedy that audiences so enjoyed.

Arbuckle was out of work when, in 1913, he wandered into the Keystone film studio headed by Mack Sennett. The 250-pound (113-kilograms) Arbuckle was given the nickname "Fatty" and put to work as a well-meaning, but oafish, hero involved in many funny scrapes. Arbuckle spent three years as part of the Keystone Cops comedy troupe, starring in many short films. He was particularly popular for the "Fatty and Mabel" series, in which he costarred with actress Mabel Normand.

In 1917 Arbuckle joined with producer Joseph Schenk to start a film company called Comique. He spent the next few years directing a string of hit comedies, including *The Butcher Boy* (1917), *Out West*

(1918), and *Back Stage* (1919). Arbuckle's popularity with the public led to his signing a contract with the Paramount studio to appear in six feature films. He soon found, however, that his schedule was overly hectic and that he had little creative control over his work. In the early 1920s, he appeared in such films as *Brewster's Millions* and *Traveling Salesman* (both made in 1921).

In September 1921 Arbuckle took a short vacation to San Francisco, California. During a wild party in the St. Francis Hotel, a young actress named Virginia Rappe collapsed. Arbuckle helped her to a bed and called for medical help. Four days later, Rappe died of a ruptured abdomen. Based on the word of another actress, Arbuckle was accused of raping Rappe and causing her death. He was charged with murder.

Even before the trial began, the public was quick to condemn Arbuckle. Theater owners refused to show his films, religious leaders called him a symbol of Hollywood's evil, and the film industry banned him from appearing in any more movies. After three trials, Arbuckle was found innocent of the murder charge. The Hollywood ban was lifted, but it was too late. Arbuckle's career was ruined.

Arbuckle lived for eleven more years and did manage to find work as a director, operating under the name William Goodrich. He even appeared in a few more movies, but he never fully recovered from the stress of the scandal. He suffered from depression and alcoholism in the years leading up to his 1933 death.

for example, he would be turned upside down and used as the Human Mop. No matter what happened to him, the young Keaton maintained the same expressionless face, which would become a staple in his later work. Audiences loved the act, and the family made appearances in New York and London, among other cities.

The Keaton family act broke up in 1917, due to the alcoholism of Keaton's father. Buster was offered a job in a Broadway show, and he soon met the famous comic actor Roscoe "Fatty" Arbuckle (1887–1933). Keaton appeared in two 1917 films with Arbuckle, *The Butcher Boy* and *Fatty at Coney Island*. In 1918, Keaton was called to active duty in World War I, serving for about a year with the U.S. Army in France. Upon his return, he appeared in twelve more Arbuckle films.

Bringing order to a crazy world

Keaton's movie appearances throughout the 1920s featured a character memorable for his solemn, impassive face and his status as a calm observer of the sometimes zany events around him. Audiences seemed to appreciate the way that Keaton's persona imposed order on a chaotic world, never reacting to what happened to him, no matter how dangerous or crazy. Working with producer Joseph Schenk, who handled the finances while Keaton took creative control, Keaton both directed and starred in movies that included *One Week* (1920) and *The Playhouse* (1921). In the latter film, he used innovative special effects and a moving camera (most movies cameras operated from a fixed position).

Some of the Keaton's other films made with Schenk included *Our Hospitality* (1923), about a pair of feuding southern families; and *Sherlock, Jr.* (1924), in which a movie projectionist who wants to be a detective falls asleep and enters the movie playing on the screen. In *The Navigator* (1924), filmed aboard an ocean liner, Keaton has various adventures aboard an abandoned ship.

Over the next two years, however, Keaton's movies took dips in either critical acclaim or popularity. One of his personal favorites, *The General* (1926), was a Civil War romance, while *Steamboat Bill, Jr.* (1928) was centered on a Mississippi River boat race. Neither was a commercial success, and finally Keaton's contract was sold to Metro-Goldwyn-Mayer (MGM) Studios. Keaton found that he had no creative control over the films in which he appeared. He soon developed a drinking problem, and his career fell into a slump.

A career in decline

The advent of movies with sound further damaged Keaton's prospects, as it did those of many silent film actors. He made a series of mediocre films with MGM until his contract ended in 1933. The year before that, he had been divorced from his first wife, Natalie Talmadge. Keaton was then briefly married to nurse and playwright Mae Scrivens, but the couple split up in 1935. After appearing in several European films during the 1930s, Keaton was hired by Columbia studios, but his performances were not up to his earlier standard.

After getting his alcoholism under control, Keaton married dancer Eleanor Ross in 1940. For the next decade, he made stage appearances and wrote jokes for several movie studios. His career took an upturn in the 1950s and 1960s, when he appeared in television commercials as well as programs like *The Twilight Zone*. He also returned to films with a cameo appearance in *Sunset Boulevard* (1950) and roles in Chaplin's *Limelight* (1952) as well as such popular movies as *Around the World in Eighty Days* (1956) and *It's a Mad, Mad, Mad, Mad World* (1963).

Near the end of his life, Keaton enjoyed a revival of interest in his early work. A few months before his 1966 death, he received an enthusiastic reception at the Venice Film Festival.

Harold Lloyd

Just as Charlie Chaplin was known for his Little Tramp character and Buster Keaton for his deadpan expression, Harold Lloyd was famous for a persona all his own. He was the hard-working, sometimes nervous "nice guy" in a too-small suit, round glasses, and a straw hat. During his childhood, Lloyd's family moved more than fifteen times as his father drifted from job to job. Lloyd began acting early, whenever local theater groups needed a child actor.

Attending high school in San Diego, California, he excelled at both the intellectual sport of debate and the physical sport of boxing. He also acted in every school play as well as on local theater stages.

Lonesome Luke and beyond

After graduation, Lloyd continued with his stage work, but gradually he became interested in the movies. He moved to Los Angeles in 1913 and soon was hired as an extra (an actor who plays small parts, such as a member of a crowd scene) at Universal Studios. There he met another extra named Hal Roach (1892–1992), who was hoping to become a director. An inheritance allowed Roach to realize his dream, and he opened his own studio in 1914. He hired Lloyd to appear in a series of one-reel comedies, in which Lloyd attracted attention with a character called Lonesome Luke. Clearly modeled after Charlie Chaplin's Tramp in his social outcast status, Luke wore clothes that were too small instead of too big.

American film comedian Harold Lloyd created his own character of the bespectacled, shy, and sincere boy-next-door, anxious to make good but invariably involved with hair-raising schemes. (© Hulton-Deutsch Collection/Corbis. Reproduced by permission.)

Lloyd was lured away from Roach by the Pathe studio by the promise of better pay (fifty dollars a week instead of five dollars a day) and better roles. For a while he continued to play Lonesome Luke in simple films full of slapstick humor. Lloyd's first appearance in what would become his trademark character was in *Over the Fence* (1917). Just as he would in so many movies to come, Lloyd played the average, timid boy-next-door who is neither particularly good-looking nor wealthy but whose determination and quick thinking allow him to conquer adversity (and win the girl, of course). In many of his movies, Lloyd's character would start out with a fault, such as foolishness or laziness, but by the end of the film he would have shown his true courageousness and resourcefulness.

Lloyd developed a reputation for his physical courage and agility by pulling off daring stunts. For example, in perhaps his most acclaimed film, *Safety Last* (1923), he plays a shy store clerk who ends up hanging precariously off the face of a high clock tower. Lloyd continued to perform his own stunts even after losing a thumb and part of a finger when a stunt bomb exploded in his hand. Lloyd showcased his considerable athletic ability by scaling buildings and carrying on complicated chases involving cars and trucks.

Peak of popularity

In 1922, the appearance of *Grandma's Boy* (in which a coward gains courage from what he believes is a magic charm) marked Lloyd's shift to longer films. Between 1924 and 1930, he produced many of his own films while also still working with Roach and Pathe. His most notable movies include *Why Worry* (1923), about a rich young man who overcomes his hypochondria (when someone is unusually anxious about his or her health) to win a girl's love; and *The Freshman* (1925) which features a timid, awkward water boy for a college football team. Somehow, the unlikely hero manages to score the game's winning touchdown, thus winning the acceptance he has craved.

Lloyd's films were remarkably popular and commercially successful, making him one of the richest of the silent-film comedians. In 1923 he married actress Mildred Taylor, and the couple moved into a Hollywood mansion they called Greenacres, where they raised their three children.

The coming of sound movies signaled the end of many silent-film actors' careers. This was often due to the unsuitability of their voices for the new, so-called "talkies." But there also was the fact that audiences began to turn away from the slapstick comedy of the silent-film era toward the greater complexity and depth that spoken dialogue allowed. Lloyd did appear in a few sound films, including *Movie Crazy* (1932) and *Professor Beware* (1938), but neither was particularly popular.

Lloyd retired from acting to focus on producing films for RKO studios, but he returned to the screen a final time for the disastrous *The Sins of Harold Diddlebock* (1945), later released as *Mad Wednesday*, which was a sequel to *The Freshman*. In his final decades, Lloyd was active in community work and in Republican politics. Having invested his early earnings wisely, he enjoyed a large income until end of his life. In the 1960s, he made some films comprising scenes from his famous silent comedies. He died in 1971.

For More Information

Books

Dardis, Thomas. *Keaton: The Man Who Wouldn't Lie Down*. Minneapolis: University of Minnesota Press, 2002.

D'Augustino, Annette M. *Harold Lloyd*. Westport, CT: Greenwood Press, 1994.

Kerr, Walter. *The Silent Clowns*. New York: Knopf, 1975.

Lynn, Kenneth C. *Charlie Chaplin and His Times*. New York: Simon & Schuster, 1997.

MacCann, Richard Dyer. *The Silent Comedians*. Metuchen, NJ: Scarecrow Press, 1993.

McCaffrey, Donald W. *Great Comedians: Chaplin, Lloyd, Keaton, and Langdon*. New York: A.S. Barnes, 1968.

McPherson, Edward. *Keaton: Tempest in a Flat Hat*. New York: Newmarket Press, 2005.

Milton, Joyce. *Tramp: The Life of Charlie Chaplin*. New York: HarperCollins, 1996.

Robinson, David. *Chaplin: His Life and Art*. New York: McGraw-Hill, 1985.

Schroeder, Alan. *Charlie Chaplin: The Beauty of Silence*. Danbary, CT: Franklin Watts, 1997.

Web Sites

"Buster Keaton." *American Masters (PBS)*. Available online at http://www.pbs.org/wnet/americanmasters/database/keaton_b.html. Accessed on June 22, 2005.

Charlie Chaplin. Available online at http://www.charliechaplin.com/article.php3?id_article=22. Accessed on June 22, 2005.

"Charlie Chaplin." *American Masters (PBS)*. Available online at http://www.pbs.org/wnet/americanmasters/database/chaplin_c.html. Accessed on June 22, 2005.

"Charlie Chaplin." *The Time 100: Artists and Entertainers*. Available online at http://www.time.com/time100/artists/profile/chaplin.html. Accessed on June 22, 2005.

"Harold Lloyd." *American Masters (PBS)*. Available online at http://www.pbs.org/wnet/americanmasters/database/lloyd_h.html. Accessed on June 22, 2005.

Calvin Coolidge

Born July 4, 1872 (Plymouth Notch, Vermont)
Died January 5, 1933 (Northampton, Massachusetts)

U.S. president

"The business of America is business."

President Calvin Coolidge presided over the Roaring Twenties, a decade when a thriving U.S. economy was sometimes called Coolidge Prosperity. Thrust into the presidency when **Warren G. Harding** (1865–1923; served 1921–23; see entry) died suddenly, Coolidge soon had to confront several scandals involving members of Harding's administration. His quick, firm response helped to restore the public's faith in the nation's highest office. A man of few words, he was known as "Silent Cal," Coolidge was also a leader of little action. Deeply conservative, he believed that government should stay as far out of business affairs as possible. Although some blame the laissez-faire (hands-off), pro-business policies of Coolidge's presidency for the stock market crash (which occurred after he left office), the majority of U.S. citizens approved of his ideas at the time.

Hard work and thrift

Coolidge's ancestors arrived from Great Britain in the seventeenth century, and one of them served as a soldier in the American Revolution (1775–83). The future president was

Calvin Coolidge's quick, firm response to the scandals involving Warren G. Harding's administration helped to restore the public's faith in the office of the presidency. *(Courtesy of The Library of Congress.)*

born John Calvin Coolidge (he later dropped his first name) in the quiet Vermont village of Plymouth Notch. His father, also named John Calvin Coolidge, worked at various times as a farmer and shopkeeper and held a number of local political offices. From his father, Coolidge learned the values of hard work, honesty, and thrift and the idea of public service as a duty. His mother, Victoria Moor Coolidge, a sensitive woman who appreciated poetry and nature, died when he was twelve; a beloved sister also died in childhood.

Coolidge was a shy boy who would become a reserved, uncommunicative man. He suffered from allergies and did not make friends easily. Coolidge attended his village's one-room school until he was fourteen, when he entered Black River Academy in Ludlow, Vermont. Later he went to Amherst College in Massachusetts, where he studied hard and developed strong debating skills. It took some time for his classmates to get to know him, but eventually they came to appreciate his dry wit. Coolidge was chosen to speak at his 1895 graduation, and he also won first prize in a national essay contest.

Having decided to become a lawyer, Coolidge prepared himself by reading law in the office of two attorneys in Northampton, Massachusetts. Two years later he passed the state's bar examination (a qualifying test for lawyers). He opened his own office in Northampton, where he made a decent living but never became rich. His carefully kept records show, for example, that in the first year he earned five hundred dollars. Never one to spend much money, Coolidge never owned his own house and did not own a car until he was vice president of the United States.

Beginning a career in politics

Coolidge's father had often been involved in politics, and Coolidge seems to have considered this a natural role for himself as well. He was active in the Republican Party in 1896 and 1897, and the next year he was elected as a Northampton city councilman. For the next thirty years Coolidge would rarely be out of political office. From the beginning he took a conservative approach to the issues, but he did support two important reform measures of the period: amendments to the U.S. Constitution that would allow for the direct election of senators and give women the right to vote.

While living a somewhat lonely life in Northampton, Coolidge was renting a room across from the Clarke Institute for the Deaf. By chance he met one of the school's teachers, Grace Anna Goodhue, whose outgoing, sunny personality was in stark contrast to his own. As quoted in Nathan Miller's *New*

World Coming: The 1920s and the Making of Modern America,
Coolidge later remarked that he had hoped that, "after having
made the deaf to hear, Miss Goodhue might perhaps teach the
mute to speak." Although many people found them an unlikely pair, the two were married in 1905. About a year after their
marriage, the couple's first son, John, was born, followed in
1908 by the birth of Calvin Jr.

Despite his reserved, quiet nature, Coolidge was able to
attract the support of a variety of voters, especially those
from the working class. He was elected to the Massachusetts
House of Representatives in 1906 and again the following
year. In 1909 he was elected mayor of Northampton. In this
position he worked to make city government more efficient, to
lower taxes, and to reduce the city's debt; these are some of the
same goals he would later bring to the office of the presidency.
The voters sent Coolidge to the Massachusetts state senate in
1911, where he eventually achieved such a prominent leadership role that he was elected president of the senate. This made
Coolidge the highest-ranking Republican officeholder in
Massachusetts (the state's governor and lieutenant governor
were Democrats).

Receiving national attention

Coolidge continued his upward climb in Massachusetts
politics when, beginning in 1915, he spent three years as lieutenant governor. In 1918 he was elected governor. In this office
he attracted little national attention until 1919, when his
handling of a local crisis brought him widespread praise. In
Boston, the state's largest city, the police force had long complained of low pay, long hours, and poor working conditions.
Having received no response from the city government, they
voted to form a union under the umbrella of the American
Federation of Labor, or AFL (an organization made up of
unions from a variety of industries and professions).

After nineteen Boston police officers who had been union
organizers were suspended from their jobs, the police force
voted to stage a strike. This action caused near-chaos in
Boston, with rioting and violence erupting; three people were
killed, and much property was damaged. Boston's mayor
appealed to Coolidge for help, but at first he was told that

this was a local matter that the governor could not resolve. Eventually Coolidge did send in additional troops to help restore order. Then he informed the striking officers that they would not be allowed to return to their jobs.

In a telegram to AFL president Samuel Gompers (1850–1924), who had protested the governor's action, Coolidge made the famous statement, "There is no right to strike against the public safety by anybody, anywhere, any time." Although union leaders and members criticized this harsh response, almost everybody else in the nation approved of it. Coolidge won universal admiration (even Democratic president Woodrow Wilson [1856–1924; served 1913–21] praised him) and was easily reelected the following fall.

A quiet vice president

As the 1920 Republican Party convention (when party delegates gather to select a nominee for the presidential election) approached, Republicans around the nation had high hopes of winning the presidency. Having been made famous by the Boston police strike, Coolidge was among those discussed as a possible candidate. When the convention began, however, the Republicans nominated Ohio senator Warren G. Harding as its presidential candidate. For the position of vice president, the party leaders favored Senator Irving Lenroot of Wisconsin, but the general delegates rebelled and elected Coolidge. It was felt that this serious, unsmiling New Englander would bring balance to a ticket headed by an outgoing, friendly native of the Midwest.

The 1920 election marked a major shift in mood and focus in the United States. Following the end of World War I (1914–18), a particularly bloody and devastating conflict that seemed to shake the foundations of society, people were ready for a change. The reforming spirit of the Progressive Era (which lasted roughly from 1900 to 1914) was replaced with a strong desire both to stay out of other nations' troubles and to maintain the status quo (keep things as they are).

In this kind of atmosphere, the traditional conservatism of the Republican Party appealed to voters, and the Democrats were unable to provide an attractive alternative. The Democratic candidate, Ohio governor James M. Cox (1870–1957), was a wealthy newspaper publisher who lacked any strong ideas about what

This is an artist's rendition of the swearing-in of Calvin Coolidge at his parents' home in Vermont. The oath is being administered by Coolidge's father at 2:47 AM following the news of Warren Harding's death on August 2, 1923. *(AP/Wide World Photos. Reproduced by permission.)*

direction the United States should take. A few months before the election, Harding promised a "return to normalcy," which he later defined (as quoted in Geoffrey Perret's book *America in the Twenties*) as "a regular steady order of things.... normal procedure, the natural way, without excess." The people of the United States demonstrated their faith in Harding's philosophy, electing him by a wide margin.

As vice president, Coolidge was a quiet presence in Harding's administration. He presided over the U.S. Senate, the traditional role of the vice president, and made a few speeches. He was not part of the inner circle of a president who had surrounded himself with personal friends (which would later be to his advantage). As Harding's presidency continued, rumors of corruption at the highest levels of government began to circulate. It seems likely that Harding was aware of some wrongdoing by several members of his administration, although his own honesty has never been questioned. In any case, while touring the West in the summer of 1923, Harding died suddenly of an apparent heart attack.

Suddenly president

Coolidge was visiting his father in Vermont when, on August 2, he was awakened in the middle of the night with the news of the president's death. At 2:47 AM, Coolidge's father, who was a justice of the peace (a person authorized to perform certain legal formalities), gave him the oath of office (the official, verbal promise a president makes to fulfill the duties of his office). The oath was administered again later at an official ceremony in Washington, D.C.

Realizing that the U.S. public was shaken by the sudden death of their president, Coolidge immediately vowed to continue the policies that Harding had put into place. He also planned to keep most of Harding's appointed officials, especially such important and competent men as Treasury Secretary Andrew Mellon (1855–1937) and Commerce Secretary (and future president) **Herbert Hoover** (1874–1964; see entry). Soon after becoming president, however, Coolidge was faced with a crisis.

The scandals that had been lurking beneath the surface during the last months of Harding's presidency finally emerged. The worst of these, known as the Teapot Dome scandal because it involved oil reserves near Teapot Dome, Wyoming, was investigated during congressional hearings held in late 1923 and early 1924. It was revealed that Secretary of the Interior Albert B. Fall (1861–1944) had leased drilling rights on several government oil reserves in the West to private oil companies in exchange for money. These pieces of oil-rich land were supposed to be used only by the U.S. military, but Fall had arranged for their transfer from the Department of the Navy to the Interior Department.

Fall was convicted of bribery and was sent to prison. Another close adviser of Harding, Harry Daugherty (1860–1941), also had to leave the administration under a cloud of suspicion. Coolidge, meanwhile, had successfully distanced himself from the corruption. By moving quickly to ensure that the scandals were investigated and the wrongdoers punished, he had helped to restore U.S. citizens' faith in the office of the president. His low-key manner and reputation for honesty also did much to calm the public.

Just as he had promised, Coolidge continued with the pro-business policies that Harding had established. He backed Mellon's proposals to cut taxes, reduce the national debt, and keep tariffs (taxes on imports, which were meant to benefit U.S. companies) high. He also supported the Immigration Act of 1924, which put restrictions on the number of newcomers from other nations who could move to the United States.

Despite his reputation for being uncommunicative, Coolidge was actually quite a visible leader. He was always willing to pose for photographs, sometimes dressed in silly costumes, and he spoke to the U.S. people often through the new medium of radio. In fact, he was the first U.S. president to use radio to express his ideas and policies. Coolidge also held two press conferences a week, although he chose ahead of time the questions he would answer.

Winning a second term

As the 1924 election approached, Coolidge looked forward to a chance to become president by winning votes, rather than by circumstance. By this time, many of the people of the United States identified Coolidge with the traditional values of common sense and thrift. His honesty and integrity made him a comforting presence in a world that seemed to be changing rapidly. On top of all this, the economy was booming. It seemed that the laissez-faire approach to government that Coolidge supported was working, and it was hard for Democratic nominee John Davis (1873–1955) and Progressive Party candidate Robert La Follette (1855–1925) to prove otherwise.

Coolidge did not put a lot of effort into campaigning, partly because he did not need to and partly because, in the summer of 1924, he was grieving the loss of his youngest son. Sixteen-year-old Calvin Jr. had died from blood poisoning that resulted from a blister he received while playing tennis on the

Charles Dawes: A Distinguished Public Servant

Charles Dawes had a successful career as a businessman and public servant. His involvement in federal government culminated with the vice presidency under Calvin Coolidge. When Coolidge became president after the 1924 election, Dawes entered the vice president's seat with his usual dynamic energy, turning what had usually been a quiet role into one of strong advocacy.

The son of a Civil War hero and one-term member of Congress, Dawes was born in 1865 in Marietta, Ohio. He earned a law degree in 1886 from the Cincinnati Law School and began practicing law the next year in Lincoln, Nebraska. Dawes published an influential book on U.S. banking practices in 1894, which helped establish his reputation as a financial theorist.

In 1893 Dawes moved to Chicago, Illinois, and met William McKinley, whom he supported in the 1896 presidential election. President McKinley rewarded Dawes for his support by appointing him comptroller of the currency. This position placed Dawes in charge of the system for producing money. Dawes soon resigned the post to run for the Illinois senate. Upon his defeat, he turned his attention to business and became a prominent figure over the next decade. He served as president of a new and successful bank, was involved with many Chicago-area charities and civic organizations, and also wrote essays and lectured.

During the 1910s and 1920s, Dawes served successfully in several government posts. After being appointed to lead the new Bureau of the Budget in 1921, Dawes helped to reduce federal government spending by more than one-third. In 1923 he played an important role in the Allied Reparation Commission, established to deal with Germany's economic collapse following its defeat in World War I. Dawes earned the 1925 Nobel Peace Prize for his work on what was called the "Dawes plan," a five-year program to help Germany stabilize its economy and repay its debts.

Dawes was chosen as the Republican vice presidential nominee to run alongside Calvin Coolidge in his 1924 bid for reelection. During the campaign Coolidge, whose teenaged son had recently died, played a low-key role while Dawes made many speeches and appearances. He railed against the Ku Klux Klan and accused the Progressive Party's candidate, Robert M. LaFollette, of being a political radical.

As vice president, Dawes took his role as head of the U.S. Senate more seriously than had many of his predecessors. He actively urged action on a number of proposed laws and measures, including the Kellogg-Briand Pact, banking reform, and relief for farmers.

Dawes left the vice presidency in January 1929. He went on to serve as ambassador to Great Britain (1939–32) and then as head of the Reconstruction Finance Corporation (1932), which was established to provide relief to the banking industry following the October 1929 stock market crash and the onset of the Great Depression. Dawes served only a few months in that position before returning to his banking job in Chicago. He remained active in business affairs and charity work until his death in 1951.

White House court. Despite Coolidge's low-key approach, the campaign that had as its slogan "Keep Cool with Coolidge" was successful. The election results showed that Coolidge had won an impressive 54 percent of the popular vote, while Davis had won 29 percent and La Follette 17 percent.

In a 1925 speech to newspaper publishers, Coolidge made one of his most famous statements, declaring that "the business of America is business." He remained true to this belief. During Coolidge's second term, his cabinet continued to be dominated by conservative Republican businessmen who believed that the government did best by doing little. That meant not restricting companies by making them follow a lot of regulations. It also meant reducing income taxes, in order to give ordinary consumers more money to spend while also allowing the wealthy to make more investments. This economic strategy, known as "trickle-down economics" because the benefits are supposed to seep down through all levels of society, would become popular again in the 1980s during the administration of President Ronald Reagan (1911–2004; served 1981–89). In fact, Reagan so admired Coolidge that he replaced a White House portrait of President Harry Truman (1884–1972; served 1945–53) with one of "Silent Cal."

Domestic and foreign affairs

Despite Coolidge's general opposition to government interference in business affairs, his presidency saw the passage of some laws that imposed restrictions on two new and important industries: radio broadcasting and aviation. With the farming sector, however, Coolidge took a more detached approach. U.S. farmers had experienced a major decrease in demand for their products after World War I. Their profits had dropped drastically, and they were among those who did not share in the general prosperity of the 1920s (the coal-mining and textile industries were also suffering during this decade). Twice Coolidge vetoed (refused to sign) the McNary-Haugen Bill, which would have provided farmers with federal assistance.

Coolidge left much of the responsibility for foreign affairs to Secretary of State Charles Evans Hughes (1862–1948) and Hughes's successor, Frank Kellogg (1856–1937). He did not support U.S. involvement in the League of Nations (an organization set up after World War I to foster cooperation between countries). He opposed the effort to cancel the war debts of several European nations, which had borrowed money from the United States to pay for the conflict but were having trouble paying it back.

Coolidge's somewhat vague wish to encourage peace in the world led him to sponsor the 1927 Geneva Naval Conference, which was supposed to result in agreements to reduce the size of participating nations' naval forces. The conference was unsuccessful, though, due to several countries' inability to agree on terms. The next year, Coolidge supported the signing of the Kellogg-Briand Pact, through which fifteen countries (later joined by a number of others) renounced war as a means of resolving conflicts. Because the agreement included no means of enforcement, however, it was virtually meaning-less. The outbreak of World War II in the late 1930s would prove just how empty the promise had been.

Another foreign-affairs accomplishment of Coolidge's presidency was the restoration of good relations with Mexico after a dispute involving oil lands. Coolidge appointed a new ambassador, Dwight Morrow (1873–1931), who helped to smooth over the conflict. In a move that was criticized by those who resented U.S. interference in other countries' affairs, Coolidge sent five hundred Marines to Nicaragua to restore order after a revolution replaced that country's government with a new, more conservative administration.

As the election of 1928 approached, it seemed likely that Coolidge's popularity would ensure his reelection. While on vacation in the Black Hills of South Dakota, however, Coolidge surprised his supporters by announcing that he would not run for president. Some believed that Coolidge's depression over the death of his son, added to the physical exhaustion from which both he and his wife were suffering, had led to this decision. It has also been suggested that Coolidge foresaw the economic crisis that would soon occur. The out-of-control speculation and lack of regulation of the banking and credit industries that occurred during Coolidge's administration would be cited as major factors in the October 1929 stock market crash.

In any case, Coolidge left his successor, Herbert Hoover, to face the disaster (and to take most of the blame). After leaving office Coolidge returned to Northampton, where he spent much of his time writing newspaper and magazine articles. He died of heart disease on January 5, 1933.

For More Information

Books

Abels, Jules. *In the Time of Silent Cal.* New York: Putnam, 1989.

Ferrell, Robert H. *The Presidency of Calvin Coolidge.* Lawrence: University Press of Kansas, 1998.

Haynes, John Earl. *Calvin Coolidge and the Coolidge Era: Essays on the History of the 1920s.* Washington, DC: Library of Congress, 1998.

Kent, Zachary. *Calvin Coolidge: Thirtieth President of the United States.* Chicago, IL: Children's Press, 1988.

McCoy, Donald R. *Calvin Coolidge: The Quiet President.* Lawrence: University Press of Kansas, 1988.

Sobel, Robert. *Coolidge: An American Enigma.* Washington, DC: Regnery, 1998.

Stevens, Rita. *Calvin Coolidge: 30th President of the United States.* Ada, OK: Garrett Education Corp., 1990.

Webb, Kenneth. *From Plymouth Notch to President: The Farm Boyhood of Calvin Coolidge.* Taftsville, VT: Countryman Press, 1978.

Web Sites

"Calvin Coolidge: 30th President of the United States." *The Calvin Coolidge Memorial Foundation.* Available online at http://www.calvin-coolidge. org/index.html. Accessed on June 22, 2005.

"Calvin Coolidge." *The White House.* Available online at http://www. whitehouse.gov/history/presidents/cc30.html. Accessed on June 22, 2005.

Clarence Darrow

Born April 18, 1857 (Kinsman, Ohio)
Died March 13, 1938 (Chicago, Illinois)

Lawyer

"Your Honor stands between the past and the future. You may hang these boys; you may hang them by the neck until they are dead. But in doing it you will turn your face toward the past."

Clarence Darrow was one of the most famous lawyers in U.S. history. Always a strong defender of the underdog and a winner of seemingly lost causes, Darrow played a leading role in some of the most extraordinary courtroom dramas of the 1920s. A lifelong opponent of capital punishment, he used testimony based on the new, modern science of psychology in a successful attempt to save murderers Nathan Leopold (1904–1971) and Richard Loeb (1905–1936) from execution. In the famous court battle known as the Monkey Trial, which involved the clash of religious and scientific views of the origin of humanity, Darrow defended the right of educator John Scopes (1900–1970) to teach his students about the theory of evolution.

A young Ohio lawyer

Born in the northeastern Ohio town of Kinsman in April 1857, Darrow was the son of Amirus and Emily Darrow. His father had once been a Unitarian minister but after losing his religious faith became a carpenter and furniture maker. The elder Darrow was a book-loving agnostic (someone who doubts but does not

Clarence Darrow is one of the most famous lawyers in U.S. history and played a leading role in some of the most extraordinary cases of the 1920s. *(AP/Wide World Photos. Reproduced by permission.)*

deny the existence of God), and his wife was a supporter of women's rights. They passed their liberal social views and concern for the less privileged members of society to their son.

As a boy, Darrow enjoyed participating in outdoor activities such as fishing, sledding, and baseball with his seven brothers and sisters. He also developed a fear of death that seems to have grown out of his discomfort with his father making coffins as a carpenter. Some historians have even linked Darrow's hatred for the death penalty to this part of his past. The death of his mother when he was fourteen also cast a shadow over his youth.

Darrow was never an enthusiastic student, even though he loved to read books. After spending a year at Allegheny College in Pennsylvania, he returned to Kinsman and took a job as a teacher. He enjoyed the experience of addressing a class, but soon he decided to become an attorney. Darrow attended the University of Michigan law school for a year, and then, like many law students of the period, completed his education by working in a law office.

In 1878, when Darrow was twenty-one, he passed Ohio's bar examination (a test of qualifications for practicing law). For the next ten years he worked as an attorney in the small towns of Kinsman, Andover, and Ashtabula, Ohio. He married a quiet, reserved young woman named Jessie Ohl in 1880 (the couple would divorce in 1897, and six years later Darrow would begin a happy thirty-five-year marriage to Ruby Hamerstrom). In 1887 Darrow moved his family, which now included his only child Paul, to Chicago, Illinois, a lively, bustling city that seemed to hold exciting possibilities for a sharp young lawyer. Chicago would be Darrow's much-beloved home for the rest of his life.

Gaining fame as a labor lawyer

Darrow made many new contacts in Chicago, where he took part in Democratic Party politics and established a close friendship with John Peter Altgeld (1847–1902), a millionaire and judge who shared Darrow's interest in social reform. Following Altgeld's election as governor of Illinois in 1892, Darrow too became a prominent figure. In 1889 he was appointed the head of Chicago's legal department, but he left this job three years later to become an attorney for the Chicago and Northwestern Railway Company.

Darrow's career as a corporate (company) lawyer was short-lived. By the middle of the 1890s, he was making a name for himself in labor law. As U.S. industry had expanded in the late nineteenth and early twentieth centuries, the labor movement too had evolved as a way for workers to protect their interests. In addition to caring about such matters as fair wages and safe working conditions, Darrow believed that workers should be allowed to form unions in order to give themselves bargaining power in disagreements with owners and managers. In the early decades of the twentieth century, tensions between management and unions often resulted in conflict and even violence.

In 1894 Darrow agreed to represent labor leader Eugene V. Debs (1855–1926), a well-known Socialist (someone who believes in a political and economic system in which the means of production, distribution, and exchange are owned by the community as a whole, rather than by individuals) and president of the American Railway Union. With other union leaders, Debs had organized a massive railroad strike that made a significant impact on the nation. Lower courts had ruled that Debs and the others had conspired to obstruct trade between states and also violated a judge's order to end the strike.

Darrow took the case to the U.S. Supreme Court, but the earlier rulings were upheld, and Debs spent six months in jail. Despite this loss, Darrow gained fame as a defender of labor. He worked on labor cases for the next seventeen years, always striving to bring attention to the problems of ordinary workers. For example, while serving as a defense counsel during arbitration (a way to resolve a dispute outside the court system) of a coal miners' strike, Darrow cast light on the dangers of this kind of work and the industry's reliance on underage laborers.

Other famous cases

Another of Darrow's most famous labor cases involved his defense of William D. "Big Bill" Haywood (1869–1928), the head of the newly formed International Workers of the World (IWW) Union. Former Idaho governor Frank Steunenberg (1861–1905), who was well known for his anti-union stance, was killed when a bomb exploded outside his home. Haywood and two other union officials were charged with the murder. Despite a defense effort that was not up to the standard of most of Darrow's performances, the jury found the defendants not guilty. During the trial, Darrow had exposed the many efforts of mining company managers and local government leaders to harass union members.

Darrow tried his last labor law case in 1911, when he agreed to defend brothers Joseph and James McNamara, who were socialists and union activists. They had been charged with the October 1910 bombing of the building that housed the *Los Angeles Times,* whose publisher, Otis Chandler, was known to be antiunion. The blast killed twenty-one people and injured forty. A surprising turn of events came in the middle of the trial, when the brothers changed their plea from not guilty to guilty. Darrow had advised his clients to plead guilty so that he could work on helping them avoid the death penalty (a guilty plea meant that their fate would be decided by a judge, not a jury). This plan worked, but labor leaders were angry with Darrow. They felt he had tarnished the image of the labor movement by not winning a not guilty judgment for the McNamaras.

This was quickly followed by two charges that Darrow had tried to bribe members of the jury during the McNamara trial. Darrow was tried and found not guilty, but the publicity had damaged his reputation. He returned to Chicago to rebuild his career, a difficult task for a man already in his fifties. During the next decade, however, Darrow would make a remarkable recovery from this low point.

As World War I (1914–18; the United States entered the war in 1917) broke out in Europe, Darrow called for the United States to get involved. This was not a popular stance at first, but the United States did eventually enter the conflict on the side of the Allies (Great Britain, France, and Italy) against Germany. Before the war was over, however, Darrow had changed his mind. He disapproved of the American public's suspicion and intolerance of foreign-born people and their supposedly radical ideas that had been generated by the war, which resulted in the passage of several laws designed to keep people from expressing unpopular views. Darrow defended several clients charged with breaking these laws.

Gaining mercy for killers

Darrow gradually began taking more criminal cases, and this eventually became his specialty. Over the course of his career, he would defend more than fifty people accused of first-degree murder, and only one of these clients—his first, Robert Prendergast, whom Darrow represented only at the appeal stage—would receive the death penalty. Many of the trials took place in Chicago, but several would make front-page

Capital Punishment: Always Controversial

Clarence Darrow was one of the most eloquent opponents of capital punishment, the lawful use of death as a penalty for certain crimes. Although it has existed throughout the United States' history, this ultimate form of punishment has always been controversial.

The first European settlers to the American colonies brought with them the tradition of capital punishment. The earliest recorded execution took place in 1608 in Virginia's Jamestown colony. After gaining independence in the American Revolution (1773–89), the U.S. Constitution, under the Eighth Amendment, and the constitutions of nine of the eleven former colonies prohibited "cruel and unusual punishment," but permitted death as a penalty for crimes specified by law. This unwittingly set the stage for a debate that has continued into the twenty-first century.

What exactly did the nation's founders consider to be cruel and unusual punishment? Some maintain that the phrase prohibits torture and particularly brutal forms of execution, such as burning at the stake. Others believe the phrase includes any form of capital punishment. Critics often refer to the Eighth Amendment to support their arguments against the death penalty. Supporters claim that capital punishment deters crime, although studies are inconclusive.

Debate over capital punishment has existed since the nation's founding, but it has rarely affected the executions themselves. The number of people executed for a capital crime has grown over time, with one hundred and sixty recorded during the eighteenth century, almost fourteen hundred in the nineteenth century, and more than four thousand from 1930 to 2004. In 2002 more than three thousand prisoners awaited execution on death row.

In the 1960s opposition to the death penalty did interrupt executions while the issue was considered by the Supreme Court. In *Furman v. Georgia* (1972), the court ruled that some state capital punishment laws were applied randomly and thus were unconstitutional. The court did not, however, determine the death penalty to be a cruel and unusual punishment, and the ruling did little to end the practice. States with questionable laws quickly changed them to comply with the court's ruling.

In addition to the cruel and unusual argument, capital punishment critics charge that the practice is racially biased. Figures from the U.S. Department of Justice show that in 1997, 42 percent of those on death row were African American, even though less than 15 percent of the total U.S. population was African American. Figures also showed that between 1977 and 1995, more than 80 percent of murder victims of those sentenced to death were white, while those who killed African Americans received lesser sentences. The Supreme Court, however, ruled in *McKleskey v. Kemp* (1987) that these inequalities were only unconstitutional if they resulted from intentional discrimination, which is difficult to prove.

By the end of the twentieth century, thirty-eight U.S. states, as well as the federal government, allowed capital punishment. By the mid-1990s, polls showed that more than 70 percent of U.S. citizens supported capital punishment. As the debate continued, several states in the early twenty-first century instituted stays of executions after some death row inmates were found to be not guilty.

Nathan Leopold (left), Clarence Darrow (center), and Richard Loeb (right) listen as they are sentenced to life in prison for the murder of Bobby Franks. In an emotional and lengthy closing statement, Darrow asked the judge to spare the lives of his clients. (© Bettmann/Corbis. Reproduced by permission.)

headlines across the nation. These so-called "Crimes of the Century" would add even more excitement to a decade that seemed to thrive on sensationalism and controversy.

In 1924 Darrow was hired to defend Nathan Leopold and Richard Loeb, teenagers from wealthy Chicago families who had confessed to murdering a fourteen-year-old acquaintance. The young men had killed Bobby Franks for no other reason than to plan and execute the perfect crime, and they showed no remorse for what they had done. News of the murderers' cold-blooded approach to killing caused much public outrage, and many people believed that the boys' rich families were trying to buy their freedom.

Realizing that his only hope was to save his clients from execution, Darrow directed them to plead guilty. During the trial, he introduced an array of experts to establish that Leopold and Loeb were psychologically unstable and had never developed a sense of right and wrong. Darrow told the judge that the crime had been, as quoted in Nathan Miller's *New World Coming: The 1920s and the Making of Modern America*, "the act of immature and diseased brains." This approach to criminal defense is now common, but in the 1920s, the field of psychology was in its infancy and Darrow's technique was unusual.

In an emotional and lengthy closing statement, Darrow asked the judge to spare the lives of Leopold and Loeb. He pointed out that his clients' wealth was actually a disadvantage, because it made people less sympathetic to them. Finally, he emphasized that capital punishment was a brutal, outdated practice that would someday be condemned. "Your Honor stands between the past and the future," Darrow declared. "You may hang these boys; you may hang them by the neck until they are dead. But in doing it you will turn your face toward the past." The judge sentenced the young men to life in prison, not execution, giving Darrow another victory over capital punishment.

The Scopes Trial

About a year after the Leopold and Loeb case, Darrow was involved in one of the most famous trials in U.S. history. In early 1925 the state of Tennessee passed a law banning the teaching of the scientific theory of evolution, or any other theory that contradicted the biblical version of humanity's origin, in the public schools. A number of similar laws were being passed in other states, highlighting the struggle between traditional values and modern beliefs that was taking place in the 1920s.

Although many welcomed the technological and scientific advances that the twentieth century had brought, others feared that religious faith was threatened by scientists like Charles Darwin (1809–1882), whose theory of evolution traced the changes in human beings, animals, and plants over millions of years. Fundamentalists (those who believe that the stories told in the Bible are literally true) waged a fierce struggle against what they viewed as a coldhearted, immoral approach to humanity's origin.

A showdown between Bryan and Darrow

Soon after the passage of the Tennessee law, the American Civil Liberties Union (ACLU) offered to defend any teacher who was willing to test its constitutionality, for they believed that such a ban violated the right of freedom of speech. A group of citizens in Dayton, Tennessee, who disapproved of the ban but also hoped to bring some fame and business to their small town, persuaded a high school teacher named John Scopes to purposely break the law. In April Scopes taught his students a lesson on evolution. He was arrested, and his trial was set for July.

Almost immediately, **William Jennings Bryan** (1860–1925; see entry), a Nebraska politician, former presidential candidate, and ardent fundamentalist, agreed to join the prosecution. When he heard of Bryan's involvement, Darrow (who had sided with Bryan on many political issues and supported his presidential bids) volunteered to head the defense team. As the trial date approached, Dayton was overtaken by a circus-like atmosphere, as a host of outsiders—from reporters to street-corner preachers to souvenir sellers—invaded the town.

Bryan made a splashy arrival, stepping down from his train to an adoring crowd. He began to make appearances and speeches around town, proclaiming his willingness to stand up for religion against science. Arriving two days after Bryan, Darrow spoke at a dinner gathering where, in an attempt to stir up sympathy for his side of the issue, he recalled his own small-town roots. Most of the townspeople, however, were on Bryan's side.

An emotional trial

Closely followed by people across the nation, the trial proved to be an emotional confrontation between tradition and modernity. Knowing that Scopes' violation of the law could not be disputed, Darrow planned to show that the law itself was unconstitutional. While Bryan called witnesses simply to prove that Scopes had taught evolution, such as students from his class, Darrow's witnesses included scientists with religious beliefs, who would show that there need be no conflict between religious faith and scientific truths. The judge, however, ruled this testimony invalid, because it was unrelated to the central issue of whether Scopes had violated the law.

Frustrated and desperate, Darrow made a bold move. He called Bryan himself to the witness stand as an expert witness on the Bible. Knowing Darrow's reputation for ruthless cross-examinations (questioning of prosecution witnesses), the other prosecutors urged Bryan not to testify. Bryan, however, readily accepted the challenge. At first he held up fairly well under Darrow's questioning, but by the end of the hour-and-a-half session Darrow was in control. He grilled Bryan relentlessly about his religious beliefs, asking him, for example, if he truly believed that Jonah could have survived for three days inside the stomach of a whale. (This was a popular story in the Bible.)

Bryan ended up looking confused and foolish. The trial ended when Darrow asked the jury to find his client guilty, so that he could take the case to a higher court. The defense rested without making a final statement, which meant that Bryan was denied a chance to summarize the prosecution's position. Scopes was found guilty and fined one hundred dollars. (The sentence was later overturned, and no further attempt was made to enforce Tennessee's law. A 1968 ruling by the U.S. Supreme Court made all such bans unconstitutional.)

To most observers, it appeared that despite the outcome of the trial, Darrow had won a moral victory, delivering a major blow to the fundamentalist movement while upholding freedom of speech. Five days after the trial ended, Bryan died in his sleep, and many suggested that the trial and especially Darrow's questioning had taken a fatal toll on his health.

A quiet life

In 1929 Darrow retired from his law practice. Three years later, however, he traveled to Hawaii to represent Lieutenant Thomas Massie, a U.S. Navy officer who, along with several other defendants, was charged with murder. A Hawaiian man who had been accused of raping Massie's wife had been kidnapped and killed. The defendants admitted to the crime and were found guilty, but the charge was reduced from murder to manslaughter. They served only one hour of a ten-year sentence.

Darrow lived quietly for the rest of his life. He was in demand for lectures and debates, however, and in these forums as well as in a number of publications he continued to express his liberal views, which included a defense of agnosticism, opposition to capital punishment, and calls for reforms to the court and prison systems. Darrow died of heart disease when he was eighty years old. At his request, his body was cremated and his ashes sprinkled over a pond in a Chicago park.

For More Information

Books

Driemen, John E. *Clarence Darrow*. New York: Chelsea House, 1992.

Tierney, Kevin. *Darrow: A Biography*. New York: Thomas Y. Crowell, 1979.

Weinberg, Arthur, and Lila Weinberg. *Clarence Darrow: A Sentimental Rebel*. New York: Putnam, 1980.

Web Sites

"Clarence Darrow (1857–1938)." *Eastland Memorial Society*. Available online at http://www.inficad.com/~ksup/darrow.html. Accessed on June 22, 2005.

Linder, O. Douglas. "Who Is Clarence Darrow?" Available online at http://www.law.umkc.edu/faculty/projects/ftrials/DARESY.HTM. Accessed on June 22, 2005.

Jack Dempsey

Born June 24, 1895 (Manassa, Colorado)
Died May 31, 1983 (New York City, New York)

Boxer and businessman

Jack Dempsey was one of the first great sports heroes and a popular figure of the Roaring Twenties, which has been called the Golden Age of Sports. He joined the ranks of other leading athletes, such as baseball's **George Herman "Babe" Ruth** (1895–1948; see entry), football's Red Grange (1903–1991) and golf's Bobby Jones (1902–1971), who were admired and even worshipped by the public. Between 1919 and 1926 Dempsey reigned as the heavyweight boxing champion of the world, and for those years he seemed to embody the 1920s passion for success in all kinds of human endeavors. Even in defeat, Dempsey captured the imagination and love of the U.S. people, who would long remember his ferocious fighting style and unbeatable spirit.

"Going for a quick knockout was just common sense. I had a little motto about getting rid of my opponents. 'The sooner the safer.'"

A tough young brawler

William Harrison Dempsey, called Harry by his family, was one of eleven children born to Hyrum and Mary Dempsey. With their children in tow, the couple moved between Colorado and Utah, an area that, at the turn of the century, was still part of the wild western frontier. They made an

During the 1920s boxer Jack Dempsey captured the imagination and love of the U.S. people, who would long remember his ferocious fighting style and unbeatable spirit. *(Courtesy of The Library of Congress.)*

uncertain living through farming, ranching, and restaurant work and sometimes had to accept handouts to survive.

Dempsey left school after the eighth grade and started working, holding such jobs as shoe shiner, pig feeder, and field worker. At sixteen he went to work in the region's copper mines. Around the same time, his brother Bernie began a brief career as a boxer, calling himself "Jack Dempsey" in honor of an Irish middleweight champion with that name (who had died, coincidentally, the year of Harry's birth). The younger brother followed Bernie's example and especially his training methods, which included racing against horses to develop speed, chewing gum for extra jaw strength, and soaking his face in beef brine (broth saturated with salt) to darken and toughen it and thus make him appear fiercer.

Dempsey started fighting too, calling himself "Kid Blackie" at first. He went from saloon to saloon, challenging anyone to fight who would take him on, and usually winning. Dempsey also took to hopping freight trains and living like a hobo (the popular name for homeless, jobless men), earning anywhere from two to ten dollars per fight. He first used the name Jack Dempsey in a 1914 bout in which, substituting for his brother, he beat George Copelin in Cripple Creek, Colorado. Dempsey continued to fight his way across Colorado, Utah, and Nevada, earning a local reputation for his skill in the ring.

At the same time, Dempsey trained intensely, running six miles a day and practicing punches while inside a small cage to develop the low, crouching stance that would always mark his style. After a series of knockouts (victories achieved by knocking one's opponent unconscious) of several well-known western fighters, Dempsey traveled to New York City with his new manager, Jack Price. They visited sportswriters to publicize Dempsey's ability but generated little interest; the famous journalist Damon Runyon (c. 1884–1946), however, gave Dempsey the nickname the Manassa Mauler after seeing the young boxer beat several New York opponents.

Fighting his way toward the top

Soon Dempsey returned to the West. For a time it seemed that his boxing career might be over. On a whim, he married an older woman named Maxine Cates, who worked in a Seattle saloon. She was not with him, however, when he moved to Salt Lake City, Utah, where he washed dishes, picked fruit, dug ditches, and worked in a coal mine. Then one day a telegram arrived from John Leo McKernan, known as Doc Kearns, a California boxing manager and promoter who had seen Dempsey fight and believed he had potential.

Under Kearns's direction, Dempsey began working hard to gain speed and power in the ring. After six months of intense training, he started fighting again. His victories over such well-known boxers as "Gunboat" Smith and Carl Morris drew both crowds and praise, and he continued to take on better and better fighters, building an impressive knockout rate of 60 percent. At this point, Dempsey's goal was to challenge the reigning heavyweight champion, Jess Willard (1881–1968). A towering fighter known as the "Pottawatomie Giant," Willard had held the title since 1915, when he had beaten the great Jack Johnson (1878–1946), the first African American heavyweight champion.

Dempsey still had to prove that he was worthy of meeting Willard in the ring. He did that when, in July 1918, he managed to knock out Fred Fulton (ranked second behind Willard) within the first eighteen seconds of the first round of the fight. Kearns now began an intensive campaign to portray Dempsey as a savage warrior with an aggressive style that featured fast punches and relentless stalking of his opponent. Describing his approach to fighting, Dempsey later recalled, as quoted in Nathan Miller's *New World Coming: The 1920s and the Making of Modern America*, "Going for a quick knockout was just common sense. I had a little motto about getting rid of my opponents. 'The sooner the safer.'"

Heavyweight champion of the world

As the 1920s began, the image of boxing was undergoing a rapid transformation. In the late eighteenth and early nineteenth centuries, most people had considered this a violent, low-class sport, and in some places it was even against the law. But after World War I (1914–18) many of the laws banning boxing were overturned, and new commissions established rules to govern the sport and prevent criminals from influencing it. Boxing gained respectability and became one of the most popular events for spectators from all levels of society. It was also becoming a profitable business, as men like Kearns and George "Tex" Rickard (1871–1929), another boxing promoter who would soon become part of Dempsey's life, fully realized.

Dempsey had now earned the right to challenge Willard for the heavyweight title. The championship match was set for July 4, 1919, in Toledo, Ohio. There were twenty thousand fans in attendance as the grim-faced, ever-crouching, quick-punching Dempsey battered Willard to the floor seven times in the first round. By the end of the third round, Willard had a broken jaw, cuts above both eyes, and six broken teeth. He was finished. Meanwhile, as described by historian Geoffrey Perret in *America in the Twenties,* "Dempsey, who was brown and hard, as if carved from mahogany, sat slumped in his corner between rounds, scowling at the canvas between his feet, his face unshaven, his forehead furrowed. He was all muscle and darkness."

At twenty-four, Dempsey was the new heavyweight champion of the world. Eager to take advantage of the young boxer's sudden fame, Kearns signed him to a fifteen-thousand-dollar-per-week contract to make appearances on the vaudeville circuit (a popular form of live stage entertainment that combined music and comedy acts). Dempsey's prospects became somewhat clouded in the early 1920s, however, when he was indicted (formally accused, based on charges made by Maxine Cates, whom Dempsey had divorced a year earlier) for dodging the draft during World War I. Although Dempsey was eventually found not guilty, the public reacted negatively to the idea that the boxer had pursued his own career while other young men had been fighting and dying in Europe.

Defending the title

Dempsey's promoters (who now included both Kearns and Rickard) made the most of his draft-dodger reputation for his July 1921 match with Georges Carpentier (1894–1975). The French fighter had a heroic record of service during World War I, and the fight was staged as a contest between good (represented by Carpentier) and evil (embodied by Dempsey). In an unusual reversal of the usual situation, U.S. citizens cheered for a foreigner to win and yelled "Slacker!" when Dempsey appeared. By the end of the fight, however, he had regained their respect with a knockout victory over Carpentier.

Dempsey's next major fight was against Argentina's Luis Firpo (1896–1960), who was known as the "Wild Bull of the Pampas" (pampas are large, treeless plains in South America). The match was held at the Polo Grounds in New York City and attracted a crowd of eighty thousand that included such celebrities as Babe Ruth, who was then at the height of his career with the New York Yankees. In a bout that lasted less than four minutes, Dempsey knocked Firpo down seven times in the first round. Firpo fought back ferociously, even knocking Dempsey

Heavyweight champion Jack Dempsey stands over challenger Luis Firpo down in the ring during the second round of their title bout at the Polo Grounds in New York City on September 14, 1923. Dempsey went on to win the match. *(AP/Wide World Photos. Reproduced by permission.)*

out of the ring at one point. Having fallen onto the press table, Dempsey was pushed back into the ring by two sportswriters. He went on to win the match in a second-round knockout.

The Dempsey-Firpo fight drew a record one-million-dollar gate (amount of ticket sales), demonstrating the huge popularity of both Dempsey and the sport of boxing. By now Dempsey had earned more than one million dollars in fight prizes (his career total would be three and a half million). He was a major celebrity, greeted by adoring fans at every public appearance. Sportswriters chronicled his every move, and newspapers found that their circulation went up before and after every Dempsey fight.

For much of the early 1920s, Dempsey took a kind of vacation from the ring. He moved to Hollywood and even married a movie actress, Estelle Taylor (1899–1958). He also broke off his relationship with Kearns, and was now represented only by Rickard.

Tunney presents a challenge, and a contrast

By 1926 it was again time for Dempsey to defend his title. The fighter who came forward to challenge Dempsey was a former Marine and veteran of World War I named Gene Tunney (1898–1978). He differed from Dempsey not only in appearance and background, for he was blond and handsome and a product of the middle class, but also in boxing style. Whereas Dempsey went for the quick knockout, Tunney liked to wait for his opponent to tire before moving in with the winning punch. As the fight approached, Tunney trained intensively and was in excellent condition, while Dempsey was not well prepared.

The match took place on September 23 in Philadelphia, Pennsylvania, attended by 120,000 spectators (the gate of $2,000,000 set another record). There were 1,200 reporters present to record the event, and an estimated 50,000,000 people were listening through the new medium of radio broadcasting. The fight went ten rounds. Dempsey's fans were stunned when Tunney emerged the winner, but Dempsey himself knew that his years of relaxing in Hollywood had dulled his edge. Meanwhile, the sophisticated Tunney, who would never become as popular with ordinary people as Dempsey, reportedly returned to his hotel after the match to enjoy a pot of tea.

Having lost his heavyweight title, Dempsey returned to the ring in July 1927 to fight Jack Sharkey (1902–), with seventy-two thousand fans on hand to watch. He won the bout, which led to a rematch with Tunney two months later. Held at Soldier Field in Chicago, Illinois, this match drew an even larger crowd than the first contest between Dempsey and Tunney. It is estimated that three of every four U.S. citizens listened to it on the radio. The crucial moment in the match occurred when Dempsey, who was being outpunched by Tunney, hit his opponent with a hard left punch, followed by a volley of lefts and rights that finally sent Tunney to the floor.

Instead of retreating to a neutral corner, a rule that both fighters had previously agreed to in the event of a knockdown, Dempsey stood over his opponent. This delayed the start of the referee's count (when a fallen boxer has ten

Speed, Strength, and Stamina: Swimming Star Gertrude Ederle

Athletes in the Roaring Twenties were often looked upon as heroes. Fans thrilled in their accomplishments and eagerly awaited their next success. Swimmer Gertrude Ederle was a popular athletic hero of the 1920s. She had an enthusiastic following and achieved fame when she became the first woman to swim across the English Channel.

Ederle was born in 1906 to German immigrants who had settled in New York City. She broke onto the swimming scene in 1922 when, as an unknown fifteen-year-old, she won first place in a 3.5-mile (5.6-kilometer) race called the Day Cup. She created a sensation by beating fifty-one other contenders, including several well-known champions of women's swimming.

Over the next few years, Ederle dominated long-distance swimming, breaking nine world records and winning six national titles. At the 1924 Summer Olympics, Ederle won a gold medal for a relay event, and bronze medals for the 100-meter (328-feet) and 400-meter (1,312-feet) races. The following summer, Ederle finished a 21-mile (33.79-kilometer) course from the New York Battery to Sandy Hook, New Jersey, and beat the existing men's record.

Having broken so many records, Ederle set her sights on what was widely considered the ultimate feat in her sport: swimming across the English Channel. At that time only five swimmers had succeeded, and they were all men. The Channel was a particularly difficult, dangerous body of water and only the strongest, most determined swimmer could attempt it. Most people believed that a woman was not capable of making the crossing.

Ederle made her first attempt to cross the Channel in August 1925. After nine hours, she became caught in a strong current and was pulled out of the water. Ederle tried again the following year. She entered the water in France on August 6, 1926, at 7:05 AM under good weather conditions and headed for Dover, England.

Although she faced dangerous crosscurrents, high winds, and waves during her swim, Ederle ignored the urgings of friends and family, following her across the channel in two tugboats, to come out of the water. After fourteen hours, thirty-four minutes and about 35 miles (56.32 kilometers) Ederle reached Dover. Despite having been sent off course by currents, Ederle beat the record of the fastest male crosser by two hours, fifty-nine minutes. Her record remained intact for almost twenty-five years.

When she returned to New York City, Ederle was greeted with a parade and an estimated two million cheering fans. She received book, movie, and stage contracts, as well as marriage proposals. The attention eventually overwhelmed Ederle, and she suffered a nervous breakdown in 1928. Later in life, Ederle taught swimming to deaf children. She was sensitive to her students because she had experienced some hearing loss due to all of her time spent in the water. Ederle died in 2003, at the age of ninety-eight.

seconds to stand and rejoin the fight), giving Tunney extra time to recover. He rose before the end of the count and went on to beat Dempsey. The fairness of this so-called "long count" would be debated for years. In any case, it only enhanced Dempsey's public image, as many fans seemed to feel that he should have won the fight.

An exciting career winds down

Dempsey's boxing career was now essentially over, despite an unsuccessful comeback attempt in 1931. He lost much of the money he had earned from his matches in the Great Depression (the period of economic downturn that began with the stock market crash in 1929 and lasted until approximately 1941), but he did find occasional work as an actor and wrestling referee. Having divorced Taylor, he married singer Hannah Williams in 1933; the couple had two daughters. During World War II (1939–45), Dempsey joined the Coast Guard and served as director of a physical fitness program.

In 1943 Dempsey divorced Williams; fifteen years later he married Deanna Piatelli. He spent several decades greeting guests at his two New York City restaurants, posing beneath photos from his boxing career. He was named to the Boxing Hall of Fame, and in 1950 he was designated the greatest fighter of the first half of the twentieth century by the Associated Press. In June 1970 he celebrated his seventieth birthday with a grand party held at Madison Square Garden (a large arena in New York City). In the early 1980s Dempsey developed heart problems, and he died in 1983.

For More Information

Books

Bacho, Peter. *Boxing in Black and White.* New York: Henry Holt, 1999.

Dempsey, Jack, with Barbara Piatelli Dempsey. *Dempsey.* New York: Harper & Row, 1977.

Evensen, Robert J. *When Dempsey Fought Tunney: Heroes, Hokum, and Storytelling in the Jazz Age.* Knoxville: University of Tennessee Press, 1996.

Kahn, Roger. *A Flame of Pure Fire: Jack Dempsey and the Roaring 20s.* New York: Harcourt Brace, 1999.

Miller, Nathan. *New World Coming: The 1920s and the Making of Modern America.* New York: Scribner, 2003.

Perret, Geoffrey. *America in the Twenties.* New York: Touchstone, 1982.

Roberts, Randy. *Jack Dempsey: The Manassa Mauler.* Baton Rouge: Louisiana State University Press, 1979.

Smith, Toby. *Kid Blackie: Jack Dempsey's Colorado Days.* Ouray, CO: Wayfinder Press, 1987.

Web Sites

The Official Jack Dempsey Web Site. Available online at http://www.cmgww.com/sports/dempsey/index.php. Accessed on June 22, 2005.

"Jack Dempsey." *Enshrinees.* The International Boxing Hall of Fame. Available online at http://www.ibhof.com/dempsey.htm. Accessed on June 22, 2005.

W.E.B. Du Bois

Born February 23, 1869 (Great Barrington, Massachusetts)
Died August 27, 1963 (Accra, Ghana)

Civil rights activist, educator, writer

W.E.B. Du Bois was the most celebrated African American leader of the firsthalf of the twentieth century. A prolific writer who produced twenty books and more than one hundred articles and essays, he was one of the first to speak out in favor of full and unconditional rights for blacks. During the Roaring Twenties Du Bois played an important role in the Harlem Renaissance, the period of cultural expression and achievement that was centered in New York City's African American community. As editor of *The Crisis,* the journal of the National Association for the Advancement of Colored People (NAACP), Du Bois provided a place for the talented young writers and artists of the period to publish their work. In addition, he made *The Crisis* into an important forum for black journalism and often used it to express his own intellectual and political views about the ongoing struggle for equality. During the 1920s, Du Bois clashed with Marcus Garvey (1887–1940), the dynamic leader of the United Negro Improvement Association, whose approach to black progress differed from his own. He also disapproved of the way some Harlem Renaissance writers insisted on portraying African American life in all its gritty, harsh reality.

> "At the dawn of the twentieth century his was the voice that was calling to you to gather here today in this cause."
>
> *NAACP leader Roy Wilkins*

During the 1920s W.E.B. Du Bois played an important role in the Harlem Renaissance and was one of the first people to speak out in favor of full and unconditional rights for African Americans. (*© Corbis. Reproduced by permission.*)

A brilliant student

William Edward Burghardt Du Bois was born in Great Barrington, Massachusetts, a mostly white town that had, nevertheless, a strong tradition of racial tolerance and abolitionism (the belief that slavery should be illegal). His father was Alfred Du Bois, a barber of mixed French and African racial descent who left his family soon after his son's birth. His mother, Mary Salvina Burghardt, supported herself and her son by working as a maid. Du Bois contributed to the family income by doing odd jobs such as delivering groceries, mowing grass, chopping wood, and even writing articles for several newspapers.

During his school years Du Bois was one of very few black students, but he impressed both teachers and classmates with his intelligence and willingness to work hard. When he graduated from high school, he was chosen as his class's valedictorian (who delivers the farewell address at graduation). Du Bois wanted very much to attend college, and Harvard University was his first choice. His high school education, however, had not provided the kind of preparation he needed for Harvard.

Du Bois's advisors, including his high school principal, recommended that he attend Fisk University, a black school in Nashville, Tennessee. Du Bois received a full scholarship to Fisk, where he studied a variety of subjects that included classical literature and languages, philosophy, chemistry, and physics. He also edited the school's literary magazine.

Broadening his perspective

For the first time in his life, Du Bois was living in the South, where relations between blacks and whites were very different from those in his native New England. Following the American Civil War (1861–65) and the Reconstruction Era (1865–77), a system of legalized segregation (separation of the races) had been put into place through the so-called "Jim Crow" laws. African Americans living in the southern states were forced to attend separate and inferior schools and could not use the same public facilities—such as restaurants, restrooms, and drinking fountains—as whites. Not surprisingly, Du Bois found life under these circumstances very difficult. He responded by avoiding segregated places like movie theaters and streetcars, spending most of his time on campus. He also developed a shy, aloof manner that was often interpreted as coldness or arrogance.

During his college years, Du Bois spent his summers teaching in black schools in rural eastern Tennessee. This proved to be a life-changing experience, for Du Bois witnessed firsthand the hardships and suffering endured by poor African

Americans living in a racist society. Yet Du Bois also gained new insight into the richness of his heritage and resilience of his people through his exposure to the spirituals (religious songs) he heard. His awareness of the ways in which blacks used music and other means to lift their spirits and endure their circumstances made him feel both proud and hopeful.

In 1888 Du Bois graduated from Fisk, and he immediately entered Harvard. He majored in philosophy and earned another bachelor's degree in 1890, and he was one of only five students chosen to speak at his graduation ceremony. Du Bois stayed at Harvard another year to earn a master's degree in history and economics. Then he spent two years abroad, studying sociology and economics at the University of Berlin in Germany. During this period he also visited Switzerland, France, Austria, Italy, Hungary, and Poland, gaining a broader, more global perspective. Du Bois's money and time ran out before he could earn a degree, however, and he returned to the United States in 1894.

Recognized as a scholar

After a year spent teaching at Wilberforce University in Ohio, where he met and married Nina Gomer, who would be his wife until her death in 1950, Du Bois returned to Harvard to complete his PhD. He wrote his dissertation (a long essay, written to fulfill the requirements of a university degree) on the African slave trade, and in 1896 he became the first black student to receive a PhD from Harvard.

In 1896 and 1897 Du Bois worked as an assistant professor of sociology at the University of Pennsylvania while conducting an extensive study of the African American community in Philadelphia. Du Bois personally interviewed thousands of people, producing an extremely detailed report that exposed the poverty, violence, and crime that marred his subjects' lives. No such study had ever been done before, and the published version, *The Philadelphia Negro* (1899), was widely recognized as a major accomplishment.

In 1898 Du Bois accepted a position as professor of economics and history at Atlanta University, a black institution. For the next eleven years, he would be busy not only teaching but also directing a series of annual conferences titled Studies of the Negro Problem. The conferences focused attention on issues affecting African Americans, and they brought Du Bois more recognition as a leading black scholar. In 1899 Du Bois and his wife were saddened by the death of their toddler son, Burghardt, of an intestinal illness.

As time went on, Du Bois found himself more and more impatient as he waited for white society to grant equality to African Americans. He grew increasingly convinced that a passive approach was useless in the face of racism and discrimination and that blacks should use protest and activism to achieve their goals. In 1900 Du Bois attended a Pan African Conference in London, England, where black leaders from all over the world met to discuss their common interests. This marked the beginning of Du Bois's lifelong interest in forging ties between all people of African descent, whether they lived in the United States, Europe, the Caribbean, or Africa itself.

A new kind of leadership

A major milestone in Du Bois's career occurred in 1903 with the publication of *The Souls of Black Folk.* This book of fourteen essays collected Du Bois's writings on such topics as the devastating effects of racism, the remarkable resilience of black people, and the confusing sense of double consciousness experienced by those who considered themselves both black and American. The book would prove very influential, and it would also drive an even larger wedge between Du Bois and Booker T. Washington (1856–1915), another important African American leader of the early twentieth century.

During the last quarter of the nineteenth century, Washington had emerged as the most prominent black leader in the United States. The founder of the Tuskegee Institute, a school where blacks received training in a number of trades and crafts, Washington advised African Americans to endure segregation and racism quietly. They should focus, he stressed, not so much on things like higher education and voting rights as on learning how to support themselves. Economic progress would come first, and other types of equality would eventually follow.

Du Bois had neither the time for nor any faith in Washington's program. He felt that African Americans should demand all of their rights immediately and unconditionally,

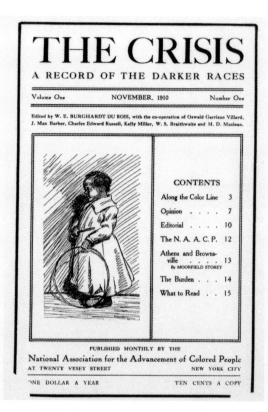

The cover of the first issue of *The Crisis,* the monthly magazine of the National Association for the Advancement of Colored People (NAACP) founded by W.E.B. Du Bois. *(© Bettmann/Corbis. Reproduced by permission.)*

and that any kind of compromise with white people seeking to limit black freedom would prevent further progress. He urged what he called the Talented Tenth, meaning the small minority of blacks who were well educated and economically successful, to lead the way.

African Americans were divided in their loyalties, with some remaining faithful to the familiar and beloved Washington and others agreeing with Du Bois's activist approach. A definite split came in 1905, when Du Bois and others who felt as he did formed the Niagara Movement. The group met in Ontario, Canada, to express support for the complete integration of blacks into U.S. society, with the same rights and privileges granted to other citizens. Washington and his supporters, who some called the "Tuskegee Machine" due to the power they wielded, opposed the movement and applied what pressure they could to weaken it.

Founding the NAACP

The Niagara Movement lasted for only about four years, when its members broke off to join other civil rights organizations. The most prominent and longest-lasting of these was the NAACP (still in existence in the twenty-first century), which Du Bois formed along with a number of white supporters. Du Bois hoped that the participation of whites would increase the organization's impact; in fact, he was the only black member of its board of directors. In late 1920 Du Bois left his job at Atlanta University and moved to New York City, the headquarters of the NAACP, to become its director of publications and research.

Du Bois immediately founded the journal *The Crisis,* which would serve as an important forum for African American voices and viewpoints. Subscription numbers grew quickly as African American readers eagerly looked to *The Crisis* for news, information, and opinions on matters of importance to the black community. From the beginning, the always outspoken Du Bois had many conflicts with the other board members, who considered him excessively radical in his views. They felt Du Bois should proceed more cautiously, while he thought the NAACP should take more aggressive steps to demand equal rights for blacks. In any case, by 1913 the journal's circulation had grown to thirty thousand and it was the nation's leading black publication.

When World War I (1914–18) began in Europe, Du Bois was initially opposed to the United States becoming involved. Once the United States entered the war in 1917, though, Du Bois strongly spoke out to encourage young black men to volunteer for military service. This was a way, he declared, to show the depth of African American loyalty to the nation that had been their home for more than three hundred years. When whites saw that blacks were willing to sacrifice their own lives for the freedom of others, for the conflict was commonly known as a war "to make the world safe for democracy," they would be sure to grant African Americans the equal rights, acceptance, and expanded opportunities they desired.

Several hundred thousand black soldiers did serve in the war, and in 1919 Du Bois traveled to France to chronicle their experiences. The issue of *The Crisis* in which his report appeared sold a record 106,000 copies. After the war ended, Du Bois urged the returning soldiers to continue the fight for equality in their own country. This kind of talk was not welcomed by whites who were already worried about the threat of economic competition and social disruption they felt blacks posed. During the summer of 1919, a number of bloody race riots broke out in several major U.S. cities, and some blamed Du Bois's strong words for helping to cause the violence.

Elder statesman to the Harlem Renaissance

During the Roaring Twenties Du Bois served as a kind of elder statesman to the younger writers, artists, and musicians who made up the Harlem Renaissance. This outpouring of cultural expression and achievement, from the jazz-inflected poetry of Langston Hughes (1902–1967) to the African-influenced murals of Aaron Douglas (1899–1979) to the innovative music of **Louis Armstrong** (1901–1971; see entry), showcased the rich culture and talent that Du Bois had long heralded. Under the direction of literary editor Jessie Redmon Fauset (1882–1961), herself an accomplished novelist, *The Crisis* provided readers with their first look at many works produced by Harlem Renaissance writers.

Nevertheless, relations were not smooth between Du Bois and all segments of the Harlem Renaissance. Du Bois disagreed with some of them on how they should portray the lives of black people. He sensed that the world was watching, and he wanted whites to see only the most upright, respectable aspects of African American life. That was the best way, Du Bois believed, to gain respect from whites and thus make them more inclined to grant blacks equality. Writers like Hughes and Claude McKay (1890–1948), however, disagreed. They wanted to convey the real sights, sounds, smells, and circumstances of the world around them. Therefore Hughes, for example, filled his poems with urban black dialect and nightclub scenes, while McKay's novel *Home to Harlem* (1928) includes characters who are prostitutes and drug users.

Du Bois also carried on a running battle with Marcus Garvey (1887–1940), a Jamaican immigrant who had gained a huge following through his calls for black pride and for a separate black state. The leader of the United Negro Improvement Association (UNIA), Garvey dressed in an elaborate military uniform and plumed hat, and he seemed to have much more appeal to ordinary blacks than the distant, intellectual Du Bois. Through articles in *The Crisis*, Du Bois tried to portray Garvey as a dangerous fake, while Garvey fought back in the pages of *Negro World*, the publication of the UNIA. Eventually, Garvey was convicted of mail fraud and sent back to Jamaica, which seemed to confirm to Du Bois that he had been right about him all along.

Du Bois's interest in the mutual concerns shared by all people of African descent led him to organize four Pan-African Congresses between 1919 and 1927. Leaders and activists gathered from all over the globe to discuss ways to improve the status and circumstances of black people. Among the most important issue of the years following World War I was what,

Marcus Garvey: A Different Kind of Black Leader

While W.E.B. Du Bois was a shining light to African American intellectuals and activists, Marcus Garvey appealed to many working-class and poor blacks with his outspoken racial pride and his efforts to improve the lives of those with African descent. Frequently at odds with Du Bois, Garvey's flamboyant style and mass appeal did not win him approval from other black leaders of the day.

Born in a small town in Jamaica in 1887, Garvey had little schooling but an intense interest in politics and an awareness of the poverty and prejudice faced by blacks around the world. This led him to found the United Negro Improvement Association (UNIA) in 1914. The organization was dedicated to helping people of African descent, no matter where they lived.

In 1916 Garvey traveled to the United States. He had long admired the work of Booker T. Washington, the African American leader who had established the Tuskegee Institute, an Alabama school where blacks learned vocational skills and trades. Garvey hoped to raise money to start a simi-lar school in Jamaica. He would spend most of the next decade in the United States, where his magnetic personality, outspoken racial pride, and plans for a glorious black future gained him a devoted following.

Garvey soon founded a magazine called *Negro World,* which he used to express his views about how black progress could best be promoted. Garvey's essays urged people of African descent to be proud of their heritage and to reject racist views of their inferiority. At the center of his beliefs was the idea that black people should join together to reclaim Africa from the European nations that had colonized the continent in earlier centuries. This concept was known as pan-Africanism.

Garvey customarily dressed in a medal-adorned military uniform and a plumed helmet. He appointed himself "Provisional President" of the all-black African nation he envisioned. On August 1, 1920, the UNIA held a convention in New York City that featured a large parade through Harlem. That evening, Garvey spoke to a crowd of twenty-five thousand followers at Madison Square Garden.

Garvey's appeal to a mass audience was not matched with similar admiration from other black leaders. Du Bois in particular resented Garvey, whom he considered to be an unrealistic and dangerous fake. Garvey and Du Bois carried on a battle of words in articles that appeared in Du Bois's *The Crisis* magazine and Garvey's *Negro World.* No one was more relieved than Du Bois when, in 1922, Garvey was convicted of defrauding people, many of them poor, who had invested in his failed shipping company. After several years in jail, Garvey was sent back to Jamaica. He died in 1940.

in the wake of Germany's defeat, would be done with that nation's African colonies. Although those in attendance pushed for these colonies to become independent nations, in the end they were treated as spoils to be divided among the European countries that had been victorious in the war (Great Britain, Italy, and France).

Disillusioned with the U.S. system

Witnessing the widespread hardship of the 1930s, when the economic downturn known as the Great Depression (1929–41) brought unemployment to millions, Du Bois became increasingly unhappy with the U.S. economic and social system. His ideas became more and more radical as he began moving away from the idea that African Americans should depend on white society for help. Instead, Du Bois began to advocate for black social, economic, and educational institutions. To the NAACP's board of directors, this sounded dangerously similar to segregation, which they had always strongly opposed. In 1934, after serving for twenty-four years as the editor of *The Crisis*, Du Bois was forced to retire from his position.

Du Bois returned to Atlanta University as chair of the sociology department and editor of a sociology journal called *Phylon*, with a special focus on the effects of racism. He also began traveling abroad to countries that offered different perspectives, such as Communist Russia and China. In 1943 he was forced into retirement from Atlanta. He then returned to the NAACP as director of special research. It is likely that the board of directors expected this to be an essentially ceremonial position for Du Bois, who was then seventy-seven years old. But that is not how he treated it, returning once again to his outspoken advocacy of extreme positions. Once again, in 1948, he was forced out.

Du Bois made an unsuccessful bid for a U.S. Senate seat as the candidate of the American Labor Party in 1950. Throughout the 1950s he was involved in exploring alternatives to capitalism (a system in which a country's trade and industry are controlled by private interests, for profit), especially communism (where all property is owned by the community and each person contributes and receives according to his or her ability and needs) and socialism (where the means of production, distribution, and exchange are owned by the community as a whole).

At this time in U.S. history, many people were concerned about the growing power of Communist countries like Russia and China. The fear that the United States itself could be invaded by Communists led to an atmosphere of suspicion and even paranoia, most dramatically demonstrated in the congressional hearings chaired by Senator Joseph McCarthy (1908–1957).

Du Bois's Communist leanings and activism got him into trouble with the U.S. government. In November 1951, after Du Bois had circulated a petition to ban nuclear weapons, he was charged with failing to register as an agent of a foreign country. Du Bois was acquitted (found not guilty), but he became even more disillusioned with the United States. At around the same time, the passports of Du Bois and his wife Shirley Graham (his first wife had died in 1950) were seized, which meant they could not travel outside the United States; the documents were not returned until 1958.

A citizen of Ghana

As soon as he had his passport again, Du Bois began a period of travel to Russia, China, and Africa. In 1961 he was invited by President Kwame Nkrumah (1909–1972) to move to Ghana, a West African country that had recently won its independence. Du Bois accepted the invitation, but before he left he made the pointed gesture of officially joining the Communist Party. He also gave up his U.S. citizenship to become a citizen of Ghana, where he began work on a history of Africa called the *Encyclopedia Africana*.

Du Bois died in 1963, one day before the March on Washington for Jobs and Freedom. This historic event was attended by more than two hundred thousand people, who gathered to call for full equal rights and opportunities for African Americans. As the news of Du Bois's death passed through the crowd, those assembled acknowledged his role in the struggle for civil rights. As quoted in Manning Marable's *W.E.B. DuBois: Black Radical Democrat*, NAACP head Roy Wilkins (1901–1981) reminded the crowd that "At the dawn of the twentieth century his was the voice that was calling to you to gather here today in this cause." In Ghana, Du Bois was given a hero's funeral and buried on the grounds of the state house.

For More Information

Books

Hamilton, Virginia. *W.E.B. DuBois: A Biography*. New York: Crowell, 1972.

Lewis, David Leavering. *W.E.B. DuBois: Biography of a Race, 1868–1919*. New York: Henry Holt, 1993.

Marable, Manning. *W.E.B. DuBois: Black Radical Democrat*. Boston: Twayne, 1986.

Rudwick, Elliott. *W.E.B. DuBois: Voice of the Black Protest Movement*. Urbana: University of Illinois Press, 1982.

Stafford, Mark. *W.E.B. DuBois*. New York: Chelsea House, 1989.

Web Sites

Hynes, Gerald C. *A Biographical Sketch of W.E.B. DuBois*. Available online at http://www.duboislc.org/html/DuBoisBio.html. Accessed on June 22, 2005.

Reuben, Paul R. "Chapter 9: Harlem Renaissance—A Brief Introduction." *PAL: Perspectives in American Literature*. Available online at http://www.csustan.edu/english/reuben/pal/chap9/9intro.html. Accessed on June 22, 2005.

F. Scott Fitzgerald

Born September 24, 1896 (St. Paul, Minnesota)
Died December 21, 1940 (Los Angeles, California)

Novelist and short story writer

F. Scott Fitzgerald was probably the most gifted and insightful literary chronicler of the Roaring Twenties. It was he who, in the title of one of his collections of short stories, coined the term "Jazz Age" to describe this decade of exuberance, creativity, and sometimes troubling change. Along with his glamorous wife, Zelda, Fitzgerald himself lived the life of excess for which the period is known. His was a tragic story in many ways, yet he also produced lasting literary masterpieces. The best of these is undoubtedly his novel *The Great Gatsby,* which has become a classic of U.S. fiction, but his numerous, finely crafted short stories are also acclaimed.

"So we beat on, boats against the current, borne back ceaselessly into the past."

An ambitious young writer

Francis Scott Fitzgerald was born in St. Paul, Minnesota, in 1896. His father, Edward Fitzgerald, was a native of Maryland, and his mother, Mollie McQuillan Fitzgerald, was from a wealthy local family; he had one younger sister. When his son was two years old, the elder Fitzgerald moved his family to the East Coast after accepting a position with the large dry

F. Scott Fitzgerald was probably the most gifted and insightful literary chronicler of the Roaring Twenties. *(Courtesy of The Library of Congress.)*

goods firm of Procter and Gamble, but they returned in 1908 when he lost this job. From then on the family lived on Mollie's inheritance. Some commentators have traced Fitzgerald's life-long anxiety about financial failure to his father's inability to support the family.

As a boy, Fitzgerald always loved writing. His first publica-tion, a detective story, appeared in the school newspaper of the St. Paul Academy, which he attended from 1908 to 1911. Poor grades forced Fitzgerald to transfer to the Newman School in Hackensack, New Jersey, where he spent the years between 1911 and 1913. During this period he especially enjoyed writing plays, several of which were produced during his summers at home by an amateur theatrical group.

Fitzgerald entered New Jersey's Princeton University in 1913. He spent much of his time writing for various campus publications, including the *Nassau Literary Magazine,* and making some lifelong friends. One of these was Edmund Wilson (1895–1972), who would later become a famous and well-respected literary critic. Fitzgerald neglected his academic work, however, and had to leave Princeton in 1915. He returned the next year, but he would never graduate. When, in 1917, the United States entered World War I (1914–18), Fitzgerald joined the army. He was made a second lieutenant and sent to an army base near Montgomery, Alabama.

This was a crucial period in Fitzgerald's life, for it was in Montgomery that he met and fell in love with Zelda Sayre, the daughter of an Alabama Supreme Court judge. The couple became engaged, but Zelda belonged to a wealthy, upper-class social set, and Fitzgerald felt he could not marry her until he had achieved some success. During his fifteen months of military service, he was never sent overseas, but he did begin work on his first novel, an autobiographical work that he initially titled *The Romantic Egoist.*

Fitzgerald sent his manuscript to the Scribner publishing company. It was rejected but returned with an encouraging note to revise the novel and submit it again. After a brief period as an advertising copywriter in New York City, Fitzgerald went home to St. Paul to work on rewriting his novel. Following another rejection and another revision, Scribner finally accepted the novel, which was renamed *This Side of Paradise.*

The fast life of the Roaring Twenties

This Side of Paradise chronicles the life of Amory Blaine, a Princeton undergraduate who bears a notable resemblance to his creator. Among the experiences shared by both are a failed romance (Fitzgerald's had been with Ginevra King, a wealthy girl after whom he would model Daisy Buchanan, one of his most famous creations), problems with bad grades, and an interest in literature. The novel also features a female character who embodies the flapper ideal of the Roaring Twenties: these young women were known for such bold, unconventional behaviors as drinking and smoking in public and wearing short skirts and bobbed (short) hair. Generally, the novel was considered a truthful portrait of postwar youth, who rebelled against their elders and disregarded tradition. Because it included patches of poetry and pieces of short stories and plays that Fitzgerald had previously written, its structure seemed original and vaguely sophisticated.

This Side of Paradise was published in March 1920 and quickly gained popularity; by the end of the year, it had sold forty thousand copies. A week after its publication Fitzgerald married Zelda, and the two began an adventurous life of travel, parties, and outrageous antics. They were known, for example, for having ridden up New York City's Fifth Avenue on the roof of a taxicab. Meanwhile, Fitzgerald continued to write steadily, publishing his short stories in such well-known national magazines as *Smart Set* and the *Saturday Evening Post.* His first short story collection, *Flappers and Philosophers* (1920), appeared soon after *This Side of Paradise.*

Throughout his career, Fitzgerald would fall back on the more profitable practice of publishing short stories (in 1922, for example, most of the $22,000 he earned came from short story writing) to bolster his income. Nevertheless, many of his short stories are finely written. This first collection contained several of Fitzgerald's best stories, including "The Ice Palace" and "Bernice Bobs Her Hair"; the latter centered on a girl accepting her friends' challenge to take the daring and modern step of cutting her long hair.

After a short period in Europe, the Fitzgeralds returned to St. Paul for the birth of their daughter, Frances Scott Fitzgerald (called Scottie). Afterward they plunged right back into their fast-living ways. They never owned a home, preferring to stay in expensive hotels or rent large houses.

Fitzgerald's second novel appeared in 1922. *The Beautiful and the Damned* centers on a beautiful, glamorous couple, Anthony and Gloria Patch, who live on inherited money. They spend freely, drink heavily, and quarrel often as their lives gradually fall apart. The novel is distinguished by its strongly cynical tone and emphasis on the negative effects of

The Expatriate Scene in Paris

It was an unusual circumstance of the Roaring Twenties that many of the creators of the most exciting artistic developments in the United States lived in Paris, France, during this period. There were several reasons for this expatriate migration. World War I had exposed many young people to Europe, and life was cheaper there and offered an escape both from Prohibition and from what many considered the intolerance and small-mindedness of U.S. society. There also were more opportunities to have one's work published in Paris.

Although a great number of the expatriates in France during the 1920s were merely posing as artists, some genuinely talented artists and writers lived there as well. Such classic works as *The Great Gatsby* by F. Scott Fitzgerald and *The Sun Also Rises* by Ernest Hemingway were written in France. These and other serious authors were welcomed by three older figures who had arrived several years earlier: writer and literary critic Gertrude Stein, who hosted a popular literary salon; poet Ezra Pound (at least until his departure in 1924); and Sylvia Beach, who owned a famous bookstore called Shakespeare & Company. It was Beach who, in 1922, published James Joyce's groundbreaking modernist novel *Ulysses.*

Other authors were able to publish their work through such Paris-based companies as the Contact Press, the Three Mountains Press, and the Black Manikin Press, or in literary journals like *The Little Review, Gargoyle,* and the *Transatlantic Review.* Paris also attracted musicians, some of whom—like composers Virgil Thomson and Aaron Copland—studied with French composer Nadia Boulanger, dancers, and visual artists. Painters like Marc Chagall, Joan Miro, and Pablo Picasso were on the scene, as were journalist Djuna Barnes and poets e.e. cummings and Hilda Doolittle.

too much money. Although the critics gave it low marks, *The Beautiful and the Damned* sold well.

That same year, another collection of Fitzgerald's short stories was published. *Tales of the Jazz Age* (the author's nickname for the Roaring Twenties, which would become widely used) contains some of his most popular and frequently anthologized (compiled) stories, such as "The Diamond as Big as the Ritz," "May Day," and "Winter Dreams." Most of the stories in the volume, however, are not up to the standard of Fitzgerald's best writing.

A masterpiece of twentieth-century literature

Despite the success of his books and the considerable amount of money Fitzgerald had made through selling his short stories to magazines, the couple's extravagant lifestyle landed them in debt. They rented a house on Long Island (near New York City), where Fitzgerald wrote a play called *The Vegetable* (1923) that he hoped would ease their financial troubles. Instead, the play was a flop.

Searching for a less expensive place to live, the Fitzgeralds moved to Europe again, renting a villa on the French Riviera (a coastal region in southern France). There they entered a circle of U.S. expatriates (those who live outside their native country). Despite the demands of their active social life, and the heartache and tension caused by Zelda's affair with a French pilot, Fitzgerald wrote the novel that is usually considered his masterpiece.

The Great Gatsby is a relatively short, tightly written work with a complex structure and compelling characters. Fitzgerald used symbolism masterfully to illustrate and explore the novel's themes, which include the clash between traditional values and modern culture, the shallow pursuit of wealth and the tarnishing of the so-called "American dream," and the stubborn persistence of hope.

The novel takes place on Long Island. Its hero is Jay Gatsby, born Jimmy Gatz, whose pursuit of a wealthy, out-of-reach young woman leads him to amass a huge fortune through bootlegging (the selling of alcoholic beverages, which had been made illegal by Prohibition, the Eighteenth Amendment to the U.S. Constitution). The object of Gatsby's blind devotion, Daisy Buchanan, is a shallow creature who has married the rich but insensitive Tom Buchanan. The couple has a young daughter. Meanwhile, Tom is involved with the wife of a mechanic whose shop is along the road to New York City.

The Great Gatsby is narrated by Nick Carroway, a native of the Midwest and Daisy's cousin, who has rented a cottage near Gatsby's estate. Fitzgerald successfully employs this disillusioned but sensitive narrative voice to tell the story of Gatsby's downfall. He paints a vivid, detailed portrait of life in the Roaring Twenties, from the fancy parties attended by flappers and shady underworld characters to the ash heaps that exist just outside the glittering world of the wealthy.

Despite critical acclaim, the novel was not a popular success; it sold only twenty-five thousand copies in 1925. In fact,

Mia Farrow as Daisy Buchanan and Robert Redford as Jay Gatsby in the 1974 film version of F. Scott Fitzgerald's *The Great Gatsby*.

(© Bettmann/Corbis. Reproduced by permission.)

The Great Gatsby would not attain its status as a classic of U.S. literature until after Fitzgerald's death.

A nomadic life and a new novel

The Fitzgeralds lived in Europe through 1926. During this period, Fitzgerald befriended Ernest Hemingway (1899–1961), who was on his way to becoming one of the most celebrated writers of the twentieth century. Fitzgerald greatly admired Hemingway both for his literary talent and his bold, adventurous personality. Meanwhile, Zelda was starting to show some signs of mental disturbance as she searched for her own creative outlet, experimenting with painting, ballet, and eventually writing. Both Fitzgeralds were drinking heavily.

In 1926 Fitzgerald's short-story collection *All the Sad Young Men* appeared. One of the stories included was "Rich Boy," which explored some of the same themes as *The Great Gatsby*. This volume, however, actually sold more copies than the novel. That same year, the Fitzgeralds returned to the United States, spending a brief period in Hollywood, California (the center of the new, expanding film industry), where Fitzgerald worked as a screenwriter. Then they settled for two years in Delaware, with Fitzgerald supporting the family by writing short stories, mainly for the *Saturday Evening Post*. At this point he was earning as much as four thousand dollars per story.

The ever-nomadic Fitzgeralds returned to France in 1929. There Fitzgerald continued work on a novel that he had begun earlier, now incorporating details and characters drawn from the expatriate scene around him. As the 1930s began, Zelda's psychological problems finally resulted in a total breakdown. She spent a year and a half being treated in a Swiss sanitarium (a kind of hospital and rest home for chronically ill people), which would be the first of a long series of hospitalizations. From now on, Zelda's illness would exert not only emotional but also financial stress on Fitzgerald.

The Fitzgeralds returned to the United States in 1931. After a brief period of recovery, Zelda had another breakdown, brought on by the news of her father's death. She would never be well again. Despite the turmoil of his personal life, Fitzgerald continued to work, and two years later he published a third novel.

Tender is the Night is filled with much autobiographical material. It tells of the gradual disintegration of Dick Diver, a talented psychiatrist who has given up a promising career to marry and continue treating a young female patient, Nicole Warren (a character with many similarities to Zelda). Like the Fitzgeralds, the Divers and their three children live on the French Riviera, supported by Nicole's family wealth. As the novel progresses, the couple, whose past lives are chronicled in a section placed in the middle of the book, rather than in chronological order, grows increasingly troubled. Nicole has an affair with a French naval officer, and Diver falls in love with a young actress. The marriage ends, and Diver retreats to practice in a small town in the United States.

Some commentators interpreted *Tender Is the Night* as an indictment of the shallowness and excess of the Roaring Twenties. Others found it a more complex chronicle that highlights the loss of innocence experienced by those who came to adulthood during and just after World War I. In any case, the novel was published in the middle of the Great Depression (the period of economic downturn and hardship that lasted from the 1929 stock market crash until the beginning of World War II), and readers were not particularly interested in reading about the problems of the wealthy. *Tender Is the Night* received mixed critical reviews, but it was not popular with the public.

A faltering career

During the last decades of his life, pressed with the demands of paying for both Zelda's treatment and Scottie's college education, Fitzgerald continued to write and sell his short stories. He also accepted a position as a screenwriter at Metro Goldwyn Mayer (MGM), one of the most successful of the Hollywood film production companies. Fitzgerald earned one thousand dollars per week, but he was not particularly successful. He felt that he was wasting his talent, and he was drinking heavily. The only bright spot was provided by his stable relationship with gossip columnist Sheilah Graham.

Fitzgerald did not entirely abandon his literary work, as he began a novel based on his experiences in the movie industry. The protagonist of this book, which Fitzgerald never finished, is Monroe Stahr, the powerful, self-made head of a Hollywood studio. Eventually published under the title *The Last Tycoon* (1941), the novel tells the story of Stahr's ill-fated romance with a young actress. Some critics believe that it would have been Fitzgerald's best work if he had lived to finish it. Instead, Fitzgerald died of a heart attack at the age of forty-four. At the end of his life, he considered himself a failure, but he has since come to be recognized as one of the finest writers of the twentieth century.

In 1975, the bodies of both Fitzgeralds (Zelda died in 1948 in a mental hospital fire) were buried together in the cemetery of St. Mary's Church in Rockville, Maryland. The epitaph on their gravestone is the final sentence of *The Great Gatsby*: "So we beat on, boats against the current, borne back ceaselessly into the past."

For More Information

Books

Bruccoli, Matthew. *Some Sort of Epic Grandeur: The Life of F. Scott Fitzgerald.* New York: Harcourt, 1981.

Bruccoli, Matthew, and Jackson R. Bryer, eds. *F. Scott Fitzgerald in His Own Times: A Miscellany.* Kent, OH: Kent State University Press, 1971.

Lehan, Richard. *The Great Gatsby: The Limits of Wonder.* Boston: Twayne, 1990.

Medlow, James R. *Invented Lives: F. Scott Fitzgerald and Zelda Fitzgerald.* New York: Houghton Mifflin, 1984.

Meyers, Jeffrey. *Scott Fitzgerald: A Biography.* New York: HarperCollins, 1994.

Web Sites

The F. Scott Fitzgerald Society. Available online at http://www. fitzgerald society.org/. Accessed on June 22, 2005.

"A Brief Life of Fitzgerald." *USC: F. Scott Fitzgerald Centenary Home Page.* Available online at http://www.sc.edu/fitzgerald/biography.html. Accessed on June 22, 2005.

Henry Ford

Born July 30, 1863 (Springwells, Michigan)
Died April 7, 1947 (Dearborn, Michigan)

Industrialist

The important role of the automobile in contemporary U.S. culture really began in the Roaring Twenties. It was during this decade that owning an automobile began to seem like a necessity, for it allowed freedom and convenience and affected such issues as where people worked and lived and what they did for fun. The man who was largely responsible for this trend was Henry Ford. Rising from a Michigan farm boy to become one of the richest people in the world, Ford was a popular hero to millions. He revolutionized the infant automobile industry by producing a reliable car that a wide variety of people could afford to buy. Yet Ford was a man of personal contradictions. He paid his workers more and cut their hours, but he also forced them to follow his own rules of morality and behavior, and he fiercely resisted their efforts to unionize (join labor unions, which allowed workers to negotiate for higher wages and better working conditions).

"An idealist is a person who helps other people to be prosperous."

A young engineer

Born on a farm in Springwells, Michigan (near what is now Dearborn), Henry Ford was the first of six children born to

Henry Ford revolutionized the automobile industry by producing a reliable car that a wide variety of people could afford to buy. *(© Underwood & Underwood/Corbis. Reproduced by permission.)*

William and Mary Ford. He was expected to help with the work on the family farm, but he did not like it much. Instead, he was fascinated with gadgets and liked to spend his time taking things apart. Through tinkering with various farm machines, Ford became a self-taught mechanic. He quit attending his one-room village school when he was fifteen, and the next year he walked to Detroit, a thriving city about 8 miles (12.9 kilometers) from Springwells.

First Ford became an apprentice in a machine shop that made valves and fire hydrants, working twelve hours a day, six days a week. In his next job, he worked on steam engines, which burned fuel to create the steam that, in turn, powered the pistons that made the engine work. But Ford was more interested in a new invention called the internal combustion engine, which burned fuel inside the cylinder that housed the piston, creating energy more efficiently than by using steam. Ford learned more about internal combustion engines when, in 1882, he became an engine expert for the Westinghouse Company. His job was to travel around southeastern Michigan and repair farm machinery.

In 1888 Ford married Clara Bryant, a young woman he had met at a country dance. His father offered him 40 acres (16 hectares) of tree-covered land next to the family farm, so Ford settled into cutting and selling lumber and firewood. Five years later, his son Edsel was born. Meanwhile, Ford had set up a small engineering workshop in his back yard, and he spent as much time as he could there, conducting experiments with both steam- and gas-driven engines. His first attempt to create a motor-powered vehicle resulted in a two-cylinder internal combustion engine that he mounted on a bicycle.

An ambitious inventor

Bored with rural life, Ford moved his family to Detroit in 1891. His skills made it easy for him to get a job at the Detroit Illuminating Company, an electrical company headed by inventor Thomas Alva Edison (1847–1931). Ford started out making an impressive one hundred dollars per month, and by 1895 he had been made chief engineer and had befriended Edison himself, with whom he would maintain a close relationship for many years to come. Ford continued to experiment with making what were then called "horseless carriages," early versions of automobiles.

In June 1896 Ford produced a vehicle he called a Quadricycle, testing it on the streets of Detroit to the amazement of onlookers. It weighed only 500 pounds (225 kilograms) and rolled on bicycle wheels. It had two speeds but no reverse gear, and it was steered with a tiller, like a boat. The Quadricyle was not the first automobile in existence, however.

Earlier models had already been produced by the Duryee brothers of Massachusetts and by German engineer Gottlieb Daimler (1834–1900).

Three years later Ford joined with wealthy businessman William Murphy to form the Detroit Automobile Company. Even though the company failed, it gave Ford some valuable experience in manufacturing automobiles. By 1901 he had produced a racing car called the 999 that, with Ford at the wheel, won a race against what was then the fastest automobile in the world. This feat caught the attention of another wealthy investor, coal dealer Alexander Malcomson, who offered to finance Ford's next venture. This led to the founding of the Henry Ford Company, which became the Cadillac Motor Car Company after Ford's 1902 departure.

The next year Ford used resources pooled from several investors to form the Ford Motor Company, through which he finally achieved success. At first he continued to produce racing cars, which tended to attract positive publicity. Eventually, though, Ford's company moved toward making ordinary street cars, although these were still large, expensive vehicles that only rich people could afford. Ford's Model A was very popular, selling seventeen hundred cars in 1904. The company produced more models, all named after letters of the alphabet, and by 1907 it had made more than one million dollars in profits.

The Tin Lizzy

Ford was not satisfied, though. He believed that he could make and sell smaller, cheaper automobiles that would appeal to a much wider market of average U.S. citizens. These cars, he knew, would have to come with inexpensive, easily replaceable parts. The answer came in 1907, when Ford released the Model T. Fondly known as the Tin Lizzy, this car would dominate the automobile industry for the next two decades. Ford sold 8,000 Model Ts the first year and 730,000 in 1916, the year of its highest production.

The Tin Lizzy was a light, durable car that was perfectly suited to travel on bad roads (and thus particularly loved by farmers). People joked that it was available in any color, as long as that color was black. It came with no extras, such as windshield wipers, and tended to break down a lot, but its simple design made repairs fairly easy. The Model T's most attractive feature, though, was its price tag: at its cheapest (in 1924), it was available for $260, and a used Model T could be bought for as little as $50.

The phenomenal success of the Model T could be attributed in large part to Ford's reforms in both manufacturing and management. Finding it difficult to keep up with the demand for the Model T, he had looked for ways to streamline and speed up production. Ford was intrigued by the theory of "scientific management" that had been proposed by industrial engineer Frederick Taylor (1856–1915), who had done careful studies to determine both the most effective ways to manage employees and the most efficient uses of workers' time and motions. Ford put these practices to work in his Detroit factory, and he introduced another innovation: the assembly line.

Innovative approaches

The assembly line had already been used in the manufacture of small machines like typewriters, but never on such a large scale or for a machine that had five thousand parts, as an automobile did. The assembly line moved the parts along a waist-high conveyor belt past workers, each of whom performed a single task. This greatly improved the speed of production while lowering costs. Meanwhile, Ford forbade his workers from doing anything, such as talking or sitting down, that distracted them from their jobs. He walked around the factory constantly, looking for ways to improve procedures even more.

These changes allowed Ford to reduce production time on the Model T from one car every twelve and a half hours to one every ninety minutes or better (in 1924, the company released 10,000 cars per week, and on the day of its highest production, October 31, 1925, Ford produced 9,109 cars, or one every ten seconds). The lower costs for the company allowed Ford to do something even more revolutionary than the assembly line. Determined to build up a steadier, more loyal workforce, he offered workers $5 a day rather than the usual $2.60, a move that other employers harshly criticized. But Ford did not stop there. He also reduced his workers' workday from nine to eight hours.

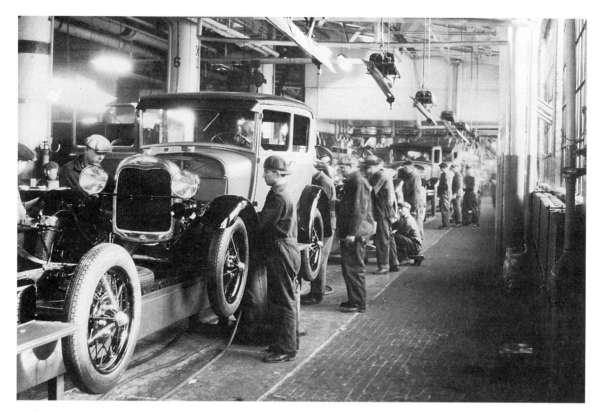

Assembly line workers inside the Ford Motor Company factory at Dearborn, Michigan, in 1928. Although working conditions on the line were unpleasant, men lined up to apply for jobs with Ford. *(Hulton Archive/ Getty Images. Reproduced by permission.)*

Working in a Ford automobile plant was not easy, not only due to the boss's rigid rules and the sometimes unpleasant conditions, but also because of the depressing boredom of working on an assembly line. In addition, the company's notorious Sociological Department tried to control workers' lives by checking up on their behavior outside work. Ford disapproved of smoking and alcohol use, and he expected his workers to accept his ideas about morality. Nevertheless, men lined up to apply for jobs with Ford, and, once hired, they tended to stay for years. Ford was strongly admired, in fact, for the way he had risen from farm boy to billionaire despite a lack of formal education. And he had done so by making sure that the workers who toiled in his factories could afford to buy the cars they built there.

Building wealth and influence

By 1916 war was raging in Europe as Germany continued its drive to take over areas controlled by other nations. Although some called for the United States to become involved on the side of the Allies (Great Britain, France, and Italy), Ford was not among them. Always a committed pacifist (someone who believes that war and violence are never justifiable), he decided to employ his considerable wealth and influence in a bid for peace. He sponsored a mission of pacifists who sailed on a ship called the *Oskar II* to Sweden, intending to hold peace talks with all of the European nations. When Germany refused to participate, however, the mission failed.

In 1918 Ford made his son Edsel president of the Ford Motor Company (although he still wielded control from behind the scenes) while he ran on the Democratic ticket for the U.S. Senate. Ford was not elected, and he returned to running his company. His desire to control all aspects of the automobile manufacturing process was realized in 1919, when he opened his state-of-the-art Rouge River plant, the largest such facility in the world. By this time Ford was growing his own rubber on plantations in Brazil, and he owned ships, coal and iron-ore mines, and thousands of acres of woodlands. Thus he brought all of his own raw materials to his plant, which was equipped with a steel mill and glass factory as well as the usual assembly shops. Nearly 100,000 workers were employed at the Rouge River plant.

The rise of the automobile

During the 1920s, the automobile first assumed the major role in U.S. life that it has continued to play. And during that crucial decade, Ford made 60 percent of all U.S. cars. The automobile industry provided jobs for about five million people, who worked not only in the actual manufacturing of vehicles but also in the making and selling of parts and supplies, in the gasoline industry, and in service stations.

The suburbs expanded, as automobiles allowed people to live farther from their workplaces. Recreation opportunities also increased, as families took outings and vacations in their cars, and young people found their social lives vastly improved by the greater mobility and privacy afforded by the automobile. The

Federal Highway Act of 1921 made funds available to the states to replace or improve the nation's network of terrible roads, many of them unpaved and built for horses, not cars. From now on, the United States would be a car-driving, car-loving nation.

A new model

During the late 1920s it became clear that the public's enthusiasm for the Model T was starting to dwindle. Ford had concentrated all his efforts on only one car, but now consumers were looking for more choices and more style. The other major automobile companies, General Motors and Chrysler, were gaining quickly on Ford. In response to this competition, Ford halted production on the Model T and went to work on a new car called the Model A.

Car fanciers across the nation were abuzz with speculation about the new model. On the day of its unveiling, December 2, 1927, Ford ran full-page advertisements in newspapers and magazines. Dealers all over the country reported huge crowds gathering in showrooms to get a glimpse of the Model A. In New York City, the largest dealership had to move its exhibition to Madison Square Garden (a large arena) to accommodate the crowds. The Model A did not disappoint, for it was available in a range of colors from Florentine Cream to Niagara Blue, and it could reportedly go as fast as 75 miles (120 kilometers) per hour. Best of all, of course, was its low cost. At $495, it was less expensive than General Motors' most popular model, the Chevrolet.

Although the Model A sold well (a million and a half in 1929), the Chevrolet was soon in the lead again. Meanwhile, Ford was busy with other pursuits. The most positive was the establishment of Greenfield Village in Dearborn, Michigan. This museum began when Ford moved his childhood home out of the way of a planned highway. He brought in other historic buildings—such as the courthouse in which President Abraham Lincoln (1809–1865) had once practiced law and Edison's workshop—arranged them around a village green, and filled them with antiques.

Less positive was Ford's role in a scandal involving the *Dearborn Independent,* a newspaper he owned. In the early 1920s the newspaper had published a series of articles that were harshly

The *Dearborn Independent* Scandal

By 1919 Henry Ford was one of the most famous men in the United States, much admired by the public for having lifted himself out of a working-class background and into the highest ranks of wealth and status. Looking for a way to share his views with the public, Ford bought a weekly local newspaper called the *Dearborn Independent*. Although he was not the editor, the newspaper served as a vehicle for his own opinions.

One of Ford's strongly held beliefs was Jewish people were a threat to Christian society, and his anti-Semitism (anti-Jewish sentiments) were expressed in the newspaper. A series of articles in the *Independent* between May 1920 and December 1921 alleged that Jews had caused World War I and were planning to overthrow Christian civilization. The newspaper also began to publish a translation of *The Protocols of the Elders of Zion*, which claimed to describe Jewish plans for the destruction of Christianity. The document was actually a fake, originally produced by the secret police of czarist Russia in order to divert public attention away from that nation's corrupt government.

The Jewish community in the United States was divided over how to respond to the *Independent*'s articles. One group, led by the American Jewish Committee, preferred a nonconfrontational approach. The second group, spearheaded by the publishers of the magazine *American Jew,* supported a more aggressive response, such as a boycott of Ford products.

In early 1922 the *Independent* stopped printing anti-Semitic material, but its earlier articles were published in a book titled *The International Jew: The World's Foremost Problem* (1922) and circulated around the world. Adolf Hitler, the Nazi dictator of Germany and an outspoken anti-Semite, was a known admirer of the book.

The *Dearborn Independent*'s anti-Semitic campaign resumed in 1924 with an attack on a Jewish lawyer who had organized farm cooperatives. A cooperative is a collaborative arrangement in which people in a business or community work together to mutual benefit. The lawyer sued the newspaper and Ford for defamation, or publishing false information that damages one's reputation. The case came to trial in 1927, but Ford was spared from testifying when he was injured in an automobile crash the day before he was to appear in court. When a juror later spoke to a newspaper reporter about the trial, the judge declared a mistrial.

Concerned about the possible effect of negative publicity on his ailing company, Ford met with a representative of the American Jewish Committee. He agreed to take back the anti-Semitic statements published in the *Independent,* and he issued an apology to Jews. Ford soon closed down the newspaper, but he renewed Jewish anger and distrust during the late 1930s when he accepted a prize from Hitler.

critical of Jewish people, blaming them for many of the world's problems and accusing them of a plot to take over the world. Among the admirers of these articles was Adolf Hitler (1889–1945), the anti-Jewish leader of Nazi Germany, who would soon lead his country into World War II (1939–45). When a Jewish attorney who had been directly named in the article threatened to sue Ford, he apologized, but he had already gained a reputation as an anti-Semite (a person who dislikes Jews).

Resisting change

With the Great Depression, the period of economic downturn and hardship that lasted from the 1929 stock market crash until approximately 1939, came some major changes in U.S. society. One of these was the strengthening of the labor movement, as workers began to make more demands for better pay, benefits, and working conditions. This was a change, however, that Ford was unable to accept. His large security force repeatedly harassed and intimidated leaders and potential members of the United Auto Workers (UAW), the union that was working to organize the auto industry.

Ford was one of the last companies to become unionized, and it did so only after several violent worker strikes and, in 1941, a court order allowing workers to join the union if they wished. Seventy percent of Ford's workers voted to join the UAW. Ford also resisted the efforts of President Franklin D. Roosevelt (1882–1945; served 1933–45) to ease the effects of the Depression. Ford would not go along with either the National Recovery Act, which encouraged industries to work together to ease economic problems, or the National Labor Relations Act, which provided various benefits to workers.

After suffering a stroke in 1938, Ford again handed over the reins of his company to his son. Although Ford had opposed U.S. involvement in World War II, once the U.S. naval forces at Pearl Harbor, Hawaii, were bombed (the event that triggered the United States' entry into the war), he quickly converted his factories to manufacture airplanes and weapons. At Ford's Willow Run plant, eight thousand Liberator bomber planes were produced.

When Edsel died in 1943, Ford came out of retirement one last time. At this point, due to Ford's stubborn one-man rule and generally poor management, the Ford Motor Company was in decline. But in 1945 Ford's grandson Henry Ford II took over the company, and under his leadership it began a slow upward climb. At the beginning of the twenty-first century, it was the second-largest automobile manufacturer in the world. And since its founding in the late 1930s, the company's Ford Foundation has offered many billions of dollars in charitable grants.

Two years after his last retirement, at the age of eighty-three, Ford died at his Fair Lane mansion. His grand, final home was located only a few miles from the farm on which he had grown up.

For More Information

Books

Batchelor, Ray. *Henry Ford, Mass Production, Modernism, and Design.* Manchester, UK: Manchester University Press, 1994.

Burlingame, Roger. *Henry Ford: A Great Life in Brief.* New York: Knopf, 1969.

Collier, Peter, and David Horowitz. *The Fords: An American Epic.* New York: Simon & Schuster, 1987.

Lacy, Robert. *Ford: The Men and the Machine.* Boston: Little, Brown, 1986.

Miller, Nathan. *New World Coming: The 1920s and the Making of Modern America.* New York: Scribner, 2003.

Nevins, Allan, and F.E. Hill. *Ford: The Times, the Man, the Company.* New York: Scribner, 1954.

Perret, Geoffrey. *America in the Twenties.* New York: Touchstone, 1982.

Web Sites

"Henry Ford." *Education on the Internet and Teaching History Online.* Available online at http://www.spartacus.schoolnet.co.uk/USAford.htm. Accessed on June 23, 2005.

"Henry Ford, 1863–1947." *A Science Odyssey: People and Discoveries.* Available online at http://www.pbs.org/wgbh/aso/databank/entries/btford.html. Accessed on June 23, 2005.

Iacocca, Lee. "Builders & Titans: Henry Ford." *The Time 100.* Available online at http://www.time.com/time/time100/builder/profile/ford2.html. Accessed on June 23, 2005.

The Life of Henry Ford. Available online at http://www.hfmgv.org/exhibits/hf/default. Accessed on June 23, 2005.

George Gershwin

Born September 26, 1898 (Brooklyn, New York)
Died July 11, 1937 (Hollywood, California)

Composer and pianist

"George Gershwin died on July 11, 1937, but I don't have to believe that if I don't want to."

John O'Hara, U.S. novelist and short story writer

George Gershwin was one of the best-known and most important figures in the musical history of the United States. He played a key role in the Roaring Twenties, for his music played an important part in this exciting decade. Writing for the Broadway stage, Gershwin (along with his brother Ira [1896–1983], who provided the lyrics) kept people humming along to such songs as "I Got Rhythm," "Let's Call the Whole Thing Off," and "They Can't Take That Away from Me." In fact, many of the songs the Gershwins made popular in the 1920s are still sung and enjoyed today. Gershwin's more serious compositions, especially his most famous, the acclaimed *Rhapsody in Blue,* combined the older traditions of classical and operatic music with elements of the new musical forms of jazz and blues. Gershwin helped to establish and promote these uniquely American contributions to the world's musical heritage.

The talented child of immigrants

Part of what makes George Gershwin's story so interesting is his status as the child of immigrant parents who came to the United States in search of better lives for their children. Gershwin

George Gershwin was one of the best-known and most important figures in the musical history of the United States. *(Hulton Archive/Getty Images. Reproduced by permission.)*

is a shining example of how such dreams can come true. His parents were Russian immigrants who settled on New York City's Lower East Side. They named their second son Jacob, but everybody called him George. His father ran a number of businesses, including a stationery store, several restaurants, a bakery, a pool hall, and a boardinghouse. The family was well-off.

Gershwin enjoyed playing games and roller-skating with his friends in the city streets. He much preferred sports to academics, and he was not particularly interested in music either. When he was ten years old, he happened to hear some violin music coming out of the window of a school building. Entranced, he learned that the music was coming from the violin of his classmate Maxie Rosenzweig (who would later perform under the professional name Max Rosen). Gershwin befriended Maxie, who introduced him to classical music.

When Gershwin was twelve, his parents bought a piano, mostly because their oldest son, Ira, had expressed an interest in playing. But the younger brother also had an inclination to play; he learned quickly and soon began putting his own tunes together. Gershwin's parents arranged for him to take music lessons. He studied with a teacher named Charles Hambitzer, who recognized his talent, taught him about technique and harmony, and guided him to the work of classical composers like Frederic Chopin (1810–1849) and Franz Liszt (1811–1886).

Working as a "song plugger"

At the same time, however, Gershwin was an enthusiastic admirer of popular music, which included romantic ballads and comedy songs as well as occasional jazz music. At this time jazz was in its infancy. Born out of a rich blend of influences—including African rhythms and instruments brought by slaves to the United States, and elements of the folk music sung and played by the nation's earliest settlers, who came from Great Britain—jazz first took the form of ragtime piano tunes with a unique, syncopated rhythm pattern (created when the weak beat is stressed in place of the usual strong one).

Gershwin started writing his own songs in 1913. That summer he worked as a pianist in a resort in New York's Catskills Mountains. Determined to make a career for himself in music, the fifteen-year-old Gershwin dropped out of school and became a song plugger (someone who tries out new songs on the piano) on Tin Pan Alley. This was the name for an area in New York City, running along Twenty-Eighth Street, between Broadway and Fifth Avenue, where many music publishers were turning popular songs into a big, profitable business.

Gershwin worked first for the Remick publishing house, at a salary of fifteen dollars a week. In 1916, he published his first song, "When You Want 'Em, You Can't Have 'Em," with lyrics by Murray Roth. Next Gershwin went to work for T.B. Harms, the nation's leading publisher of sheet music,

Irving Berlin: A Beloved Songwriter

Irving Berlin was one of the most prominent composers of popular songs during the Roaring Twenties and the mid-twentieth century. Though he had no formal musical training and could not read sheet music, over the course of his career Berlin wrote more than nine hundred songs, as well as scores for eighteen films and nineteen Broadway musical plays. His work is still being heard in the early twenty-first century.

Berlin was born Israel Baline in Tyumen, Russia, in 1888. He arrived in the United States at age five and settled with his family in New York City. After his father's death Berlin worked to help support the family, making money as a street singer and, in 1905, as a singing waiter in a saloon. It was in this job that Berlin wrote his first song, "Marie from Sunny Italy," to compete with a bartender at a rival bar. When Israel Baline's name was misspelled as Irving Berlin on the sheet music, he thought it sounded more American and he kept it. In 1911 he wrote "Alexander's Ragtime Band," the song that propelled him to fame.

Between 1912 and 1916 Berlin wrote more than 180 songs. After composing tunes for the 1911 *Ziegfeld Follies,* he started writing entire Broadway musicals, including *Watch Your Step* (1914) and *Stop! Look! Listen!* (1915).

When World War I broke out, Berlin decided to become a U.S. citizen. He was drafted into the army and completed basic training near the town of Yaphank on New York's Long Island. While there he wrote one of his most popular songs, "Oh! How I Hate to Get Up in the Morning!"

Once out of the army Berlin returned to writing songs. When new technology allowed movies to incorporate sound in the 1920s, he wrote scores for films, including *Puttin' on the Ritz* (1929); *Cocoanuts* (1929); and *Top Hat* (1935). Perhaps his best known film score was for *Holiday Inn* (1942), which featured the classic Berlin song "White Christmas." In 1954 this song and several other Berlin favorites would be included in the movie *White Christmas.*

When World War II began in Europe in the late 1930s, Berlin revived a peace-oriented song he had written during World War I and never used. "God Bless America" was sung by Kate Smith on a radio broadcast that aired on November 11, 1938. It became an immediate favorite of the U.S. people.

Berlin continued to write popular songs throughout his career. *Annie Get Your Gun* (1946), which was loosely based on the life of western figure and entertainer Annie Oakley, was the most successful of his Broadway shows. It featured a number of popular songs, including "I Got the Sun in the Morning" and "There's No Business Like Show Business." Berlin who died in 1989, was acclaimed as a towering figure in American music.

making an impressive thirty-five dollars a week. Two years later Gershwin's career took an upward leap when he wrote the complete score (all the musical numbers) for a Broadway show called "La La Lucille."

The first page of Gershwin's manuscript of *Rhapsody in Blue.* COPYRIGHT 1924 BY NEW WORLD MUSIC CORPORATION. USED BY PERMISSION

The first page of the music for George Gershwin's famous composition *Rhapsody in Blue.* *(©1924, renewed WB Music Corp.*

A promising young composer

Another break came for Gershwin in 1919, when he wrote a song called "Swanee" (with lyrics by Irving Caesar). The Broadway singer and actor Al Jolson (1886–1950) heard Gershwin perform the song at a party, and he subsequently included it in his show *Sinbad*. A year later, Jolson recorded the song. This success helped to bring Gershwin into the spotlight as a promising young composer.

Between 1920 and 1925, Gershwin wrote the scores for each yearly edition of George White's *Scandals,* popular productions that featured spirited singing and dancing. It was during this period that Gershwin's grounding in classical music, his interest in jazz, and his talent for popular music began to come together. The cultural explosion known as the Harlem Renaissance—when African American writers, artists, intellectuals, and musicians made New York City's black community a center of cultural achievement—was in full bloom. Gershwin was often seen in Harlem's nightclubs, speakeasies (establishments where alcohol, made illegal by the passage of the Eighteenth Amendment, was sold and entertainment offered), and rent parties (informal gatherings in private homes). He was fascinated by the innovative jazz and blues being played in so many venues, by so many talented musicians.

Their influence is evident in *Blue Monday,* a twenty-five-minute jazz opera that Gershwin wrote in 1922. Although the piece was not successful (it was considered too gloomy for the lighthearted *Scandals*), it represented Gershwin's first attempt to incorporate African American musical influences and characters into his work. A little over a decade later, Gershwin would develop this idea more fully in *Porgy and Bess* (1935).

Rhapsody in Blue

Gershwin was not the only white musician of the period who was interested in the new musical forms coming out of African American culture. One of these was bandleader Paul Whiteman (1891–1967), who would later be incorrectly labeled the "King of Jazz" (the label is more appropriately applied to some of the true founders of jazz and blues, such as Ferdinand "Jelly Roll" Morton [1885–1941] or W.C. Handy [1873–1958]).

Determined to show off the wide range of popular music, Whiteman planned a major concert to be held at New York City's Aeolian Hall on February 12, 1924. He asked Gershwin to contribute a jazz concerto that would serve as the show's centerpiece. The result was *Rhapsody in Blue,* which was an immediate hit and which has since become one of the most familiar, beloved, and frequently performed American compositions. This work firmly established Gershwin's position as a serious composer.

Rhapsody in Blue marked the first time that jazz rhythms and blues-tinged melodies had been blended with classical elements. Though some critics fault the piece as cliche-ridden and repetitive, most agree that it is infused with an inspiration and openness deeply rooted in U.S. culture. *Rhapsody in Blue* helped to increase international respect for U.S. musicians and musical forms. Further, it freed other classical composers, such as Aaron Copland (1900–1990) of the United States and Maurice Ravel (1875–1937) of France, to follow Gershwin's lead and incorporate elements of jazz and blues into their own works.

Later in 1924 Gershwin scored his first hit Broadway musical, *Lady Be Good.* Gershwin's brother Ira, with whom he would collaborate frequently over the next two decades, wrote the lyrics for the show's songs, which included such classics as "Fascinating Rhythm" and "The Man I Love." Some of the most famous shows they scored were *Oh, Kay!* (1926), *Funny Face* (1927), and *Girl Crazy* (1930). *Of Thee I Sing* (1931) was especially notable for its unusual element of political satire, and it was the first musical comedy to win a Pulitzer Prize (a prestigious yearly award for literature and writing of various kinds).

Music both serious and lighthearted

For the rest of his life, Gershwin alternated between writing music for the Broadway stage and composing serious pieces for the concert stage. The latter category includes *Piano Concerto in F* (1925), *Three Preludes* (1926), and *An American in Paris* (1928). In 1932 Gershwin produced both *Second Rhapsody for Piano* (1932), which he hoped would be as successful as his first *Rhapsody*, and *Cuban Overture*. Neither work was particularly well received. During the 1930s he also wrote film scores for several popular movies, including *Damsel in Distress* and *Shall We Dance?* The latter starred the renowned screen dancers Fred Astaire (1899–1987) and Ginger Rogers (1911–1995) and featured such memorable songs as "Let's Call the Whole Thing Off" (which the two stars performed on roller skates).

In 1925 Gershwin had read the best-selling novel *Porgy* by DuBose Heyward, which was set in the poor black community of Charleston, South Carolina. He was immediately interested in turning this story into a jazz opera, especially after the 1927 stage adaptation of the book became a huge hit. Gershwin finally realized this dream in 1935 when *Porgy and Bess* premiered. Amid complaints that it was an overly long, awkward blend of jazz, opera, and popular music, the show flopped. Some critics also noted that *Porgy and Bess* contained numerous stereotypes of black people. Nevertheless, the composition that Gershwin called a "folk opera" was one of the first attempts to portray African American life for mostly white audiences.

Gershwin's belief in the value of *Porgy and Bess* never wavered, but it was not until 1942 (five years after Gershwin's death) that a revival of the show became a Broadway hit. It has since been performed often in the United States and other countries and is considered a classic work of U.S. musical theater. In addition, many songs from *Porgy and Bess,* such as "Ol' Man River" and "Summertime," continue to be widely recognized and enjoyed.

Gershwin was a handsome, athletic, energetic, and charming man, but his confidence in his own talent and his devotion to his art made him somewhat self-absorbed and occasionally arrogant. Although he was involved in a number of romances, he never married. In 1937 he began experiencing some troubling health symptoms. While performing his *Concerto in F* with the Los Angeles Philharmonic Orchestra, his mind went blank, and he later suffered from frequent headaches. Medical tests revealed a brain tumor, and on July 11 he underwent surgery. He died five hours later, at the age of thirty-eight.

For More Information

Books

Jablonski, Edward, and Lawrence D. Stewart. *The Gershwin Years.* Garden City, NY: Doubleday and Co., 1973.

Kimball, Robert, and Alfred Simon. *The Gershwins.* New York: Atheneum Publishers, 1973.

Rosenberg, Deena. *Fascinating Rhythm: The Collaboration of George and Ira Gershwin.* New York: Dutton, 1991.

Schwartz, Charles. *Gershwin: His Life and Music.* Indianapolis, IN: Bobbs-Merrill Co., 1973.

Web Sites

"George." *George and Ira Gershwin: The Official Web Site.* Available online at http://www.gershwin.com. Accessed on June 23, 2005.

"George Gershwin." *American Masters (PBS).* Available online at http://www.pbs.org/wnet/americanmasters/database/gershwin_g.html. Accessed on June 23, 2005.

George Gershwin. Available online at http://www.gershwinfan.com/biogeorge.html. Accessed on June 23, 2005.

Warren G. Harding

Born November 2, 1865 (Corsica, Ohio)
Died August 2, 1923 (San Francisco, California)

U.S. president

"Let us stop to consider that tranquillity at home is more precious than peace abroad, and that both our good fortune and our eminence are dependent on the normal forward stride of all the American people. . . ."

Warren G. Harding was elected to the presidency on the promise of returning the nation to what he called "normalcy" after the turmoil of World War I (1914–18). His term in office, which lasted from 1921 until his unexpected death in 1923, ushered in not only the general economic prosperity that characterized the Roaring Twenties but also the dominance of the Republican Party during this decade. Charming and personable, Harding was much loved by the ordinary people of the United States during his presidency, but history has not been as kind. His reputation was marred by revelations after his death that his administration had been riddled with corruption.

Finding his way

Warren Gamaliel Harding was the eldest of eight children born to George Tyron Harding, a Civil War veteran, a farmer, and a doctor, and Phoebe Dickerson Harding, a gentle, very religious woman who eventually went into medical practice with her husband. Harding attended a one-room school and performed his farm chores without much enthusiasm. The

Warren G. Harding's term as president ushered in the general economic prosperity that characterized the Roaring Twenties. *(Courtesy of The Library of Congress.)*

family moved to a farm outside the small town of Caledonia when Harding was ten years old. Here Harding learned to play the cornet, spent his summers working in a sawmill, and worked as a printer's "devil" (helper) at a newspaper, where he learned the basics of a trade with which he would be involved for a long time to come.

When Harding was fourteen he entered Ohio Central College, a two-year academy with a rather weak academic

Florence Harding: A Formidable First Lady

Florence Kling Harding, wife to U.S. president Warren G. Harding, was a strong individual who supported her husband's career to the White House but could not escape the rumor that she was some how involved in his death. A dynamic woman, Florence inspired a range of opinion about her character and her relationship to her husband.

Born into a wealthy family in Marion, Ohio, in 1860, Florence studied music for one year before returning home. The nineteen-year-old soon became pregnant by a local boy, Henry "Pete" De Wolfe. Although they were said to have eloped, a marriage may not have actually taken place. Son Eugene was born in 1880, and De Wolfe left his young family soon after the birth. Florence, struggling as a single mother, gave the baby to her parents to raise.

At age thirty, Florence met Warren G. Harding, who had recently bought Marion's *Daily Star* newspaper. Although her father disapproved, the two married in July 1881. Their marriage produced no children.

After their marriage, Florence took over the newspaper's circulation department, where she was known as a demanding but effective manager. Meanwhile, Harding became active in politics, supported and encouraged by his wife. He served first as an Ohio state senator, and in 1914 was elected to the U.S. Senate.

As the 1920 election approached, Harding's campaign manager urged him to run for president. Florence had reservations but supported her husband. She was actively involved in her husband's campaign by courting the press and endearing herself to female voters by speaking out on women's rights. With the Nineteenth Amendment, granting women the right to vote, that had recently come into law, Florence became the first

program. He served as co-editor of the school newspaper before graduating in 1882. Shortly before his graduation, Harding's family had moved to Marion, and he joined them there that summer. He worked as a teacher but lasted only one semester, claiming later that it was the hardest job he had ever had. Next he read law in an attorney's office (the common method, in the early twentieth century, for training to become a lawyer), but he did not like this kind of work either. Jobs as an insurance agent and a part-time reporter for the weekly *Mirror* newspaper also did not work out.

Meanwhile Harding helped to organize a town band, and he started forming the conservative Republican beliefs that he would hold for the rest of his life. In November 1884, when he was nineteen, Harding got together with two friends to buy, for three hundred dollars, a small, ill-equipped daily newspaper wife of a presidential candidate to cast a vote for her husband.

Harding won the presidency by a large margin. Upon moving into the White House, Florence immediately ordered the mansion to be opened to tourists. As First Lady, she hosted many teas, receptions, and state dinners. These festivities were well covered by the media, and newspapers often printed Florence's remarks in favor of women competing in sports and running their own businesses. Behind the scenes she encouraged her husband to speak out more forcefully on racial equality and religious tolerance. Florence was also known to serve as bartender at the poker games hosted by her husband, who served illegal liquor at these private gatherings.

Although Florence made significant contributions to her husband's career, their marriage does not appear to have been happy. It was widely known, though not reported by the press, that the president indulged in extramarital affairs. After the death of both Hardings, a book written by Nan Britton claimed that her daughter had been fathered by Harding.

By 1923 rumors were circulating that the Harding administration was riddled with corruption. The Hardings were aware of these growing concerns when they set off on a trip to Alaska and the West Coast that was billed as "a Voyage to Understanding." During the journey Harding became ill and, on August 2, 1923, suddenly died. Florence refused to allow an autopsy, which later led to allegations that she had somehow been involved in his death, but these were never proven.

After the funeral, Florence destroyed many of Harding's presidential papers, most likely to protect his reputation. She lived for only another year and a half, dying of kidney disease on November 21, 1924.

called the Marion *Star*. Eventually Harding became the *Star*'s sole owner, and under his care the newspaper became increasingly successful. Within five years, in fact, it was Marion's leading publication.

At the same time, Harding was becoming a prominent citizen of Marion. He was appointed to the boards of directors of several companies, served as a trustee of his Baptist church, and belonged to a number of community organizations. In 1881 he married Florence "Flossie" Kling (1860–1924), who was five years older than Harding. Her father initially disapproved of the marriage because he had heard rumors that one or more of Harding's ancestors had been black. At this period in U.S. history, many people not only considered African Americans inferior to those of European ancestry but also strongly disapproved of intermingling between people of different races. This issue would continue to be raised from time to time during Harding's career.

In any case, it seems that Harding's marriage to Flossie, whom he called "Duchess" due to her dominant personality, was unhappy, and over the course of their married life he would have several extramarital affairs. Nevertheless, Harding's wife believed in his potential for success and encouraged his progress in both publishing and politics. Soon after their marriage she took over the *Star*'s circulation department, and her able leadership helped to make the newspaper a thriving, profitable operation.

A popular Ohio politician

Harding had a natural gift for public speaking and an ability to say little of substance in an important-sounding, pleasing way. Thus he seemed well suited to run for political office. In 1899 he was elected as a Republican state senator, an impressive feat in a state dominated by Democrats. In this position he gained a reputation as someone who could mediate between the two different groups of Republicans within the Senate, who often squabbled with each other. During his second term as senator, Harding was chosen for the prestigious role of Republican floor leader. It was during this period that he met Harry Daugherty (1860–1941), a Republican politician, lawyer, and lobbyist (someone who tries to influence legislators on a particular issue) who would play a major role in his presidential administration.

Harding was elected to the largely ceremonial office of lieutenant governor of Ohio in 1902. Eight years later he ran for governor, but he was defeated and returned to Marion to run his newspaper. Harding gained some national attention in 1912 when he made a speech introducing William Howard Taft (1857–1930) as the nominee of the Republican National Convention. Two years later Harding was elected to the U.S. Senate.

He spent six years in the Senate, where he was well liked but accomplished nothing notable. In fact, Harding was present for less than one-third of the votes taken during his term. He consistently avoided taking any firm stands on the issues of the day, such as the prohibition of alcoholic drinks (which would become law in January 1920 after the passage of the Eighteenth Amendment to the U.S. Constitution) and whether women should be allowed to vote (the Nineteenth Amendment, passed in 1920, would win them this right).

Harding did, however, serve as chairman of the Republican National Convention in 1916, when Charles Evans Hughes (1862–1948) was chosen to run against President Woodrow Wilson (1856–1924; served 1913–21), the Democratic Party's candidate. Hughes lost to Wilson, who led the nation into war the next year despite his earlier promises to keep the United States out of the conflict.

An inoffensive candidate for president

As the 1920 election approached, Republicans knew that they were in a good position to win. Embittered by the failure of his effort to get the United States to join the League of Nations, an international organization formed to encourage cooperation and peace between countries, and weakened by illness, Wilson had decided not to run for reelection. The only question was whom the Republicans should nominate. At first the top contenders did not include Harding, but his old friend Daugherty persuaded him to put himself forward as a candidate. Daugherty began drumming up support for Harding's candidacy.

At the Republican convention, held that summer in Chicago, Illinois, the inability of party members to agree on a nominee made Harding seem an attractive candidate. Almost everyone could agree that he had some ideal qualities: he was from an important state, he was a loyal Republican (and thus more easily controlled), he had an friendly personality, and he had never taken any controversial stands on anything. The night before Harding was nominated, a group of senators met in what came to be called a "smoke-filled room" (meaning a behind-the-scenes setting), where they expressed their approval for Harding's candidacy.

The next day he was nominated on the tenth ballot; unlike today's conventions, those in the early part of the century often featured multiple votes before a candidate was chosen. Massachusetts governor **Calvin Coolidge** (1872–1933; see entry), an unsmiling, upright man known as "Silent Cal," was

Warren G. Harding and his cabinet. Several of the men that Harding appointed would later betray his trust. (© *Corbis. Reproduced by permission.*)

chosen as the vice-presidential candidate. The Republican platform (statement of positions on various issues) centered on cutting government spending, lowering taxes, and imposing more restrictions on immigration. The Democrats, meanwhile, chose as their candidate another Ohio native, the rather bland Senator James M. Cox (1870–1957), with Assistant Secretary of the Navy (and future president) Franklin Delano Roosevelt (1882–1945) as his running mate.

Harding conducted a relaxed campaign, inviting anyone who wanted to talk with him to visit his home in Marion. Standing on his own front porch, he conducted what he called "bloviating," delivering the kind of fancy-sounding, cliche-loaded speeches for which he was famous. Yet Harding avoided taking any clear stands on the issues, such as U.S. involvement with the League of Nations. In a famous speech delivered in

May 1920, he promised a "return to normalcy," which, as quoted in Geoffrey Perret's *America in the Twenties,* he later defined as "a regular steady order of things.... normal procedure, the natural way, without excess."

Elected by a landslide

That promise undoubtedly appealed to the desire of many voters for peace and calm at an uncertain, confusing time. The election ended in a landslide victory for Harding, who won 61 percent of the popular vote. This was the widest winning margin any U.S. presidential candidate had ever achieved.

Harding's first task as president was to appoint the individuals who would make up his cabinet, the group of officials who head each department of the federal government. Some of the men he chose were very respectable and competent, including Secretary of State Charles Evans Hughes (1862–1948), Secretary of the Treasury Andrew Mellon (1855–1937), and Secretary of Commerce (and future president) **Herbert Hoover** (1874–1964; see entry). But Harding also rewarded several of his close friends for their support by appointing them to high offices. Known as the "Ohio gang" because many came from Harding's home state, these men—including Daugherty, who became attorney general; Veteran's Bureau director Charles Forbes; and Secretary of the Interior Albert Fall (1861–1944)—would eventually betray Harding's trust.

As Harding's first term began, he took steps to deliver on his campaign promise of "Less government in business and more business in government," setting off a trend of laissez-faire (hands-off) government that would last throughout the 1920s. Backed by Treasury Secretary Mellon, he set into motion a program of lowered taxes, especially for the nation's wealthiest citizens, and decreased government spending, as well as an increase in tariffs (taxes other nations had to pay to import their products to the United States). He also vetoed a bonus for World War I veterans that Congress had passed and indicated his support for new measures to restrict the number of immigrants allowed to come to the United States.

On the other hand, Harding supported the Sheppard-Towner Act, which gave federal aid to the states to help reduce infant mortality, and he helped to end the steel industry's twelve-hour workday. He signed the 1921 Federal Highway Act, which provided funding for road construction and improvement, as well as legislation creating offices to handle public welfare and the federal budget. In addition, Harding pardoned many individuals who had been imprisoned during the war for beliefs then considered traitorous; the most famous of these was labor leader Eugene V. Debs (1855–1926).

Harding's most notable accomplishment in the realm of foreign affairs was organizing the Washington Conference in 1921. This gathering of representatives from the United States, Great Britain, France, Italy, and Japan resulted in these nations agreeing to reduce the size of their navies. Harding also came out in favor of full repayment of debts owed the United States by countries that had borrowed money during World War I (some thought these debts should be forgiven), and he worked to restore better relations with Mexico and the Central American nations.

During the first year or so of Harding's presidency, the economy took something of a downturn due to the sudden dip in manufacturing and employment caused by the end of the war. But by 1922 things were looking up again. Between that year and 1927, the economy would grow by an impressive 7 percent per year, as most U.S. citizens grew more prosperous and gained more buying power.

Rumors plague a popular president

On the personal front, Harding and his wife worked hard to infuse the White House with a new spirit of cheer and welcome after the rather dreary days of Wilson's presidency. They opened the front gates and window shutters so that ordinary people could catch a glimpse of what was going on inside, and they allowed the public to tour the White House, during which Flossie Harding herself would sometimes greet visitors. They hosted many teas, receptions, and holiday parties, not to mention the weekly poker games that Harding enjoyed (a glass of illegal liquor at his side) with a select group of friends. The president also liked getting away from work to play golf and attend baseball games, and he claimed to take true pleasure in the dull process of standing in reception lines and chatting with people.

Perhaps because of his long involvement with the newspaper publishing business, Harding enjoyed an especially friendly relationship with the press. For their part, the journalists who covered the White House never publicly mentioned something that was widely known: the president carried on extramarital affairs. The relationship that lasted the longest was with Carrie Phillips, the wife of a Marion friend, with whom (as proved by letters discovered after Phillips's death) Harding was involved from 1905 to 1920. Harding is also thought to have had an affair with Nan Britton, a woman thirty years younger than he was, who would later claim to have given birth to Harding's daughter.

As the summer of 1923 approached, a different kind of rumor began to circulate. Whispers of corruption in the Harding administration seem to have reached the president himself; he probably knew, for example, that Forbes was strongly suspected of having stolen funds from the Veteran's Bureau and that others close to Harding may also have been lining their pockets with government money. There is evidence that Harding was worried about these rumors, even as he set out on what he called a "Voyage of Discovery" in June. Along with Mrs. Harding, the president was scheduled to take a 1,500-mile (2,414-kilometer) journey as far west as Alaska (becoming the first president to visit that future state) in order to talk with U.S. citizens about his support for the League of Nations' World Court.

To those around him during this period, Harding seemed weary and depressed. While traveling on a train bound for San Francisco, California, he suffered what is now thought to have been a mild heart attack. After reaching San Francisco, he seemed to be recovering. On August 2, however, he died suddenly in his hotel room, with Mrs. Harding by his side. Within a few days Calvin Coolidge had been sworn in as president. The death of their beloved president came as a shock to the people of the United States. Thousands lined the route of the train that carried Harding's body back to Marion. Florence Harding, who had been ill for a long time, died only sixteen months after her husband.

Despite his great popularity at the time of his death, Harding's reputation had become tarnished within a year. Congressional investigations held during late 1923 and early 1924 revealed the nature and extent of the wrongdoing that had occurred during his presidency. Some of the culprits were among those closest to Harding. Daugherty, for example, had taken bribes from former clients in exchange for political favors, while Forbes had funneled thousands of Veteran's Bureau dollars into his own bank account. The worst offenses, however, soon became known as the Teapot Dome scandal.

Drilling for oil

Teapot Dome was the name of an area of Wyoming where some government oil reserves (land rich with oil, which was intended to fuel navy ships) were located. It turned out that Secretary of the Interior Albert Fall had arranged for this and other western reserves to be transferred from the Department of the Navy to his own department. Then Fall had granted the right to drill for valuable oil on these lands to several of his friends who were oil company executives. Fall was eventually convicted of bribery and sent to prison, becoming the first cabinet member in U.S. history to serve time in jail. Although never convicted of a crime, Daugherty and Forbes were both forced to resign, while two other government officials connected to the scandals committed suicide.

Harding's reputation was further damaged by the publication of *The President's Daughter* (1927), a book by Britton in which she detailed her affair with the president and revealed that he had fathered her daughter, Elizabeth. Public disapproval of both the corruption scandals and Harding's illicit affairs have tended to overshadow the more positive aspects of his presidency, especially the deep bond of affection he forged with the majority of U.S. citizens.

For More Information

Books

Dean, John, and Arthur M. Schlesinger. *Warren G. Harding.* New York: Times Books, 2004.

Downes, Randolph C. *The Rise of Warren Gamaliel Harding: 1865–1920.* Columbus: Ohio State University Press, 1970.

Kent, Deborah. *Warren G. Harding: America's 29th President.* New York: Children's Press, 2004.

Landau, Elaine. *Warren G. Harding.* Minneapolis, MN: Lerner, 2004.

Murray, Robert K. *The Harding Era: Warren G. Harding and His Administration.* Minneapolis: University of Minnesota Press, 1969.

Perret, Geoffrey. *America in the Twenties*. New York: Touchstone, 1982.

Russell, Francis. *The Shadow of Blooming Grove: Warren G. Harding in His Times*. New York: McGraw-Hill, 1968.

Trani, Eugene P., and David L. Wilson. *The Presidency of Warren G. Harding*. Lawrence: Regents Press of Kansas, 1977.

Web Sites

Warren G. Harding. Available online at http://www.whitehouse.gov/query.html?col=colpics?=warren+harding. Accessed on June 23, 2005.

"Warren G. Harding." *American Presidents Life Portraits*. Available online at http://www.americanpresidents.org/presidents/president.asp?PresidentNumber=28. Accessed on June 23, 2005.

Herbert Hoover

Born August 10, 1874 (West Branch, Iowa)
Died October 20, 1964 (New York, New York)

U.S. president

> "I have no fears for the future of our country. It is bright with hope."

Herbert Hoover began the Roaring Twenties as secretary of commerce under President **Warren G. Harding** (1865–1923; served 1921–23; see entry). By the end of the decade, he had himself been elected president. Although he was much admired by the public in the years leading up to the 1929 stock market crash, Hoover's reputation took a steep downturn as the Great Depression (the economic crisis that would last until approximately 1939) took hold of the nation. Despite the considerable achievements of his earlier career, Hoover was faulted for not doing more to ease the suffering experienced by so many during this period.

A determined young man

Herbert Clark Hoover was born into a Quaker family (a religious sect that is also known as the Society of Friends) in West Branch, Iowa, located about 25 miles (40 kilometers) from Iowa City. His father, a blacksmith named Jesse Hoover, died of a heart attack when Hoover was six. Three years later, his mother, Hulda Hoover, died of typhoid (a serious infectious disease). The couple's three children were sent to live with various relatives.

Although much admired by the public before 1929, Herbert Hoover's reputation began to decline as the Great Depression gripped the United States. *(Courtesy of The Library of Congress.)*

Hoover spent the rest of his childhood in the home of his uncle, Henry John Minthorn, who lived in the Quaker village of Newport, Oregon. He attended a school run by his uncle and worked as an office boy in a real-estate office his uncle had established. It was during this somewhat lonely time in his life that he developed a reserved, disciplined nature and a determination to make his own way in the world. He decided that more than anything, he wanted to be financially independent.

In 1891 Hoover became part of the first class to enroll at brand-new Stanford University (then called Leland Stanford Junior University), which was located just south of San Francisco in what would become the town of Palo Alto, California. A good but not outstanding student, he was active in student government and was elected student-body treasurer. At Stanford Hoover met his future wife, Lou Henry. An athletic young woman who was as outgoing as Hoover was shy, she was the school's first female engineering student.

Becoming a millionaire

After four years Hoover graduated with a degree in mining engineering. At this period in U.S. history, the mineral resources hidden in the vast expenses of the western states were just beginning to be tapped, so this must have seemed like a very promising field. Hoover got his first job in a Nevada City, California, gold mine, pushing gold ore carts for ten hours a day and making a daily wage of only two dollars. A year later he began working as a clerk in the office of the Louis Janin mining firm, and in 1897 he was made assistant manager of the company's mining operation in New Mexico. His work also took him to the states of Arizona, Nevada, and Wyoming.

When Hoover was twenty-three, he was hired by a British mining company called Bewick, Moering. He went to work in the firm's remote mining camp in Australia, traveling by horse and camel over miles of dusty land and enduring blistering heat and insects. The company sent him to China in 1898. The next year he married Lou Henry. She joined him in China, just in time for the beginning of a conflict called the Boxer Rebellion, an uprising by people dissatisfied with the country's troubles and convinced that foreigners were to blame. Hoover took part in the defense of Tientsin when the city was attacked, while his new wife helped tend to the wounded.

Hoover rose through the ranks at Bewick, Moering and was sent to numerous locations in Asia, Europe, and Africa, usually leading teams that opened or operated mines. Hoover had become a millionaire by the time he was forty years old. Beginning in 1901, the main residence for Hoover and his family, which eventually included sons Herbert Jr. and Allan, was a large country house near London, England, complete with servants and extensive grounds. Retired from mining, Hoover had begun to feel restless when, in 1914, World War I broke out in Europe. This conflict involved a group of nations called the Allies (Great Britain, France, and Italy) that fought against Germany in its bid to expand its territory.

Gaining a reputation for competence

In the opening days of the war, a large number of U.S. citizens, most of them tourists, found themselves stranded in England. The U.S. government called on Hoover to try to resolve the situation, and within six weeks he had helped 120,000 people return to the United States. His reputation for competence and action soon led to his appointment as head of the Committee for Relief in Belgium (that country had been occupied by Germany, and many refugees were streaming across its borders into other nations). By the end of the war, Hoover's group would provide food to eleven million Belgian and French refugees, and he would help to raise two hundred million dollars in donations to assist the cause.

In 1917 the United States entered the war, and President Woodrow Wilson (1856–1924; served 1913–21) made Hoover head of the U.S. Food Administration. In this position he coordinated the production and supply of two million bushels of wheat to the starving people of war-torn Europe, while also urging food conservation in the United States. When the war ended, Hoover took part in the Paris Peace Conference of 1919, serving as an advisor to Wilson, among other roles. Two years later he directed a program to help ease suffering caused by a famine in the Soviet Union.

By this time Hoover had become a beloved figure to many Europeans, who sent cards and letters to thank him for the "Hoover lunches" they had received during the war. In Finland it became common to use the word "Hoover" to describe acts of kindness.

As the 1920 election approached, Hoover, who was a Republican, was seen as a possible candidate by both political parties. In the end, however, the Republican nomination went to Harding, who appointed Hoover secretary of commerce (the department that oversees trade and business concerns).

He would remain in this position after Harding's unexpected death in 1923, when Vice President **Calvin Coolidge** (1872–1933; served 1923–29; see entry) became president.

One of the most active commerce secretaries ever

Hoover was a strong believer in individualism, equal opportunity, and self-reliance, values he explained in his 1922 book *American Individualism*. At the same time, he felt that business should be concerned not just with profit but also with public service and social responsibility. His vision of what he called "cooperative capitalism" tempered the laissez-faire approach (the belief that government should loosen its control of the economy and society in general) that dominated the 1920s with a concern for the less fortunate members of society.

Hoover poured all of his considerable energy and intellect into his job, becoming one of the most active commerce secretaries in the nation's history. Calling for cooperation instead of intense competition, he encouraged businesses and industries to voluntarily form trade associations; he also promoted the establishment of cooperative farm markets and sought to expand markets for U.S. products overseas. Under Hoover's direction, a new Division of Housing was set up and the Bureau of Standards was strengthened. He pushed for regulation of the fledgling radio and aviation industries and encouraged several states to cooperate in the construction of the huge, much-needed dam on the Colorado River that bears his name.

An outspoken advocate of efficiency in government, Hoover also made evident a genuine concern for others. During the devastating flood of the Mississippi River in 1927, 25,000 square miles (64,750 square kilometers) of land were underwater, and a million people were left homeless. Hoover took a very direct role in relief efforts, coordinating the provision of food, clothing, and housing and personally overseeing the construction of tent cities and rescue and evacuation boats. It was through actions like these that Hoover earned the nickname "the Great Humanitarian."

As the 1928 election approached, Coolidge surprised everyone by declining to run for reelection. The Republican Party soon put Hoover forward as a candidate, and he easily

From Hoover Lunches to Hoovervilles

Prior to his election to the presidency, Herbert Hoover earned the nickname of the Great Humanitarian for his efforts on behalf of people facing big crises. By the 1930s, however, his name was used to refer with scorn to poor, makeshift items.

As head of the U.S. Food Administration, Hoover spearheaded the effort to supply two million bushels of wheat to starving Europeans ravaged by World War I. Grateful Europeans referred positively to the food received from these efforts as "Hoover lunches." In 1917, as commerce secretary, he coordinated relief efforts after the Mississippi River flooded and left one million people homeless, ensuring that food, clothing, and housing were available to the flood's victims. But by the early 1930s Hoover's name no longer brought to mind charity and goodwill.

The United States was caught in the early years of the Great Depression, a long period of economic decline, rising unemployment, and hardship. Thousands of people found themselves out of work, unable to find new jobs, pay their bills, or buy food for their families. President Hoover believed that the nation's economy was best handled without government interference. At the same time, the general belief of the day was that people

were responsible for their own success or failure. Aid for the unemployed, homeless, or hungry did not exist, and Hoover refused to grant government money to help those most affected by the Depression.

Unable to make a living or maintain their homes, tens of thousands of people were forced to live in shantytowns and scavenge for food. These shantytowns, made of scrap metal, wood, and whatever else could be fashioned into a shelter, came to be called "Hoovervilles," an insult to the president who was seen as doing little to help the U.S. people. Hoover's name was also attached in an uncomplimentary manner to other items. The homeless covered themselves with "Hoover blankets," which were old newspapers. Jackrabbits caught for food were called "Hoover hogs." Broken-down automobiles drawn by mules were "Hoover wagons."

Hoover's inability to meet the changing needs of the nation as it suffered through its worst economic crisis in its history changed his reputation and his popularity with the public. Despite his significant humanitarian efforts earlier in his career, he was unable to lead the nation through this dark time. Franklin D. Roosevelt succeeded Hoover to the presidency after the 1932 election. He was elected under the promise to use government funds to help put people to work and to provide assistance with food and housing for those in need.

won the nomination. After a campaign during which Hoover pledged to continue with the same policies as the Coolidge administration—lowering taxes, reducing the national debt, and maintaining an isolationist stance (staying out of other nations' problems) in foreign affairs—Hoover beat the Democratic candidate, New York governor Al Smith (1873–1944), by more than six million votes.

A presidency overshadowed by disaster

Clearly, voters had closely associated Hoover with the general prosperity that most of the nation had enjoyed throughout the Republican-dominated 1920s. Hoover forecast only good times for the nation in his March 1929 inaugural speech. As quoted in Erica Hanson's book *The 1920s,* he declared, "I have no fears for the future of our country. It is bright with hope."

For many years Hoover's presidency would be closely linked to the economic disaster that occurred before the end of its first year. Few now remember Hoover's significant accomplishments, especially in domestic affairs. A consistent advocate for conserving natural resources, he oversaw the expansion of national forests and parks. He boosted the budget for highway construction and promoted prison reform, improved child welfare, ensured better treatment for African Americans, and oversaw the growth of the aviation industry.

In foreign affairs Hoover advocated good relations with the Latin American nations and made a goodwill tour of that region early in his presidency. He tried to promote international peace through two disarmament conferences (meetings at which country representatives discussed reducing weapons), in London in 1930 and in Geneva, Switzerland, in 1932, but these were ultimately unsuccessful. When Japan invaded the Chinese region of Manchuria in 1931, Hoover directed Secretary of State Henry Stimson (1867–1950) to issue a condemnation of the action, but he did not impose economic sanctions (penalties) on Japan; some saw this as a mistake that allowed Japan to gain more power, leading to the outbreak of World War II (1939–45). In order to help the struggling European economies, Hoover arranged a one-year moratorium (temporary postponement) of debts owed to the United States from World War I.

Generally, though, Hoover's presidency was overshadowed by the events that began in October 1929. The 1920s had been dominated by a mood of optimism and prosperity, but as the end of the decade approached, some observers suggested that the economy could not continue to expand like this forever. Warning signs included a decline in construction and in consumer demand for some products, such as automobiles, coupled with a ballooning tendency for people to buy things on credit. Also very troubling was the tremendous rise in stock prices.

People who buy stocks in various companies are giving those businesses money with which to operate, in the hope of sharing in the profits when the company performs well. An increase in the price of a stock means that more people want to buy that stock, making it more valuable. When the price decreases, the stock loses value and investors may lose money. During the 1920s more U.S. citizens than ever before were investing in the stock market. Some were using their own savings, while others were borrowing money or buying stocks "on the margin" (with loans from stockbrokers that had to be repaid immediately if the stock lost value).

Many investors hoped to make a fortune on the stock market and believed that prices would continue to rise indefinitely. The New York Stock Exchange was trading six million to seven million shares (or stocks) per day by 1928, compared to a more normal rate of three million to four million. The high prices of stocks did not reflect their real value or the real earning capacity of companies. In the fall of 1929 stock market prices began dipping. Worried investors began selling off their stocks, which led to a general mood of panic. On October 24, a day known as Black Thursday, orders to sell stocks rose dramatically, while prices fell at the same steep rate. Public hysteria mounted, and five days later, on Black Tuesday, the crash was complete. Numerous banks were left with no cash to pay back loans, and many depositors lost their life savings.

Unable to ease the nation's woes

The nation was profoundly shaken by this financial collapse. In the days immediately following the crash, Hoover issued statements that were meant to comfort people and restore calm. But the situation only worsened. In response, Hoover followed his lifelong instincts, focusing on voluntary action rather than government intervention. He urged industry leaders not to cut jobs and wages, and he asked banks to join

President Herbert Hoover meeting with members of the Reconstruction Finance Corporation. Hoover created the group to provide emergency loans to banks and businesses during the Great Depression. *(© Corbis. Reproduced by permission.)*

together to help other banks in trouble. Hoover called on charity organizations and local governments to help those who were unemployed, homeless, or hungry.

It soon became clear that the nation was in a full-blown economic depression. Meanwhile, Hoover put most of the blame for the nation's weak economy on outside sources, especially the poor European economies. He signed the Hawley-Smoot Tariff, which raised the rates that other countries had to pay to import their goods into the United States. This, however, only caused resentment and led to a decline in exports leaving the United States, which some said made the depression worse.

By 1931 Hoover was forced to take more drastic steps. He established the Reconstruction Finance Corporation, which provided emergency loans to banks and businesses such as insurance companies. He supported legislation that would provide more loans for home construction. Yet he remained steadfastly opposed to the idea of starting big public works projects to give people jobs, as the Democrats were suggesting. Hoover feared that this would lead to a disastrous budget deficit (an excess in government spending). Further, he firmly believed that offering people such help from the federal government would chip away at the self-reliance and love of freedom that he valued so highly.

Meanwhile, people were suffering as the unemployment rate rose steadily, businesses closed their doors, and families could not make ends meet. The man who had always been called the Great Humanitarian now seemed uncaring. The final blow to Hoover's reputation came in the spring of 1932, when about seventeen thousand veterans of World War I marched to Washington, D.C., to demand immediate payment of the bonuses they had been promised for their military service. The Senate defeated their proposal and most returned to their homes, but some remained in the makeshift village of shacks that had been built for them. An attempt to make them leave resulted in the deaths of two veterans and two police officers. In response, Hoover called out federal troops to evict those who remained, a measure that many people saw as unnecessarily harsh.

As the 1932 election campaign got under way, 23 percent of U.S. workers were unemployed. The Democratic candidate was the dynamic Franklin Delano Roosevelt (1882–1945; served 1933–45), who promised voters a program he called a "New Deal" to ease the nation's woes. Hoover warned that the changes Roosevelt was proposing were too radical, but he seemed to have lost the public's confidence. Roosevelt won the election by a landslide, gaining 22.8 million votes to Hoover's 15.7 million.

After leaving office, an embittered Hoover continued to criticize Roosevelt's policies, describing them in his 1934 book *The Challenge to Liberty* as threats to freedom and free enterprise. Tensions between Hoover and the Republican Party leadership made his quiet bids for the Republican nomination in 1936 and 1940 unsuccessful. Although he continued to write and lecture, Hoover was not again active in government until 1947, when President Harry S Truman (1884–1972; served 1945–53) appointed him to preside over the Committee on Reorganization of the Executive Branch, which researched ways to make government more streamlined and efficient. He served in the same position again under President Dwight D. Eisenhower (1890–1969; served 1953–61).

By the time of his death in 1964, Hoover had become something of an elder statesman, respected for his experience and recognized for his contributions.

For More Information

Books

Burner, David. *Herbert Hoover: A Public Life.* New York: Knopf, 1978.

Clinton, Susan. *Herbert Hoover: Thirty-First President of the United States.* Chicago, IL: Children's Press, 1988.

Fausold, Martin. *The Presidency of Herbert C. Hoover.* Lawrence: University Press of Kansas, 1985.

Hanson, Erica. *The 1920s.* San Diego, CA: Lucent Books, 1999.

Hoff-Wilson, Joan. *Herbert Hoover: A Public Life.* Boston: Beacon, 1984.

Hoff-Wilson, Joan. *Herbert Hoover, Forgotten Progressive.* Boston: Little, Brown, 1975.

Nash, George H. *The Life of Herbert Hoover, Vol. I.* New York: Norton, 1983.

Nye, Frank T., Jr. *Doors of Opportunity: The Life and Legacy of Herbert Hoover.* West Branch, IA: The Herbert Hoover Presidential Library Association, 1988.

Polikoff, Barbara G. *Herbert C. Hoover: 31st President of the United States.* Ada, OK: Garrett Educational Corporation, 1990.

Web Sites

"Herbert Clark Hoover (1929–1933)." *American President.* Available online at http://www.americanpresident.org/history/herberthoover/. Accessed on June 24, 2005.

"Herbert Hoover." *The White House.* Available online at http://www.whitehouse.gov/history/presidents/hh31.html. Accessed on June 24, 2005.

Zora Neale Hurston

Born January 7, 1891 (Eatonville, Florida)
Died January 28, 1960 (Fort Pierce, Florida)

Author and folklorist

Zora Neale Hurston was a key figure in the Harlem Renaissance, one of the most important cultural movements of the Roaring Twenties. This explosion of African American achievement in the written, visual, and performing arts was centered in the black community of Harlem in New York City. Hurston was part of a group of younger writers, whose members included Langston Hughes (1902–1967), Claude McKay (1890–1948), and Jean Toomer (1894–1967). This group's works helped to celebrate and explore African American life. Although Hurston is best known for works written in later decades (especially her novel *Their Eyes Were Watching God*), her vibrant personality and sense of humor made her a popular and vital participant in the Harlem Renaissance. The short stories that she published during this period revealed her knowledge and appreciation of the black folk tradition that she had enjoyed since childhood. She was among the first to make use of this rich resource, through both her fiction and her work as a folklorist.

"I have touched the four corners of the horizon, for from hard searching it seems to me that tears and laughter, love and hate make up the sum of life."

Zora Neale Hurston was one of the key figures of the Harlem Renaissance, a cultural movement during the Roaring Twenties. *(Courtesy of The Library of Congress.)*

A lively and curious young woman

Zora Neale Hurston was born in the central Florida town of Eatonville, which was one of the first in the United States to be incorporated as an all-black town. She was the fifth of eight children born to John Hurston, a carpenter, Baptist preacher, and three-time mayor of Eatonville. Hurston's mother, Lucy Ann Hurston, was a former schoolteacher who seems to have appreciated her daughter's lively nature and encouraged her to

Alain Locke: A Harlem Renaissance Guiding Light

Writer, editor, and educator Alain Locke was dedicated to preserving and celebrating African American culture. He believed in nurturing the talents of young black writers and artists. During the Harlem Renaissance, Locke was one of several people who served as mentors to a new generation of cultural stars, including Zora Neale Hurston and Langston Hughes.

Descended from an African American family that had been freed from slavery before the Civil War, Locke was born in Philadelphia, Pennsylvania, in 1886. The son of a law professor and a teacher, he excelled in his studies and entered Harvard University in 1904, developing an interest in philosophy.

After graduating in 1907, Locke became the first African American to be chosen as Rhodes Scholar. This honor allowed him to attend England's famed Oxford University. Three years at Oxford were followed by a year each at universities in Germany and France.

Locke returned to the United States in 1912, and became a professor at Howard University in Washington, D.C. He would remain employed at Howard, one of the nation's leading black universities, for most of the next forty years. In 1916 Locke returned to Harvard University to earn his PhD in philosophy, becoming the first African American to receive a doctoral degree from Harvard.

As an educator, Locke had extensive contact with young people, and he encouraged them to excel. In 1916 he established a literary magazine at Howard called *Stylus,* to showcase the work of promising writers. Locke was one of the first to sense in the early 1920s that an explosion of African American arts was beginning, centered in the black community of Harlem in New York City.

Locke had a prominent role in the Harlem Renaissance, particularly with his editorship of the *The New Negro: An Interpretation.* This anthology began as a special issue of the *Survey Graphic,* a white publication whose editor had asked Locke to compile a work that highlighted the talents of African American writers and artists. The result was a collection of poems, stories, essays, and visual art by thirty-four contributors that was published in March 1925 to wide acclaim. Later that year, *The New Negro* appeared as a book, with an introduction and four essays by Locke.

In his introduction, Locke proclaimed the arrival of a new phase in African American history. Blacks were now ready to step up and take their rightful place as equal members of U.S. society, he announced. They were taking renewed pride in their racial heritage, and sharing this with the rest of the world. Unfortunately, Locke's vision would take many more decades to be fully achieved. By the end of the 1920s the Harlem Renaissance was essentially over.

Locke later remembered the Harlem Renaissance as a time of independence and self-respect for its participants. He spent his final decades busy with teaching, writing, and speaking engagements. Locke died in New York City in 1954.

pursue her dreams. An imaginative, curious child, Hurston especially enjoyed sitting on the front porch of a country store and listening to the stories told there.

Hurston's happy childhood came to an end with mother's death when she was nine. Hurston's father sent her and several of her siblings away to attend a school in Jacksonville. He soon remarried, and Hurston found herself in frequent conflict with both her father and his new wife. By the age of fourteen, Hurston was living on her own. She survived for several years by working as a maid, until she was hired as a wardrobe assistant for a traveling theatrical company. With help from her sympathetic white employer, Hurston enrolled at Morgan Academy (the high school division of what is now Morgan State University) in Baltimore, Maryland.

After graduating in 1918, Hurston entered Howard University, one of the nation's most respected black universities, in Washington, D.C. Over the next six years, she attended classes while working as a manicurist and waitress to support herself. It was during these years that she began to write short stories, publishing one called "John Redding Goes to Sea" in Howard's *Stylus* magazine in 1921. By this time Hurston had met Alain Locke (1886–1954), a professor of philosophy at Howard who would soon become one of the influential older leaders of the Harlem Renaissance.

Locke brought Hurston's story, which incorporated many details from her small-town childhood, to the attention of Charles Johnson (1893–1956), the editor of a leading black publication called *Opportunity*. Johnson encouraged Hurston to move to New York City, where an exciting period of achievement for African American writers, artists, and performers was beginning. Hurston arrived in the black community of Harlem in early 1925. In her autobiography, *Dust Tracks on a Road* (1942), she recalled that she was equipped only with "$1.50, no job, no friends, and a lot of hope."

Part of a cultural explosion

A few months later, Hurston literally burst onto the scene with an exuberant appearance at an awards dinner for *Opportunity*'s first literary contest. She was thrilled to have won second place for a short story called "Spunk" and a play called *Color Struck.* The judges had been impressed with Hurston's firsthand knowledge of, and ability to recreate, the daily lives and speech of central Florida's black people. This was an important evening for Hurston because she met two very influential people. The famous white novelist Fannie Hurst (1889–1968) offered her a job as her personal secretary (Hurston's role would shift to that of a chauffeur when her lack of secretarial skills became known), and Annie Nathan Meyer (1867–1951), one of the founders of New York's Barnard College, arranged for Hurston to attend Barnard on a scholarship.

Enrolling in the fall of 1925, Hurston became Barnard's first and only black student. Meanwhile, she was quickly accepted as an important figure in the Harlem Renaissance. Her wit and storytelling ability were enjoyed by all but especially, some said, by the white people whose fascination with African American culture drew them to Harlem. In fact, some of Hurston's own friends, such as Hughes and Wallace Thurman (1902–1934), suspected that Hurston deliberately played on white stereotypes about blacks in order to win their approval.

Hurston won praise for the stories she wrote during these years, including "Drenched in Light," about a lively eleven-year-old girl with big dreams, and "Sweat," about the destructive relationship between a man and a woman living in rural poverty. The latter story was published in the single issue of a magazine called *Fire* that Hughes, Hurston, and Thurman produced.

An interest in anthropology

At Barnard, Hurston took an anthropology course (the study of human societies and cultures) with renowned anthropologist Franz Boas (1858–1942), an experience that changed her life. For the first time, she recognized the African American folk songs, stories, and customs that she had grown up with as something of special interest to many people. Boas too realized that Hurston's background, interests, and talents made her the ideal person to research African American culture, about which little was yet known. He helped her get a grant from the Carter G. Woodson Foundation to fund a research trip in the southern United States. This first journey proved a failure, though, probably because Hurston made the mistake of speaking to the rural people she met in an educated, East Coast voice that made them uncomfortable.

In May 1927 Hurston married a fellow student named Herbert Sheen, but the two lived together for only eight months and were divorced in 1931. Hurston's devotion to her career proved stronger than her commitment to the marriage. In September 1927 Hurston met Charlotte Mason (1854–1946), a wealthy white woman known as "Godmother" because she provided financial support to a number of Harlem Renaissance writers and artists (including Hughes and sculptor Richmond Barthe [1901–1989]). Mason offered to fund Hurston's anthropological research, and Hurston signed a contract that gave Mason the right to review all the material she collected. Equipped with a movie camera, an automobile, and a two-hundred-dollar-per-month salary from Mason, Hurston set out on another journey into the South.

She spent the next three years traveling around (mostly in Alabama and Florida), gathering a huge amount of material that included songs, dances, tales, superstitions, and notes on the speech patterns and slang used by the African Americans she encountered. Hurston found it difficult to get her material published, though, and she finally broke off her relationship with Mason after finding the older woman too controlling. It was at this time that Hurston's friendship with Hughes came to an end after a dispute about *Mule Bone,* a play the two had been working on together.

Success as a novelist

Hurston worked for part of 1932 at Rollins College, a black school located in Winter Park, Florida, that hired her to organize a concert program of African American arts. When that project was finished, she returned briefly to New York City and then moved back to her hometown. She was living in Eatonville when she wrote "The Gilded Six Bits," which is considered one of her best pieces of writing and which helped to boost her career. Published in *Story* magazine in 1933, it centers on a young couple whose happiness is briefly but not permanently shattered by the arrival of a slick city-dweller in their rural town. The story attracted the attention of the Lippincott publishing company, whose representatives asked

Hurston if she had written a novel. She had not, but she said that she had, then quickly wrote one.

The central character in *Jonah's Gourd Vine* (1934), John "Buddy" Pearson, was modeled after Hurston's father. He is a carpenter and preacher who often finds himself at the mercy of his very human weaknesses, especially a tendency to be unfaithful to each of three successive wives. The book sold well, as readers were drawn to its rich language and emotional power, but some commentators accused Hurston of overlooking the racial strife that, they felt, formed an inescapable part of black life. For her part, Hurston always claimed that she did not believe that constantly focusing on the negative aspects of the African American experience told the whole story.

The novel's popularity led to the publication, at long last, of Hurston's collected folklore in *Mules and Men* (1935), with an introduction written by Boas. Although almost everyone recognized the book as an important work of anthropology, some faulted Hurston for writing in a tone that seemed too light and carefree and for again ignoring racial issues. Hurston spent the next several years touring with musical shows based on her stories, including *From Sun to Sun* and *The Great Day,* which were performed in Florida and in Chicago, Illinois. She was offered a fellowship to pursue a doctoral degree in anthropology at Columbia University in New York City, but she turned it down when she found the terms too restrictive.

In 1936 Hurston received a Guggenheim Foundation fellowship that allowed her to conduct more folklore research, this time in the West Indies. She traveled to Haiti and Jamaica,

The cover of Zora Neale Hurston's novel *Jonah's Gourd Vine.* **The central character in the book was modeled after Hurston's father.** *(Copyright 1934 by Zora Neale Hurston; renewed © 1962 by John C. Hurston. Reprinted by permission of HarperCollins Publishers.)*

publishing the results in *Tell My Horse* (1938), a book that was especially noted for providing new insights into the voodoo religion practiced in those places.

After returning to the United States, Hurston began work on the novel that would be her most acclaimed work, *Their Eyes Were Watching God*. Published in 1937, the novel tells the story of strong, passionate Janie Woods, who recounts her three marriages: the first to a much older man chosen for her by her grandmother, the second to a handsome and ambitious man, and the third to Vergible "Tea Cake" Woods. The eighteen months of happiness that Janie finds with Tea Cake comes to a sad end with his death from rabies, but she continues to feel optimistic and satisfied. At the time of its publication, some critics faulted the novel for catering to white people's expectations about black characters, but later commentators have seen it very differently. This story of a black woman's quest for fulfillment has inspired readers of African American and other ethnicities, and such famous authors as Alice Walker (1944–), Toni Morrison (1931–), and Jamaica Kincaid (1949–) have cited its influence.

A gradual sinking into poverty

In the fall of 1939 Hurston became a drama instructor at the North Carolina College for Negroes in Durham. She also married Albert Price III, a man fifteen years younger than herself whom she would divorce in 1943. Hurston's next book, *Moses, Man of the Mountain,* was published in 1939, casting the biblical figure of Moses, who led the enslaved Hebrews to freedom, as an African American in a story that featured an uneasy balance between humor and seriousness.

Hurston spent late 1940 and early 1941 in southern California, living with a wealthy friend while writing her autobiography, *Dust Tracks on a Road*. The story of how she had "touched the four corners of the horizon" in her life was well received by readers, even though some considered it an overly flattering and not entirely accurate portrayal. Magazines such as the *Saturday Evening Post* and *Reader's Digest* invited Hurston to submit articles, in some of which she seemed to be saying that black and white people needed to live separate lives. This apparent advocacy of segregation angered some critics.

During the last two decades of her life, Hurston wrote little. She did produce one more novel, *Seraph on the Suwanee* (1948), which centers on a poor white woman named Arvay Henson; Hurston claimed that she wanted to prove that an African American author could successfully portray white characters. Having purchased a houseboat, Hurston enjoyed traveling up and down Florida's Halifax and Indian Rivers. She found it difficult to support herself, however, and survived for a time by borrowing money from friends while occasionally selling articles and stories.

In 1950 Hurston took a job as a maid for a white family. She later worked as a librarian, a newspaper reporter, and a substitute teacher. After many years of poor health, she suffered a stroke in 1958 and was forced to enter the Saint Lucie County Welfare Home, a place where low-income people could receive long-term care, in Fort Pierce, Florida, where she died in early 1960. Hurston's friends and family had to take up a collection to cover her funeral expenses, and she was buried in an unmarked grave.

In 1973 novelist and poet Alice Walker placed a memorial on what she believed was Hurston's final resting place. On the headstone was carved a line written by another Harlem Renaissance figure, Jean Toomer: "A Genius of the South."

For More Information

Books

Bloom, Harold, ed. *Zora Neale Hurston.* Broomall, PA: Chelsea House, 1986.

Hemenway, Robert. *Zora Neale Hurston: A Literary Biography.* Chicago: University of Illinois Press, 1977.

Howard, Lillie P. *Zora Neale Hurston.* Boston: Twayne, 1980.

Hurston, Zora Neale. *Dust Tracks on a Road.* Philadelphia, PA: Lippincott, 1942.

Lyons, Mary E. *Sorrow's Kitchen: The Life and Folklore of Zora Neale Hurston.* New York: Scribner Book Company, 1990.

Porter, A.P. *Jump at de Sun: The Story of Zora Neale Hurston.* Minneapolis, MN: First Avenue Editions, 1992.

Yanuzzi, Della. *Zora Neale Hurston: Southern Storyteller.* Hillside, NJ: Enslow Publishers, 1996.

Yates, Janelle. *Zora Neale Hurston: A Storyteller's Life.* Staten Island, NY: Ward Hill Press, 1992.

Web Sites

"Zora Neale Hurston." *Women in History.* Available online at http://www.lkwdpl.org/wihohio/hurs-zor.htm. Accessed on June 24, 2005.

"The Zora Neale Hurston Plays." *Manuscript Division, Library of Congress.* Available online at http://www.memory.loc.gov/ammem/znhhtml/znhhome.html. Accessed on June 24, 2005.

Sinclair Lewis

Born February 7, 1885 (Sauk Centre, Minnesota)
Died January 10, 1951 (Rome, Italy)

Novelist

S inclair Lewis may have been the most popular novelist of the Roaring Twenties. In such best-selling works as *Main Street* and *Babbitt,* he captured many details of daily life while exposing the dullness, conformity, and hypocrisy of average, middle-class citizens of the United States. Part of what made Lewis such an effective chronicler of this era was his great skill in imitating the speech of ordinary people. Some critics felt that his harsh social criticism reflected his internal struggle between a desire for respectability and a yearning for deeper meaning and discovery.

"In any strict literary sense, he was not a great writer, but without his writing one cannot imagine modern American literature."

Biographer Mark Schorer

A restless wanderer and writer

Almost all of Sinclair Lewis's fiction features characters and settings drawn from the midwestern setting he knew so well. Born Harry Sinclair Lewis in the village of Sauk Centre, Minnesota, he was one of three sons of a physician. His mother died when he was six, and his father soon remarried. Lewis remembered his father, who sometimes allowed his son to accompany him when he visited patients, as stern and dignified, and he admired his dedication to hard work. Nevertheless,

Sinclair Lewis may have been the most popular novelist of the Roaring Twenties. *(© Corbis. Reproduced by permission.)*

Lewis felt an early dissatisfaction with small-town life. When he was only thirteen, he made an unsuccessful attempt to run away from home to become a soldier in the Spanish-American War (1898).

Lewis grew into a tall, slim, book-loving young man with a face scarred by acne, a factor that no doubt contributed to his shyness. In 1903 he enrolled in Yale University (located in New Haven, Connecticut), where he felt like an outsider but contributed many stories, poems, and essays to various campus publications. During his first summer vacation, he sailed to England on a cattle boat, thus beginning a pattern of restless travel that would last his entire life.

Lewis returned to Yale in the fall, but he left in 1906 and spent several months as a janitor at a utopian community (based on the ideal of communal living, in which every member is equal) run by the famous novelist Upton Sinclair (1878–1968). After short periods spent in New York City and the Central American country of Panama, Lewis returned to Yale in December 1907 and graduated the following June.

For the next few years he wandered between Iowa, New York, California, and Washington, D.C., working as a newspaper reporter and occasionally selling his short stories. Despite all of his travels, however, he always felt the pull of his native Midwest. While living in New York in 1914, Lewis married Grace Hegger. Five years later the couple's son Wells was born (he would be killed in World War II [1939–45]).

A changing society

As the 1920s approached, U.S. society was changing. For the first time in the nation's history, more people were living in towns and cities than on farms; the population was becoming more diverse as immigrants streamed in; and new developments in science, technology, and industry were dramatically altering the ways in which people lived, worked, and thought. Literature was changing too, as some leading writers practiced a new kind of realism while others offered the comfort of romanticism, sentiment, and an escape from ordinary life. In his own writing, Lewis was influenced both by contemporary trends and by the great authors of the nineteenth century, such as Charles Dickens (1812–1870) and H.G. Wells (1866–1946). The works of these authors feature a concern for social issues, satire, and sentimentality, qualities that would be evident in Lewis's writing as well.

Having settled in New York in 1910, Lewis began a period of experimentation and development, writing short stories in a conventional style marked by a light, humorous tone. After selling stories to such magazines as the *Saturday Evening Post,* he published his first novel, *Our Mr. Wrenn: The Romantic*

Adventures of a Gentle Man (1914). Like Lewis himself, the hero of this book ships out for England but eventually returns to an ordinary existence in the United States.

The Trail of the Hawk (1915) also involves a young man's quest for fulfillment. In *The Job: An American Novel* (1917), the story of an ambitious young woman's experiences in work and love, Lewis attempted for the first time to re-create the speech of the salesmen he had encountered during his frequent travels. Generally, however, these early novels are not considered as accomplished as his later works.

Exposing small-town dullness and hypocrisy

The first of Lewis's truly distinguished novels appeared, very appropriately, in the first year of the 1920s. *Main Street* (1920) centered on what Lewis would term "the village virus," meaning the negative effects of life in the stifling atmosphere of a small U.S. town. It takes place in Gopher Prairie, Minnesota, closely modeled after Lewis's hometown, where young, idealistic college graduate Carol Kennicott has gone to live after marrying an older doctor. She has imagined Gopher Prairie as a charming village full of good-hearted folk, but she finds the actual town dreary and run-down and the people dull, ignorant, and hypocritical. They are not interested in her ideas about bringing culture and improvements to their town. Carol leaves for a year to live in Washington, D.C., but she finally returns to Gopher Prairie and settles back into her old routines.

Despite its harsh criticism of U.S. society, the book was a best-seller. Readers were both shocked and fascinated by this new view of familiar places and people, and they rushed to buy the book. Lewis became a literary celebrity, a stature he would maintain throughout the decade. He was particularly praised for his ability to accurately imitate the speech patterns of ordinary U.S. citizens.

Main Street was soon followed by *Babbitt* (1922), which most commentators consider Lewis's best work. The central character is businessman and booster (someone who enthusiastically, and rather mindlessly, promotes mainstream culture) George Follansbee Babbitt, the middle-aged, middle-class manager of a real-estate office in the fictional town of Zenith.

In detailed prose that paints a vivid picture of daily life in the 1920s, Lewis tells the story of Babbitt's vague dissatisfaction with his conservative, proper life and his dreams of escape as he begins an extramarital affair and flirts with liberal political views. In the end, however, Babbitt returns to his wife and family, adhering once again to his old habits and views.

Though some critics question whether Lewis was successful in blending within one character the opposing strands of conformity and rebellion, *Babbitt* was as popular with readers as *Main Street* had been. Lewis was lauded for his portrayal of many of the major issues and themes of the 1920s, including Prohibition (the popular name for the Eighteenth Amendment to the U.S. Constitution, which banned the manufacture and sale of alcoholic drinks), consumerism, and the conflict between parents and children. In addition, the word "Babbitt" became a permanent part of the U.S. vocabulary, signifying someone who is an uncultured, narrow-minded conformist.

Many readers were angered by Sinclair Lewis's book *Elmer Gantry* **because of its extremely negative view of fundamentalism.** *(Henry Groskinsky/Getty Images. Reproduced by permission.)*

Lewis produced another unflattering portrayal of U.S. society in his next novel, *Arrowsmith* (1926), which also takes place in and around Zenith. The title character is a brilliant medical researcher who struggles between his yearning for meaningful work and the demands of both his materialistic society and his own family. Lewis was named the winner of the Pulitzer Prize (a prestigious yearly award) for *Arrowsmith*, but he declined it on the grounds such awards were corrupting to writers. Probably the main reason that Lewis declined the Pulitzer, however, was because he was still angry over the judges' failure to award it to *Babbitt* four years earlier.

More success, and then a decline

Lewis's next major novel offered an extremely negative view of the fundamentalism (a form of Christianity that includes the belief that the stories in the Bible are literally true) that had gained strength during the 1920s. This was a time when many people, shaken by perceived threats to traditional values in their fast-moving society, turned to such dynamic and deeply conservative religious leaders as **Aimee Semple McPherson** (1890–1944; see entry). The title character of *Elmer Gantry* (1927) is a fraudulent evangelist (someone who tries to persuade others to follow his or her own religious beliefs) who engages in a series of deceptions, including adultery. Many readers were angered by the book, and a number of critics felt that Lewis's portrayal of Gantry was too extreme.

After writing *The Man Who Knew Coolidge* (1928), a series of monologues by a shallow, hypocritical character named Lowell Schmaltz (another resident of Zenith), Lewis turned to the theme of the U.S. citizen abroad. In *Dodsworth* (1929) he chronicled the travels and soul-searching of the central character, a wealthy automobile manufacturer who travels through Europe with his wife and is stirred by the art and history he encounters there. By the end of the novel, Dodsworth has left his shallow wife and formed a relationship with a calmer, more serious woman, and he has made plans to become a builder of artistically designed homes.

Lewis's success in capturing with accuracy and power both the material details and the deeper themes of the Roaring Twenties was confirmed in 1930, when he became the first U.S. citizen to win the Nobel Prize for Literature. In accepting this honor, Lewis praised a number of other promising young writers, including Ernest Hemingway (1899–1961) and William Faulkner (1897–1962). Those who expected Lewis to achieve new heights of accomplishment after the 1920s were disappointed, however, for his career now began a steady decline.

During the remaining two decades of his life, Lewis seemed to run out of ideas and insights. His later work lacked the satire and realism of his earlier novels and became increasingly sentimental. Neither critics nor readers were enthusiastic about *Ann Vickers* (1933), the story of a woman's search for fulfillment, or *It Can't Happen Here* (1935), in which the United States is taken

Pioneering Journalist Dorothy Thompson

Married to novelist Sinclair Lewis in 1928, Dorothy Thompson was a talented and celebrated writer herself. Her articles, radio broadcasts, and weekly newspaper columns made her one of the best-known journalists in the United States.

Thompson was born in 1894 in Lancaster, New York. She was an adventurous and sometimes rebellious child who did not get along with her stepmother. Sent to live with her aunts in Chicago, Illinois, Thompson finished high school there and then attended Syracuse University in New York. She graduated in 1914, determined to become a writer.

In 1920 Thomson traveled to Europe. While crossing the ocean on a ship, she met a group of Zionists, people who were working to establish a Jewish state in the Middle Eastern land of Palestine. She convinced a news service to let her write an article on the subject, beginning her career as one of very few female journalists working in Europe.

Thompson covered such stories as worker strikes in Italy and the Irish independence movement. Assigned to head the *New York Evening Post*'s Berlin office in 1925, Thompson moved to Germany, where she would live for varying periods over the next nine years. After several failed efforts, in 1931 she met and interviewed Adolf Hitler, leader of the Nazi Party.

In the article Thompson wrote about Hitler for *Cosmopolitan* magazine, Thompson described him as unimpressive and incapable of ruling Germany. Over the next few years, Hitler gained more and more power, eventually becoming Germany's leader. This greatly alarmed Thompson. Her articles denouncing Hitler, and particularly his hatred for and harsh treatment of Jews, resulted in her being forced to leave Germany in 1934.

Meanwhile, Thompson had married Sinclair Lewis in 1928 and given birth to a son two years later. The relationship, however, grew strained under the pressure of two careers. The couple would divorce in 1942.

In 1936 Thompson began writing a column called "On the Record" for the *New York Tribune*. She used this forum, as well as frequent radio broadcasts, to issue urgent warnings about the troubling developments in Europe, particularly the growing flood of refugees and the rising power of the Nazis. The next year, Thompson began writing a column for the *Ladies Home Journal* that would appear for the next twenty years. She also wrote articles for such publications as the *Saturday Evening Post* and *Foreign Affairs,* building a reputation as one of the most influential U.S. journalists.

During World War II Thompson advised President Franklin D. Roosevelt on the refugee problem and reported on the war, also making radio broadcasts into Germany to urge its people to rebel against Hitler. In the decades following the war she wrote about such issues as tensions between Arabs and Israelis, the women's movement, and the dangers of nuclear weapons. She died in 1961.

over by a tyrannical ruler. In his subsequent novels—including *Gideon Planish* (1943), *Cass Timberlane* (1945), *Kingsblood Royal* (1947), and *The God-Seeker* (1949)—Lewis tried unsuccessfully to breathe life into such themes as fraudulent charity organizations, marriage, and racial prejudice.

Meanwhile, Lewis's personal life also disintegrated as he succumbed to alcoholism and restless wandering. He had married journalist Dorothy Thompson in 1928 (having divorced his first wife) and fathered another son, Michael, born in 1930; the two were divorced in 1942.

Lewis died of a heart attack in Rome, Italy, in 1951. Despite the disappointments of his later career, Lewis is still considered an important figure in literature and especially of the 1920s. His biographer, Mark Schorer, has suggested that, "In any strict literary sense, he was not a great writer, but without his writing one cannot imagine modern American literature."

For More Information

Books

Dooley, D.J. *The Art of Sinclair Lewis*. Lincoln: The University of Nebraska Press, 1967.

Fleming, Robert E., and Esther Fleming. *Sinclair Lewis: A Reference Guide*. Boston: G.K. Hall, 1980.

Grebstein, Sheldon N. *Sinclair Lewis*. New York: Twayne, 1962.

Hutchisson, James M. *The Rise of Sinclair Lewis, 1920–1930*. University Park: Pennsylvania State University Press, 1996.

Lingeman, Richard R. *Sinclair Lewis: Rebel from Main Street*. New York: Random House, 2002.

Love, Glen A. *Babbitt: An American Life*. New York: Twayne, 1993.

Schorer, Mark. *Sinclair Lewis: An American Life*. New York: McGraw-Hill, 1961.

Web Sites

"Sinclair Lewis and His Life." *The Sinclair Lewis Society Web Page*. Available online at http://www.english.ilstu.edu/separry/sinclairlewis/. Accessed on June 24, 2005.

"Sinclair Lewis—Autobiography." *Nobelprize.org*. Available online at http://www.nobelprize.org/literature/laureates/1930/lewis-autobio.html. Accessed on June 24, 2005.

Charles A. Lindbergh

Born February 4, 1902 (Detroit, Michigan)
Died August 26, 1974 (Maui, Hawaii)

Aviator

One of the most popular heroes of the Roaring Twenties, Charles Lindbergh caught the world's imagination with his flight from New York City to Paris, flying solo across the Atlantic Ocean in a little less than thirty-four hours. A pioneer in the brand-new field of aviation, Lindbergh helped to transform airplane travel from the realm of daredevil stunt flyers and military pilots to a common mode of transportation for ordinary people. To the people of the 1920s, he seemed to embody both the traditional values of courage and self-reliance and the technological miracles of the future.

A boy in love with airplanes

Charles Augustus Lindbergh was born in Detroit, Michigan, but he was raised mostly in Minnesota, where his paternal grandfather had settled after immigrating from Sweden. His father, Charles August Lindbergh, was a farmer and lawyer, and his mother, Evangeline Land, had been a high school science teacher before her marriage. The couple built a home on 110 acres (44.5 hectares) of land near Little Falls, Minnesota, where their only child enjoyed the outdoor life of fishing and hunting.

"When I was a child on our Minnesota farm, I spent hours lying on my back . . . staring into the sky. . . . How wonderful it would be, I'd thought, if I had an airplane—wings with which I could fly up to the clouds and explore their caves and canyons. . . . Then, I would ride on the wind and be part of the sky.

Charles Lindbergh became one of the most popular heroes of the 1920s and helped to make airplane travel a common mode of transportation for ordinary people. (© Bettmann/Corbis. Reproduced by permission.)

Lindbergh's father was elected to the U.S. House of Representatives in 1906 and served until 1917, when his strong isolationist stance (someone who believes in staying out of other nations' affairs) on the entry of the United States into World War I (1914–18; the United States entered the war in 1917) finally led to his defeat. The elder Lindberghs were unhappily married, and young Charles spent various periods living with either his father in Washington, D.C., or his mother in Minnesota. Although not particularly interested in school, Lindbergh loved gadgets and scientific experiments. When he was twelve, his father took him to watch some military pilots practicing maneuvers, and he developed a passion for airplanes and flying. It would be another ten years, however, before he took his first flight. Meanwhile, Lindbergh later remembered lying on the ground, looking up at the sky, and thinking, according to Barry Denenberg's *An American Hero: The True Story of Charles A. Lindbergh,* "how wonderful it would be . . . if I had an airplane—wings with which I could fly up to the clouds and explore their caves and canyons. . . . Then, I would ride on the wind and be part of the sky."

Because of the extra demands on farmers during World War I, Lindbergh left school at sixteen in order to help run his family's farm, and he missed his senior year of high school. But the government began a program that allowed boys who had missed school for this reason to enter college. Lindbergh enrolled in the University of Wisconsin, where he planned to study civil engineering. His solitary manner and lack of interest in girls or parties made him something of a social outcast, although he did enjoy such pursuits as pistol and rifle shooting (at which he excelled) and performing daring feats on his motorbike.

Becoming a stunt and air mail pilot

After three semesters of college, Lindbergh dropped out and headed for Nebraska to take flying lessons. He remembered his first flight, which he took as a passenger on April 9, 1922, as the biggest thrill he had yet experienced. Having finished a mere eight hours of instruction, Lindbergh went to work with a veteran barnstormer named Erold Bahl. These daring pilots from the earliest days of aviation appeared at country fairs and carnivals, performing various stunts and offering short rides. Lindbergh's job was to walk out on the airplane's wing while it was airborne, waving to the crowd below. He also did some parachuting.

Lindbergh's dream, however, was to fly solo, which he would not be able to do without his own plane. In 1923 this dream came true when a five-hundred-dollar loan from his father allowed him to buy a World War I-era airplane called the Jenny. For a while he continued his barnstorming career, but he knew that this was a limited pursuit. Eager for more training, Lindbergh enrolled in 1924 in the Cadet Program offered by the U.S. Army Air Service (there was not yet a separate Air Force). This very difficult program, which took place at an army base in San Antonio, Texas, featured courses in twenty-five subjects. Lindbergh studied aerodynamics, meteorology, and radio communications and received instruction in aviation skills like flying in formation, combat maneuvers, and special takeoffs and landings.

Lindbergh graduated first in his class and emerged as a second lieutenant in the Air Service Reserve. He was soon hired to fly the airmail route between St. Louis, Missouri, and Chicago, Illinois. At this point in the history of aviation, such work was extremely dangerous. Landing strips were few and often in bad condition, weather reports were unreliable, and many airplanes were not up to the job. Scores of airmail pilots were killed in crashes, and Lindbergh himself had many close calls; he even set a record by making four emergency jumps out of airplanes. It was during this period that he began to earn the nickname by which he would long be known: "Lucky Lindy."

Taking a chance on a transatlantic crossing

In the fall of 1926 Lindbergh heard about the Orteig Prize, a $25,000 award that had been offered by New York City hotel owner Raymond Orteig to the first pilot to succeed in flying from a major U.S. city to a major European city. Several unsuccessful attempts had already been made, and several lives had been lost in the process. Lindbergh thought that those pilots had failed because their planes had been too weighed down with extra crew members and supplies. He believed that only a light, single-engine plane carrying a lone pilot could make the trip.

Overcoming his natural shyness, Lindbergh persuaded a group of nine St. Louis businessmen to back him in a try for the Orteig Prize. Hoping to make their city a center of aviation, they agreed to fund the airplane that Lindbergh had in mind, which would be built by Ryan Airlines of San Diego, California. Lindbergh went to San Diego to assist in the design and construction of his airplane, which he named the *Spirit of St. Louis* in honor of his sponsors. Construction took six months.

Pioneering Woman Aviator Amelia Earhart

Charles Lindbergh was one of the most celebrated heroes of the Roaring Twenties. Another such innovator, and an inspiration to subsequent generations of women, was pilot Amelia Earhart. She set several aviation records of her own in the 1920s, and went on to even greater fame before her life ended mysteriously in the late 1930s.

Born in 1897 in Atchison, Kansas, Earhart's interest in aviation was sparked at the age of eighteen when she attended a military airplane exhibition. Though she worked to support herself at various jobs over the course of her life, from volunteer nurse's aide to social worker, flying was Earhart's passion. She signed up for flying lessons after experiencing a joyride at an air show. With a loan from her mother and income from her job at a telephone company, Earhart soon purchased a small plane. In 1922 she made her first solo flight, setting an altitude record by flying at 14,000 feet.

In April 1928 she received an offer to become the first female passenger to cross the Atlantic Ocean in an airplane. She made the trip in June, flying aboard the *Friendship* with a male pilot and navigator. The story of Earhart's flight made international headlines.

Eager to cross the Atlantic as a pilot rather than a passenger, Earhart took off from Newfoundland, Canada, in May 1932 and headed for France. A variety of problems caused an early landing in Northern Ireland, but Earhart had made it safely across the ocean. When she returned to New York, she was greeted with a parade and enthusiastic fans.

Over the next several years, Earhart pursued and achieved several other firsts in aviation history, and she was always looking for a new challenge. In February 1937 Earhart announced that she planned to fly around the world at or near the Equator. She left from San Francisco, California, on March 17, making the trip to Hawaii in a record sixteen hours. When she tried to take off from Hawaii, her plane crashed. After a five-week delay, she decided to fly from west to east, and was accompanied by a new navigator, Fred Noonan. Earhart left Miami, Florida, on June 1, 1937. She flew toward Brazil, then headed east over the Atlantic, flying over Africa, parts of the Middle East, Pakistan, India, and Burma.

Earhart's plane reached New Zealand on June 30. She soon took off again, with plans to land on tiny Howland Island in the middle of the Pacific Ocean. Earhart and Noonan never arrived at their destination, and no trace of them or their airplane was ever found. Some people have speculated that Earhart may have been captured by the Japanese, who believed she was a spy. This theory has never been proven, and their disappearance remains a mystery.

The result was a compact plane a little more than 9 feet (2.7 meters) high and 28 feet (8 meters) long, with a 46-foot wingspan. It weighed only 2,000 pounds (907 kilograms) without fuel, but 5,200 pounds (2359 kilograms) with a full tank. To increase the plane's fuel capacity, Lindbergh had stripped it of all equipment that was not absolutely necessary, so that it had no radio, parachute, navigational lights, or gas gauge. It also had no windshield, only side windows, so that Lindbergh had to use a special periscope to see what was directly in front of him. Lacking many navigational instruments, Lindbergh would depend on maps, geological landmarks, and the stars in the sky to find his way across the Atlantic. To prepare for the long flight, he practiced going without sleep.

A long and dangerous flight

On May 10, 1927, Lindbergh set off from San Diego to St. Louis, flying at a then-amazing speed of more than 100 miles (161 kilometers) per hour. Continuing on to Long Island, New York, where he landed after a total flight of twenty-one hours and twenty minutes, he set a record for the fastest transcontinental flight to date. From there Lindbergh planned to fly to Le Bourget field in Paris, France. He spent about a week making final preparations and nervously waiting for good weather. On the evening of May 19, indications seemed to be good for a take-off the next morning. That night, Lindbergh got hardly any sleep.

May 20 was a rainy day in New York, but Lindbergh was ready to go. Having packed only five sandwiches and some water to sustain him during his trip, he took off at 7:52 AM. The runway was muddy and there was a strong wind blowing, and the *Spirit of St. Louis* nearly clipped a tractor and some overhead wires as it lifted into the air. Lindbergh flew north, following the coast of New England to Nova Scotia. After crossing the easternmost tip of Newfoundland, he headed out over the Atlantic Ocean, knowing that he would not see land again until he reached the coast of Ireland. By this time he had already been in the air for eleven hours.

Crossing the ocean was by far the most dangerous part of Lindbergh's journey. He had to fight storms, fog, and ice, but his worst enemy was his own fatigue, which caused him to hallucinate and to worry that he could not possibly make it to his destination. At times his plane dipped dangerously close to the ocean's surface. After twenty-eight hours Lindbergh spotted the Irish coast. Now he knew that he was on course. He flew south, crossing the English Channel (which separates England and France) and followed the River Seine to Paris. When he reached the city, he circled the Eiffel Tower (one of the most famous landmarks in Paris) and headed for Le Bourget field.

An international hero

Lindbergh had no idea that many well-wishers had been following his progress since his plane was spotted over Ireland. Thousands of people streamed toward his intended landing spot, causing the biggest traffic jam in French history. As the shy, handsome pilot, a slim twenty-five-year-old with a modest manner, emerged from the *Spirit of St. Louis,* he was initially bewildered by the crowd and wondered if something had gone wrong. Lindbergh soon realized that all the people were there to greet him and express their joy in his success. They quickly grabbed him and carried him around the field on their shoulders.

At a time in which people were wild about celebrities and the press eager to publish every detail about them, Lindbergh immediately became an international hero. In the days following the flight, he made appearances around Europe and received several medals. Although Lindbergh had planned to continue flying, President **Calvin Coolidge** (1872–1933; served 1923–29; see entry) persuaded him to put himself and his airplane aboard the U.S.S. *Memphis* (a U.S. Navy ship) and come back to the United States. In Washington, D.C., Coolidge presented Lindbergh with the Distinguished Flying Cross and the Congressional Medal of Honor.

In New York City, he was the center of the largest ticker-tape parade (a term that refers to the long, narrow strips of paper from counting machines that people threw into the air during these events) ever held, during which he was cheered by an estimated four million people. The nation simply could not get enough of Lindbergh. His image appeared on an airmail stamp and parks, schools, streets, and countless babies were named after him. Within a few weeks of his famous flight, he wrote a brief account of the adventure, called *We* (1927), in reference to himself and his airplane, that was an instant best-seller.

President Calvin Coolidge presenting Charles Lindbergh with the Distinguished Flying Cross and the Congressional Medal of Honor after Lindbergh's historic flight. (© Bettmann/Corbis. Reproduced by permission.)

Marriage, a family, and more flying

Lindbergh's next project was an extensive flying tour of the United States. He made appearances in more than seventy-five cities, promoting to the millions of spectators who flocked to see him the notion of air travel as safe and reliable. He is credited with sparking the increased use of airmail and the big boom in airport construction that soon began. Indeed, airplane travel would become so popular that, by 1930, a variety of airlines would transport passengers more than 73 million miles (more than 117 million kilometers) per year.

Having traveled around the United States, Lindbergh accepted the invitation of Mexico's president and made a twenty-seven-hour, nonstop flight to that country. There he attended a reception in the home of the U.S. ambassador, Dwight Morrow, where he met Morrow's daughter Anne. A romance began, and the two were married on May 27, 1929. Anne Morrow Lindbergh soon learned how to pilot and navigate an airplane so that she could accompany her husband on his flights. In fact, the couple set a new transcontinental record when Anne was seven months pregnant with their first child.

Charles Lindbergh Jr. was born in June 1930. About a year later the Lindberghs left their baby with Anne's parents and flew across the Arctic to China in order to investigate possible commercial airline routes and also to assist flood victims there. They returned to the United States when they received news of the death of Anne's father. Anne was again pregnant, and, hoping to shield his family from the public's intense curiosity, Lindbergh bought a home in isolated Hopewell, New Jersey. He began work as a technical adviser to several new airlines.

Tragedy strikes

The Lindberghs' quiet life was shattered in March 1932 by a tragedy that seemed to affect the entire nation. Their two-year-old son was kidnapped from his bedroom by someone who left a crudely written ransom note demanding fifty thousand dollars for his safe return. Lindbergh paid the ransom, and a wide array of law enforcement officers and private citizens worked to find the child, but no clues were uncovered. Seventy-two days after the child had disappeared, his body was found in a wooded area not far from the Lindbergh home. It seemed likely that he had been killed soon after the kidnapping.

A German immigrant and unemployed carpenter named Bruno Hauptmann (1899–1936) was arrested and charged with the kidnapping. He was convicted, and, in April 1936, he was executed for the murder. Hauptmann maintained his innocence to the end, and some thought that the evidence against him had been unconvincing. Regardless, the Lindbergh case, which was one of several dubbed the "Crime of the Century" during the 1920s, led to the passage of a law that made kidnapping a federal offense.

Fearing for the safety of his family (which would eventually include five children), Lindbergh moved them to Europe in late 1935. They settled first in the English countryside, but after two years they moved to an island off the coast of France. There Lindbergh worked with French scientist Alexis Carrel (1873–1944) on the development of a device that would pump life-giving fluids through the heart during surgery.

Unpopular views

In the late 1930s Lindbergh was invited to visit Germany to evaluate that nation's newly developed air force, called the *Luftwaffe*. He was very impressed and warned that Germany was much better equipped militarily than England or France. In October 1938 Lindbergh received the Service Cross of the German Eagle from Hermann Goering (1893–1946), a high-ranking official of the Nazi government. Many U.S. critics felt he should return the medal, particularly after the public began to learn about the brutal crimes committed by the Nazis against Jews. Lindbergh refused, leading many to assume that he was an anti-Semite (someone who has prejudice against Jews).

Lindbergh's reputation suffered even more when, like his own father in the period leading up to the first World War, he began speaking out against U.S. involvement in World War II (1939–45). Lindbergh became a major spokesperson for a group called the America First Committee, a group of isolationists. Once the United States entered the war, however, Lindbergh tried to volunteer to serve with the Army Air Corps. His offer was refused due to the controversial statements he had previously made.

In the end Lindbergh did contribute to the war effort. He helped to design the B24 Liberator bomber airplane at industrialist **Henry Ford's** (1863–1947; see entry) manufacturing plant at Willow Run, Michigan. In 1944 he also went to the Pacific region of war activity, supposedly as a civilian observer; secretly, however, Lindbergh flew a number of combat missions.

An improving reputation

In the years following the war, Lindbergh served as an adviser to the U.S. Air Force and to various commercial airlines, testing new airplanes and helping to design the Boeing 747. He had long been interested in the possibility of space travel. In 1928, in fact, he had persuaded the Guggenheim Foundation to fund the work of physicist Robert Goddard (1882–1945), who was developing rockets, and he would closely follow the progress of this area of exploration over the next several decades.

Lindbergh's reputation with the U.S. public improved gradually over the years. President Dwight D. Eisenhower (1890–1969; served 1953–61) made him a brigadier general in the Air Force in 1954, the same year his autobiography, *The Spirit of St. Louis* (1953), won a Pulitzer Prize.

In the 1960s Lindbergh became interested in and involved with a number of environmental issues. He worked to preserve endangered whales and birds, for example, and he opposed the use of supersonic jets (aircraft that move at a speed faster than that of sound), which he believed were too damaging to the environment. In 1972 Lindbergh was diagnosed with lymphatic cancer. He returned to his family's winter home on the island of Maui in Hawaii. He died there in August 1974 and was buried in a simple grave.

For More Information

Books

Berg, Scott. *Lindbergh*. New York: Putnam, 1998.

Crouch, Tom D., ed. *Charles A. Lindbergh: An American Life*. Washington, DC: Smithsonian, 1977.

Denenberg, Barry. *An American Hero: The True Story of Charles A. Lindbergh*. New York: Putnam, 1998.

Kent, Zachary. *Charles Lindbergh and the Spirit of St. Louis in American History*. Berkeley Heights, NJ: Enslow Publishers, Inc., 2001.

Milton, Joyce. *Loss of Eden: A Biography of Charles and Anne Morrow Lindbergh*. New York: HarperCollins, 1993.

Perret, Geoffrey. *America in the Twenties*. New York: Touchstone, 1982.

Randolph, Blythe. *Charles Lindbergh*. New York: Franklin Watts, 1990.

Web Sites

Charles Lindbergh Biography. Available online at http://www.allsands.com/History/People/lindberghairpla_ek_gn.htm. Accessed on June 24, 2005.

"Charles Lindbergh Biography." *Charles Lindbergh: An American Aviator*. Available online at http://www.charleslindbergh.com/history/index.asp. Accessed on June 24, 2005.

Aimee Semple McPherson

Born October 9, 1890 (Ingersoll, Canada)
Died September 27, 1944 (Oakland, California)

Evangelist and church founder

"I am not the healer. Jesus is the healer. I am only a little office girl who opens the door and says, 'Come in.'"

The Roaring Twenties was a decade of major changes in the United States. A population shift had occurred, with more people now living in urban than rural areas. Amazing technological advances like automobiles, airplanes, and electrical appliances had brought convenience and a faster pace to daily life. These changes were exciting to some people, but others found them troubling and unsettling. Some turned to traditional religious belief for reassurance, leading to a surge in the popularity of evangelistic religious leaders (those who seek to convert others to their own faith). The most famous of these was Aimee Semple McPherson, a dynamic woman who attracted thousands of followers with her dramatic preaching and comforting message of salvation. At a time when few women took prominent roles in organized religion, McPherson founded her own church and overcame controversy to attract thousands of devoted followers.

A dynamic young religious leader

Aimee Semple McPherson was born Aimee Elizabeth Kennedy in Ontario, Canada. The daughter of farmer James Morgan Kennedy and Minnie Kennedy, a devotee of

Aimee Semple McPherson was a dynamic women who attracted thousands of followers at a time when few women took prominent roles in organized religion. *(Hulton Archive/Getty Images. Reproduced by permission.)*

the Salvation Army (a religious organization committed to helping the needy), McPherson was not a strong believer in Christianity until she was seventeen. That year, she attended a tent revival (a religious gathering held outdoors, under a tent roof) led by a Pentecostal minister. The Pentecostal religion features fundamentalist beliefs, including a literal interpretation of events in the Bible, as well as such practices as faith healing (by which illnesses and disabilities are cured through a strong belief in God) and so-called "speaking in tongues," when a person enters a kind of trance and begins speaking unknown words presumed to be from some biblical language.

In the summer of 1908 McPherson married the minister who had converted her, Robert Semple, and went out on the revivalist circuit with him. She soon found that she too had a gift for preaching and enjoyed being able to save souls (in other words, win them over to the Christian faith). In 1910 the couple traveled to China to do missionary work, which involved trying to persuade the local people there to become Christians. McPherson gave birth to a daughter, Roberta Star Semple, one month after her husband's death. Penniless, she returned to the United States and joined her mother in revivalist activities.

McPherson married Harold S. McPherson, a native of Rhode Island and a grocery clerk, in 1912, and their son Rolf Kennedy McPherson was born the next year. Soon McPherson found the call to preach too strong to resist, and she headed back on the road, leaving her husband behind. With her mother by her side, McPherson traveled up and down the East Coast in a car painted with religious slogans, such as "Jesus Is Coming—Get Ready" and "Where Will You Spend Eternity?"

McPherson gradually developed a flamboyant speaking style that was very effective, helping her to draw crowds as large as fifteen thousand in some cities. Her physical attractiveness and ability to persuade both seemed to add to her appeal. She had already attracted a considerable following when, in 1918, she and her mother traveled to Los Angeles, California. Here McPherson established her ministry, which she named the Four Square Gospel Church. She seemed perfectly suited to this city, in which so many lost-feeling residents had recently arrived from other places, and where her show-business techniques were readily accepted.

The Four Square Gospel Church

By 1923 McPherson was able to construct the huge, domed Angelus Temple, which seated more than five thousand worshippers and which was topped with an illuminated, rotating cross. Some came just to see and hear this colorful, increasingly

Billy Sunday: An Influential Evangelist

The stage for the dramatic, crowd-pleasing kind of preaching that made Aimee Semple McPherson popular was set by another revivalist preacher in the decade leading up to the Roaring Twenties. Billy Sunday won over converts in the 1910s with an entertaining style that several generations of fundamentalist leaders would imitate.

Born in Ames, Iowa, in 1862, William "Billy" Sunday was the son of a Civil War soldier who died a month after his birth. After a childhood marked by poverty, stays in orphanages, and little schooling, Sunday was on his own at the age of fourteen. He traveled around the state, supporting himself with odd jobs. Always interested in sports, Sunday started playing baseball with the local team in Marshalltown, Iowa, before being offered a position on a professional team, the Chicago Whitestockings. Sunday joined the team in 1883. After he converted to fundamentalist Christianity, Sunday began to bring his religious beliefs to the ballpark, urging his fellow players to give up drinking and other sinful practices.

In 1891 Sunday quit baseball to work for the Young Men's Christian Association (YMCA). Two years later he became an assistant to a Presbyterian evangelist named John Wilbur Chapman. Sunday's job was to set up the revival meetings at which Chapman preached. Sunday did some preaching himself, and soon after heading a revival that Chapman was unable to lead, set out on his own career as an evangelist preacher.

Ordained by the Chicago Presbytery in 1903, Sunday traveled around the country, speaking to larger and larger crowds. He became increasingly famous for his original, flamboyant style, which featured folksy, colorful language, often laced with baseball imagery and accompanied by athletic gestures. He was known for encouraging people at his services to "hit the sawdust trail," which meant that they should walk up the sawdust-covered aisle of his tabernacle (usually a temporary wooden structure) and accept Jesus Christ as their savior. Sunday also incorporated music into his services, which made them even more appealing.

The peak of Sunday's popularity came around the time of World War I. At massive rallies, he urged the passage of the Eighteenth Amendment, which banned the manufacture and sale of alcoholic beverages. He also denounced the liberal elements of society and mixed religious and patriotic terminology in support of the entrance of the United States into the war. Sunday's popularity declined in the 1920s, partly due to a scandal involving the large amounts of money he had made through his evangelist work. By the time of his death in 1935 he had led more than thirty campaigns and was said to have converted as many as three hundred thousand people to Christianity.

famous character, but many found themselves converted to her message and church. The foundation of the church included beliefs in Jesus Christ as the savior of humanity and in faith healing. In fact, the Temple housed a permanent display of canes, crutches, and braces that had been discarded by those McPherson was believed to have cured. According to Nathan Miller's *New World Coming: The 1920s and the Making of Modern America,* however, McPherson modestly insisted that she was "not the healer. Jesus is the healer. I am only a little office girl who opens the door and says, 'Come in.'"

McPherson employed music, vividly told Bible stories, costumes, and dramatic performances to deliver her message. For example, to illustrate the cost of breaking God's laws, she once rode down the Temple's front aisle on a motorcycle, dressed in a police officer's uniform.

Meanwhile, Minnie Kennedy continued her shrewd management of the business side of her daughter's ministry. In 1924 McPherson opened the first full-time religious radio station in the country, which greatly extended her reach. She also established the Lighthouse of International Evangelism, a Bible college and training school for ministry workers.

Although she was a talented publicist and powerful persuader, McPherson was also a stubborn and impulsive person. She ignored rumors that she was involved with her radio station's former engineer, a married Australian named Kenneth Ormiston. Then came an event that mystified the nation and made McPherson an even more controversial figure.

A mysterious "kidnapping"

In May 1926 McPherson went to a Los Angeles beach park to enjoy one of her favorite pastimes, swimming in the Pacific Ocean. She entered the surf and turned to wave to her secretary, who was waiting on the beach, but she never returned. A massive search was organized, with not only police, but also church members scouring the beaches for McPherson's body (two of the searchers were so upset by her disappearance that they killed themselves). It was assumed that she had drowned.

Intensive press coverage helped to sensationalize what was already a bizarre story. Then new rumors began to circulate:

McPherson had been seen in the resort town of Carmel, located farther north on the Pacific coast, in the company of a man thought to be Ormiston (whose wife had by now left the country, claiming that her husband had had an affair with McPherson). Six weeks after McPherson's disappearance, her mother received a letter demanding five hundred thousand dollars in exchange for the evangelist's safe return. Otherwise, the note threatened, she would be sold into slavery in Mexico.

Just a few days later, though, McPherson called her mother from Arizona. She had escaped from her captors, she said, after being tied up in a Mexican shack. McPherson claimed to have staggered across the desert before she was finally found. On her return to Los Angeles, McPherson was greeted by thousands of ecstatic admirers. The police, however, were less convinced that her story was true. Many residents of Carmel reported that a couple resembling McPherson and Ormiston had stayed in a hotel there for ten days. McPherson was unable to produce any evidence to back up her story, and she was forced to testify before a grand jury on charges that included conspiracy to manufacture evidence.

Eventually, the charges were dropped (some believed that McPherson had paid someone a bribe to achieve this outcome), and meanwhile McPherson had become even more famous. She took advantage of her notoriety by setting out on a revival tour of the East Coast. She was mobbed by crowds anxious to see the celebrity that they had heard so much about. McPherson started dressing more stylishly and even cut her luxurious, long red hair in a short bob. The press followed her activities eagerly, especially when she appeared in a New York City nightclub managed by a notoriously shady woman named Tex Guinan. The club's customers cheered McPherson, who invited them to come and hear her preach.

Whenever journalists or anyone else asked McPherson about her kidnapping ordeal, she repeated the same sequence of events, always insisting "That's my story and I'm sticking with it." She continued her evangelistic work, even traveling to England, France, the Middle East, and Asia. Returning to Los Angeles, she continued to run her ministry. During the Great Depression (the period of economic downturn and suffering that lasted from the 1929 stock market crash until

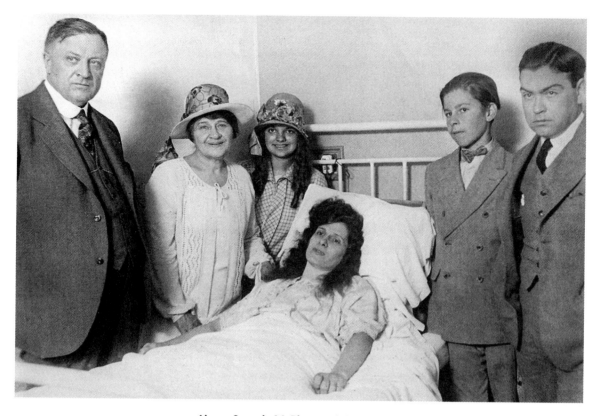

Aimee Semple McPherson is surrounded by a group of well-wishers in the hospital after her mysterious disappearance in 1926. *(© Bettmann/Corbis. Reproduced by permission.)*

approximately 1939), McPherson's church provided steady assistance to the needy, in the form of food and clothing.

As the 1930s continued, McPherson was plagued by a number of problems. She married David L. Hutton, a young choir member, in 1931, but they were divorced three years later. She was engaged in public disputes with several family members, and a total of fifty-five lawsuits were filed against her for various reasons. In addition, her church experienced some financial problems. These began to ease, however, in the 1940s, as membership was again increasing. In 1944 McPherson died of an accidental overdose of sleeping pills. Leadership of her church, which was still in existence at the beginning of the twenty-first century, with more than seven hundred branches, fell to her son.

For More Information

Books

Blumhofer, Edith. *Aimee Semple McPherson: Everybody's Sister.* Grand Rapids, MI: Eerdmans, 1993.

Epstein, Daniel M. *Sister Aimee: The Life of Aimee Semple McPherson.* New York: Harcourt, 1993.

Thomas, Lately. *Storming Heaven: The Lives and Turmoils of Minnie Kennedy and Aimee Semple McPherson.* New York: Ballantine Books, 1973.

Web Sites

Aimee Semple McPherson Resource Center. Available online at http://members.aol.com/xbcampbell/asm/indexasm.htm. Accessed on June 28, 2005.

Margaret Mead

Born December 16, 1901 (Philadelphia, Pennsylvania)
Died November 15, 1978 (New York City, New York)

Anthropologist

> "I was brought up to believe that the only thing worth doing was to add to the sum of accurate information in the world."

Margaret Mead's pioneering studies documenting the cultural influences on human development and behavior made her the most famous anthropologist (a scientist who studies human origins, cultures, and societies) of the twentieth century. It was during the Roaring Twenties that Mead produced her most famous work, *Coming of Age in Samoa* (1928). This book was based on Mead's fieldwork in that Pacific Island nation, where she lived with and studied a group of teenage girls. She found that Samoans experienced adolescence as a much less stressful transition to adulthood than did teenagers in the United States or Europe. Controversial due both to its sexual subject matter and its conclusions, *Coming of Age in Samoa* was a best-seller in an era when some found the major advances occurring in science, technology, and sociology troubling. Both Mead's work and her distinguished career, which began at a time when few women were able to reach the top of any professional field, were revolutionary.

Developing a passion for anthropology

Margaret Mead grew up in an intellectual, unconventional family. Born in Philadelphia, Pennsylvania, at the beginning of the twentieth century, she was the oldest of four children. Her

Margaret Mead's pioneering studies documenting the cultural influences on human development and behavior made her the most famous anthropologist of the twentieth century. *(Getty Images. Reproduced by permission.)*

father was a professor at the Wharton School of Finance and Commerce, her mother was a sociologist and women's rights advocate, and her grandmother—who was responsible for much of her upbringing—had been a school principal. Mead received only periodic formal schooling, for she was taught mostly at home by relatives and tutors.

The family moved often during Mead's childhood. She later said that she enjoyed being part of such an unusual

Franz Boas: Trail-Blazing Anthropologist

Margaret Mead's approach to anthropological research was strongly influenced by Franz Boas, who headed the anthropology department at Columbia University when Mead was a student there. Boas is considered the founder of modern cultural anthropology.

Born in Germany in 1858, Boas studied at the universities of Heidelberg, Bonn, and Kiel. After receiving his PhD in physics and geography, he traveled to Vancouver, British Columbia, in Canada to study the Native American cultures of the Pacific Northwest. In 1886 he immigrated to the United States. Boas subsequently taught anthropology at Clark University in Massachusetts, then at the University of Chicago and the Chicago Field Museum.

In 1896 Boas was hired to teach at New York City's Columbia University, becoming the first professor of anthropology in the United States. At the same time, he served as curator of anthropology at the American Museum of Natural History. In this position he led the effort to map and document both native North American and native Asian societies. In addition to working toward the recognition of cultural anthropology as a serious science, Boas urged the use of nontraditional research methods, especially on-site observation.

He also waged a fierce battle against those who made claims for the superiority or inferiority of particular races of people. Through his many writings Boas showed that there are many more differences among individuals than among races, and he stressed the influence of culture rather than heredity on behavior. Boas argued in favor of studying cultures as whole systems that had to be understood on their own terms, rather than in comparison to other, supposedly superior societies. These were radical assertions at a time when some so-called "scientists" were claiming that biological differences made white people superior to blacks and others of non-northern-European descent.

During his career, Boas published more than six hundred articles and a number of books, and he influenced several generations of anthropologists. He died in 1942.

family, in which the children were encouraged to have playmates of other races and economic levels, to be observant, and to enjoy creative hobbies like painting and dance. Even though Mead's parents were both agnostics (those who doubt but do not deny the existence of God), she chose to join the Episcopal Church when she was eleven years old, and she would remain a member of this denomination throughout her life.

During her senior year of high school in Doylestown, Pennsylvania, Mead became engaged to a twenty-year-old student of theology (the study of religious belief) named Luther

Cressman. She entered DePauw University in Indiana primarily to please her father, who had also attended this school. But Mead felt like an outsider in that midwestern world of sororities and fraternities (student societies), and after only a year she transferred to Barnard College in New York. There she became close friends with a group of girls with intellectual interests similar to her own.

Mead majored in psychology but found the course of her life changed in her senior year, when she took a course in anthropology from the famous Franz Boas (1858–1942). A leader in the field of anthropology, Boas took the then-radical position of denying that some races of people (especially those of western or northern European ancestry) were superior to others; he also asserted that it was environment, not genetics, that had shaped human behavior and cultures. Along with his graduate assistant Ruth Benedict, who would become Mead's close friend and mentor, Boas encouraged Mead to pursue her new interest in anthropology. In 1923 Mead graduated from Barnard and married Cressman. Then she began graduate work at Columbia University in New York City, where Boas (with help from Benedict) was the only faculty member in the anthropology department.

A pioneering study

This was an exciting and crucial period for the relatively new field of anthropology. The global conflict known as World War I (1914–18; the United States entered the war in 1917) had profoundly shaken and disillusioned people around the world with the scope of its destruction. Anthropologists were wondering whether their study of the nature of human beings and societies could be applied to contemporary issues. The theories of psychiatrist Sigmund Freud (1859–1939), who proposed that the subconscious mind and past experiences held the clues to much observed behavior, had also become highly influential. In addition, anthropologists realized that in many far corners of the world cultures would soon begin to disappear as modern life extended its reach. Boas was eager to organize detailed scientific descriptions and analyses of these cultures before they vanished.

It was with such a goal in mind that Mead, after completing her studies in 1925, set off on her own for fieldwork in Samoa. She hoped to determine whether the experience of adolescence as a time of intense emotion and conflict was universal or limited to western cultures. Inexperienced but energetic, and having learned to speak Samoan, Mead moved in with a Samoan household and stayed for nine months, becoming part of a community of fifty teenage girls and closely observing their habits and behaviors. Mead was practicing a new technique in which a so-called "participant observer" takes part in the lives of his or her subjects. She strongly believed that this was the best way to generate good data about them.

Mead found that, in contrast to the conflict-torn, stressful adolescence common in U.S. and European society, Samoan teenagers were calm, happy, and completely at ease with their blossoming sexuality. She also determined that neither monogamy (having only one spouse or sexual partner at a time) nor jealousy was valued in Samoan culture. Mead concluded that the experience of adolescence is determined not by biology but by cultural conditioning. Her conclusions pointed to a new way of looking at so-called "primitive" cultures, which had previously been seen as childlike or backward. Perhaps these people, Mead suggested, actually had a better way of approaching the transition to adulthood.

Working in New Guinea, Bali, and elsewhere

On the boat carrying her home from Samoa, Mead met and fell in love with Reo Fortune, an anthropologist from New Zealand. She returned with him to New York City, where she soon became an assistant curator at the American Museum of Natural History; Mead would be associated with the museum for the rest of her life. In 1928, the same year in which *Coming of Age in Samoa* was published, she divorced Cressman and married Fortune. She and her new husband went to New Guinea, where Mead did the research for a study on the thought patterns and fantasy worlds of children and how they are influenced by their sociocultural context. This research was published in 1930 as *Growing Up in New Guinea*. (Later, Mead would study these same children as adults.) Between 1925 and 1939, in addition to spending one summer studying the Omaha Indians of Nebraska, Mead would observe the people of seven Pacific cultures.

Mead had returned to New Guinea for further work on the differences between biological and cultural influences when, in 1932, she met British anthropologist Gregory Bateson (1904–1980). He became her third husband in 1936. Meanwhile, she published an important and controversial work called *Sex and Temperament* (1935), the result of her work among three New Guinea ethnic groups: the Arapesh, Mundugumor, and Tchambuli. Mead found that gender roles differed significantly in each of these cultures, which she considered more evidence that culture and environment, not inherited traits, determine behavior.

Mead's longtime interest in psychology led her to wonder about the cultural context of schizophrenia, a mental disorder that features a withdrawal into fantasy and delusion. Mead and Bateson traveled to the Indonesian island of Bali to study human nonverbal communication. In the Balinese culture, such practices as going into trances and becoming dissociated from reality were acceptable. Mead and Bateson employed what were then new data-gathering techniques, using still photos and motion pictures of their subjects in addition to their written notes. They took more than 30,000 photographs and used 759 of them in their subsequent book *Balinese Character*. They also edited and released several films they had made about their Bali research.

Early in her adult life, doctors had told Mead that she would not be able to have children. Nevertheless, after several miscarriages, she did become successfully pregnant. Mead agreed to allow her friend, a pioneering pediatrician named Benjamin Spock (1903–1998), to test his ideas about child

Margaret Mead carrying a child on her back during her visit to New Guinea in the 1928. *(AP/Wide World Photos. Reproduced by permission.)*

rearing on her child. He was present at the birth of her daughter, Mary Catherine Bateson, in 1939. Seven years later Spock published *The Common Sense Book of Baby and Child Care,* one of the most influential child-rearing manuals of all time.

The outbreak of World War II (1939–45) provided new opportunities for applying anthropology to public policy. During that conflict the United States found itself in contact with a wide range of people and cultures, and the government employed a number of social scientists to increase understanding about them. Because the nation was about to undergo food rationing (limited amounts would be available to individuals, due to shortages), Mead undertook a study of the eating habits of U.S. citizens. She was also sent to Great Britain to help inform the British about what to expect from the U.S. troops that were stationed there.

In studying the cultures of Germany and Japan, who were the enemies of the United States and its allies during the war, Mead had to use indirect forms of data gathering, such as watching movies, reading books, and interviewing immigrants from those nations. This work led to a series of national character studies and eventually to a book called *Cultures at a Distance* (1953). Another book from this period is *New Lives for Old* (1956), which chronicles Mead's visit to the New Guinea village she had studied twenty-five years earlier. She documented the difficulties being experienced by the adults who had grown from the children she interviewed during her first visit, as the modern world intruded on their culture.

A continuing role in contemporary thought

During the last twenty-five years of her life, Mead concentrated mostly on teaching and serving as a mentor to younger anthropologists. A longtime faculty member at Columbia University, she was at various times a visiting professor or scholar at such institutions as New York University, Fordham University, the University of Cincinnati, and the Menninger Foundation in Topeka, Kansas. Troubled by the social upheaval that occurred during the 1960s and by the so-called "generation gap" that had seemed to open between older and younger people, Mead sympathized with young people's resistance to the Vietnam War (1954–75) and their desire for a greater voice in decision-making. She expressed her views on such topics in *Culture and Commitment* (1970).

During the 1960s Mead's interest in the global problems of war, overpopulation, and threats to the environment led to involvement with such organizations as the World Council of Churches and the United Nations. In *A Way of Seeing* (1970), she made clear her stances on various issues, including her support for birth control, for the repeal of antiabortion laws, and for the right of the chronically or terminally ill to choose when to die.

Mead's most pressing concerns, however, had always had to do with families. She worried about the effects of modern life, especially the loss of the extended family and the isolation of city dwellers, on parents and children. She was particularly interested in women's issues and often spoke of the need for changing gender roles and for women to make goals and find meaningful careers. At the same time, however, she understood the ties that women felt to their husbands and children and especially valued their skills as nurturers of the young.

In 1961 Mead began co-writing, with Rhoda Metraux, a column for *Redbook,* a popular women's magazine. Here she provided advice and guidance to ordinary women, whose letters she, in turn, used as sources of information about attitudes and values. By now Mead had become an important role model to the women of the twentieth century, as they struggled with the sometimes conflicting demands of work and family.

In her last years Mead made many television and documentary film appearances. She received twenty-eight honorary degrees, and she was elected to the National Academy of Sciences in 1975. She also served as president of the American Association for the Advancement of Science. Mead died of pancreatic cancer in 1978. She was later awarded the Presidential Medal of Freedom, which her daughter accepted for her.

Following her death, some critics suggested that her work in Samoa was not as thorough as it should have been. The most prominent among these was Derek Freeman, a Mead admirer and fellow anthropologist who spent six years in Samoa and learned to speak Samoan fluently. In *Margaret Mead and Samoa: The Making and Unmaking of an Anthropological Myth,* Freeman claimed that Mead's research was shallow and imprecise and that the Samoans themselves felt she had been incorrect in her conclusions.

For More Information

Books

Bateson, Mary Catherine. *With a Daughter's Eye: A Memoir of Margaret Mead and Gregory Bateson.* New York: William Morrow, 1984.

Burby, Liza N. *Margaret Mead.* New York: Rosen, 1996.

Howard, Jane. *Margaret Mead: A Life.* New York: Simon & Schuster, 1984.

Ludel, Jacqueline. *Margaret Mead.* New York: Franklin Watts, 1983.

Ziesk, Edna. *Margaret Mead.* New York: Chelsea House, 1990.

Web Sites

Flaherty, Tarraugh. "Margaret Mead: 1901–1978." *Women's Intellectual Contributions to the Study of Mind and Society.* Available online at http://www.webster.edu/~woolflm/margaretmead.html. Accessed on June 28, 2005.

"Margaret Mead Centennial 2001." *The Institute for Intercultural Studies.* Available online at http://www.interculturalstudies.org/Mead/2001 centennial.html. Accessed on June 28, 2005.

Henry Louis H.L. Mencken

Born September 12, 1880 (Baltimore, Maryland)
Died January 29, 1956 (Baltimore, Maryland)

Writer and editor

H enry Louis (H.L.) Mencken was one of the most influential writers and editors of the twentieth century. Although he lived his entire life in the eastern coastal city of Baltimore, Maryland, his reach extended to every corner of the nation. An incredibly productive newspaper and magazine writer as well as an author of nonfiction books, Mencken produced biting social commentary on many aspects of life in the United States. He criticized not only politicians and religious leaders but also those ignorant, intolerant members of the vast U.S. middle class that he termed the "booboisie." Mencken was at the height of his career and popularity during the Roaring Twenties and is recognized as a major voice of the period. He informed, entertained, and provoked his readers, helping them to understand and judge the trends, issues, and events of this exciting but confusing time.

"The United States is incomparably the greatest show on earth. . . . I never get tired of the show."

The "maddest, gladdest" days

Henry Louis Mencken was born in Baltimore, Maryland, in 1880. He was the oldest of four children born to parents of proud German descent. His father and uncle were joint owners of a thriving cigar factory, and the family enjoyed material comfort

Henry Louis Mencken was one of the most influential writers and editors of the twentieth century, and he was at the height of his career and popularity during the Roaring Twenties. *(Courtesy of The Library of Congress.)*

and security throughout his childhood. When Mencken was three, the family moved into a three-story brick house near Baltimore's central business district. Mencken would continue to live in this same house for all but five years of his life.

His parents supported all of his pursuits, providing him with piano lessons, for example, when he began to express an interest in music. (Mencken's lifelong passion for music found an outlet when, as an adult, he was a member of the Saturday Night Club, a group of friends who got together to play classical music and socialize, for many decades.) He also developed a huge appetite for books after discovering through Mark Twain's *The Adventures of Huckleberry Finn* the joys of reading.

The importance of education was much stressed in the Mencken home. Young Harry, as he was called by his family, attended Professor Friedrich Knapp's Institute, a private school for children of German descent. He went on to a public high school, Baltimore Polytechnic High School. Mencken's father bet him that he could not graduate at the top of his class, but he did, finishing his senior year as class valedictorian (the student who gives the farewell speech for his class) and winning one hundred dollars from his father. Throughout his school years, Mencken had enjoyed writing stories, plays, and poems, and he dreamed of becoming a newspaper reporter. His favorite childhood gift, in fact, had been a working printing press that he had received for Christmas when he was eight years old.

Mencken's father, however, expected his son to go to work in the family cigar business. Mencken did so reluctantly. When his father died suddenly in 1899, Mencken went within days to the door of the Baltimore *Herald* to ask for a job. He was turned down because he lacked experience as a journalist, but having been told that he might inquire again sometime about available jobs, he went back every day. Finally Mencken was given his first assignment, which resulted in a five-line story about a stolen horse. He moved on to writing obituaries (death notices) and was eventually hired as the *Herald's* youngest staff reporter, making a salary of seven dollars per week.

In the third volume of his autobiography, *Newspaper Days, 1899–1906,* Mencken describes the life of a fledgling reporter as "the maddest, gladdest, ... existence ever enjoyed by mortal youth." He claimed that these years gave him a better education than others his age were receiving in college: "I was at large in a wicked seaport of half a million people, with a front seat at every public show." Within seven years, through his enthusiastic attitude and very hard work, including regular eighteen-hour workdays, Mencken had worked his way up to the position of editor in chief of the *Herald.*

Becoming a public personality

In 1906 the *Herald* went out of business, and Mencken was hired by the Baltimore *Sun.* It was his work for this newspaper (which would continue over the next forty-eight years) that would launch his career. Initially Mencken wrote anonymous theater reviews and editorials. In whatever spare time he could find, he worked on two nonfiction books, one about English playwright George Bernard Shaw (1856–1950) and one about German philosopher Friedrich Nietzsche (1844–1900), which were published in 1905 and 1908, respectively.

These scholarly but highly readable works attracted the attention of the editor of a leading magazine called *Smart Set,* and in 1908 Mencken was hired to write monthly book reviews for the magazine, while continuing to work at the *Sun.* It was during this period that he began a long and fruitful friendship and partnership with George Jean Nathan (1882–1958), who was a theater critic at *Smart Set.*

About two years later, Mencken was asked to write a column under his own name for the *Sun.* Now he would become a public personality, expressing his own views rather than reporting the news as a faceless, objective reporter. Mencken named the column "The Free Lance," perhaps a reference to the sharpness of his wit (since a lance is a kind of spear) as he began his assault on the supposedly respectable aspects of society. His particular targets were religious fanaticism, censorship, and other forces that he considered threatening to individual liberty.

Mencken's column ran for four years but was discontinued in 1915. At this point, a conflict was brewing in Europe, due to Germany's aggression toward other nations, that erupted into World War I (1914–18). Mencken had aggravated many people by initially siding with Germany; this controversial stance led the *Sun* to cancel his column. Once war broke out, he served briefly as a war correspondent for the newspaper, but after his return in 1917 he was given no more assignments.

An influential literary and social critic

Meanwhile, Mencken's work at *Smart Set* was establishing his status as an influential literary critic. He was credited with injecting some much-needed rigor and high standards into the field of American literature, as he called for art that questioned accepted ideas and that portrayed life with more realism and truth. He also championed the work, and thus helped establish the careers, of such groundbreaking writers as Theodore

Dreiser (1871–1945), **Sinclair Lewis** (1885–1951; see entry), **F. Scott Fitzgerald** (1896–1940; see entry), James Joyce (1882–1941), and Eugene O'Neill (1888–1953). The magazine provided these authors with a place to publish their work.

Mencken took advantage of the free time opened up by his severed relationship with the *Sun* to work on something he had long been planning. In *The American Language: A Preliminary Inquiry into the Development of English in the United States* (1919), Mencken asserted that the English spoken in the United States was actually a distinct dialect, and he showed how it had evolved over time from the language spoken by the country's first settlers. Both he and his publishers were surprised by the public's enthusiasm for the book, which sold out quickly. Over the next several decades, Mencken would publish periodic updates to this work, which became a classic of linguistic study.

Increasingly Mencken was seen as an insightful observer of and commentator on U.S. culture. Using a singular blend of scorn, humor, and well-crafted writing, he attacked politicians like President **Warren G. Harding** (1865–1923; served 1921–23; see entry), fundamentalists (conservative Christians who believe that the stories told in the Bible are literally true) like **William Jennings Bryan** (1860–1925; see entry), crooked businessmen, and the white terrorist group the Ku Klux Klan, among many other targets. Somehow he made it seem that his readers, like him, were above all of the foolishness that he was spotlighting. They were not part of the "booboisie" that bore the sharpest brunt of Mencken's scorn. Underlying all of the humor and ridicule, of course, was a serious belief in individual freedoms and especially the right of the minority to express opinions not held by the majority.

Covering the Scopes trial

During the 1920s Mencken's skill in making his own kind of sense out of a chaotic period of cultural transition made him not only the most influential editor but also one of the most important writers in the nation. In 1920 he was rehired by the *Sun* and assigned a weekly column that appeared on the newspaper's editorial page. It was in this capacity that Mencken traveled to Dayton, Tennessee, in the summer of 1925 to cover one of the most riveting events of the decade, popularly known as the "Monkey Trial."

Henry Louis Mencken became one of the most important writers in the nation while covering the trial of John T. Scopes (pictured here), a Tennessee teacher who was on trial for teaching a lesson on evolution.
(AP/Wide World Photos. Reproduced by permission.)

Earlier that year, the state of Tennessee had passed a law preventing teachers from sharing with their students the scientific theory of evolution proposed by Charles Darwin (1809–1882), a nineteenth-century scientist whose work traced the development of humans and other species over millions of years. Although the theory suggested that humans and apes may have had common ancestors, it was incorrectly interpreted by some as saying

Beloved Humorist Will Rogers

Recognized as one of the greatest and most beloved of all U.S. humorists, Will Rogers was well known during the Roaring Twenties for his dry, mocking, and witty comments on the events and trends of the period. His down-home style made him a favorite of people at all levels of society.

Rogers's roots were in the relatively untamed West of the late nineteenth century. He was born in 1879 on a ranch in Oklahoma, which was then known as Indian Territory. Both of his parents were part-Cherokee Indian, and he was proud of his Native American heritage. Rogers never graduated from high school, but he learned to ride horses and rope cattle at a very early age. In 1898 he left home to work as a cowboy in Texas. From there he traveled to Argentina, then across the ocean to South Africa, where his skill in performing rope tricks landed him a place in Texas Jack's Wild West Circus.

Rogers made his New York debut in 1905 and appeared in his first Broadway musical, *The Wall Street Girl,* in 1912. He worked regularly over the next decade, but was never a headliner. That changed when Rogers, in an effort to make his act more interesting, started telling stories and jokes and making funny comments on the news of the day. His easygoing manner and slow drawl both entertained people and put them at ease, and soon he was focusing more on comedy than roping.

Rogers soon found himself in the spotlight. He was a hit in 1916 when he had a starring role in the *Ziegfeld Follies,* and he made his film debut in 1918 in *Laughing Bill Hyde.* During the 1920s Rogers became so well known that his stock phrase, "All I know is what I read in the papers" came into widespread, general use. Beginning in 1926 he wrote a weekly, syndicated newspaper column for the *New York Times* that was read by an estimated twenty million readers. Beginning in 1930 he also shared his humorous comments on politics and daily life through weekly radio broadcasts.

In 1934 Rogers appeared in renowned playwright Eugene O'Neill's only comedy, *Ah, Wilderness!* During the late 1920s and early 1930s Rogers starred in such films as *A Connecticut Yankee* (1931), *Judas Priest* (1934), and *Steamboat 'round the Bend* (1935) and became one of the best-loved movie actors of the period.

Rogers died unexpectedly in 1935, when an airplane carrying him and his friend Wiley Post, a noted pilot, crashed en route to Alaska. On his tombstone is engraved one of his most famous sayings: "I never met a man I didn't like."

that humans had descended from apes (hence the term Monkey Trial).

The theory of evolution seemed to contradict the story of creation found in the Bible, in which God created human beings (beginning with the first man and woman, Adam and

Eve) and everything else in the world over the course of one week. Many people felt their traditional values and beliefs were threatened by the idea of evolution, and they sought to prevent it from being taught in public schools.

Soon after the passage of the Tennessee law, the American Civil Liberties Union (ACLU) offered to defend any teacher who wished to test the law's constitutionality. A high school biology teacher named John Scopes (1900–1970) volunteered, and he was arrested after teaching a lesson on evolution. His trial was set for July, and two prominent public figures had offered to represent the two sides of the issue. Leading the prosecution team was politician and fundamentalist activist William Jennings Bryan, and heading up the defense was **Clarence Darrow** (1857–1938; see entry), a well-respected lawyer famous for successfully defending underdog clients.

Mencken was on hand for most of the trial and was at his most biting. In his reports sent back to the *Sun,* he described the carnival atmosphere that had overtaken Dayton. In articles with such titles as "Homo Neanderthalensis" and "Tennessee in the Frying Pan," he portrayed the town's residents as ignorant and prejudiced, with Bryan as the central embodiment of religious fanaticism and intolerance. He sarcastically called the defendant "the Infidel Scopes" (an infidel is a person with no religion, or whose religion is not that of the majority) in order to ridicule what he saw as a vicious attack on a teacher's right to share new knowledge and theories with his students.

After reaching a peak with Darrow's merciless grilling of Bryan about his religious beliefs, the trial ended with Scopes's conviction (which would soon be overturned). By the time the trial ended, Mencken had already returned to Baltimore, but his newspaper provided the money for the fine that Scopes was ordered to pay.

More hard work and controversy

The mounting success of *Smart Set* inspired Mencken and Nathan to start a new magazine called the *American Mercury,* which was to focus more on commentary and less on literature than *Smart Set.* By the end of the year, Mencken had taken sole control of the new magazine, injecting his own brand of wit, insight, and intellectual energy into its pages. At the peak of its popularity in 1927, the *American Mercury* had a circulation of seventy-seven thousand readers. It was especially popular with the younger generation, who had come of age during or soon after World War I and who were eager to hear their own disillusionment and doubts about their increasingly prosperous, materialistic country voiced.

As busy as he was with his journalistic pursuits, Mencken found time to publish a number of books, including a collection of his articles that appeared in *Prejudices* (a series published between 1919 and 1927) and a volume of political writings, *Notes on Democracy* (1926). Critics were divided about Mencken: some praised him as one of the most talented writers in the United States, while others called his work bombastic (containing important-sounding but empty language) and shallow, with no strong or lasting message.

With the advent of the Great Depression years (1929–41), when the nation experienced a severe economic downturn and much hardship and suffering, the country's mood shifted, and so did people's taste for Mencken's outrageous style of social criticism. There were serious issues to be faced now, and his writing no longer seemed so funny. Mencken's opposition to the New Deal, the program proposed by President Franklin Delano Roosevelt (1882–1945; served 1933–45) to offset the effects of the Depression, along with his seeming lack of concern about the rise of German dictator Adolf Hitler (1889–1945), damaged his reputation. Two new books, *Treatise on the Gods* (1930) and *Treatise on Right and Wrong* (1934), were not as successful as he had expected.

In 1930 Mencken surprised those who considered him a lifelong bachelor by marrying writer and literature professor Sara Powell Haardt. Her death only five years after their marriage saddened Mencken deeply, and he moved out of the apartment they had shared and back into the house in which he had grown up. Those five years were, in fact, the only time he had lived anywhere besides his childhood home.

One arena in which Mencken's writing continued to shine throughout the 1930s and 1940s was in his coverage of political conventions. These were spectacles that he cherished, and he took joy in exposing the shallowness of the overblown rhetoric with which conventions were filled. In the late 1930s he also began writing some essays about his childhood for the *New Yorker* magazine. These were published in three volumes: *Happy Days, 1880–1892* (1940), *Newspaper Days, 1899–1906* (1941), and

Heathen Days (1890–1936). These highly personal and readable accounts of Mencken's life were very warmly received.

In 1948 Mencken suffered a stroke that left him unable to read, write, or speak clearly. This was a terrible blow to a man who had built his life around the printed word. He lived for eight more years, cared for by his youngest brother and visited by only a few close friends. He died in his sleep on January 29, 1956.

The appearance of several books published decades after Mencken's death brought him into the spotlight again. In 1989 *The Diary of H.L. Mencken* appeared, despite Mencken's wish that his journals should never be published. Some readers and critics were dismayed by evidence of anti-Semitic (prejudice against Jews) and racist views found in the diary. Mencken's defenders noted that these were commonly held opinions at the time, and that he had always been a strong defender of equal rights for all. (In fact, the last article Mencken wrote before his stroke pointed out the idiocy of a law prohibiting blacks and whites from playing tennis together.) A similar exchange of opinions about Mencken occurred upon the publication of *My Life as an Author and Editor* (1993).

For More Information

Books

Bode, Carl. *Mencken*. Carbondale: Southern Illinois University Press, 1969.

Cairns, Huntington. *H.L. Mencken: The American Scene*. New York: Vintage Books, 1982.

Manchester, William. *Disturber of the Peace: The Life of H.L. Mencken*. New York: Harper, 1951.

Mencken, H.L. *Newspaper Days, 1899–1906* (1941, reprint). Baltimore, MD: Johns Hopkins University Press, 1996.

Mencken, H.L. *Prejudices* (1927, reprint). Baltimore, MD: Johns Hopkins University Press, 1996.

Teachout, Terry. *A Life of H.L. Mencken*. New York: HarperCollins, 2002.

Web Sites

Burke, Gibbons. "Henry Louis Mencken (1880–1956)." *The H.L. Mencken Page*. Available online at http://www.io.com/gibbonsb/mencken/. Accessed on June 28, 2005.

"H.L. Mencken Room and Collection." *Enoch Pratt Free Library*. Available online at http://www.pratt.lib.md.us/slrc/hum/mencken.html. Accessed on June 28, 2005.

Edna St. Vincent Millay

Born February 22, 1892 (Rockland, Maine)
Died October 19, 1950 (Austerlitz, New York)

Poet and dramatist

Recognized as one of the most accomplished poets of the twentieth century, Edna St. Vincent Millay was an especially famous and popular cultural figure during the Roaring Twenties. Her work was widely admired by critics as well as a varied audience. Millay became a kind of spokesperson for the post-World War I generation of young people, especially women, who were expressing their rebellion against tradition and their insistence on freedom of thought and behavior. In her days as a young poet in New York's Greenwich Village artistic community, she embodied the new, sexually liberated woman of the period.

> "Millay is the poetic voice of eternal youth, feminine revolt and liberation, and sensitivity and suggestiveness."
>
> *Robert L. Gale, author of*
> *"Edna St. Vincent Millay's Life."*

A budding talent

Edna St. Vincent Millay was born in Rockland, Maine, but spent most of her childhood living with her mother, Cora Buzzelle Millay, and two sisters in the nearby town of Camden. Millay was fondly called "Vincent" by her family and friends because her parents had planned to name their son Vincent. When they instead had a girl, they gave her the middle name of Vincent. The inability of Millay's father, Henry Tolman Millay, to act responsibly and support his family led to her parents' divorce

Recognized as one of the most accomplished poets of the twentieth century, Edna St. Vincent Millay was an especially famous and popular cultural figure during the Roaring Twenties. *(Courtesy of The Library of Congress.)*

when she was eight, and she rarely saw her father after that. Millay's strong-willed, independent mother worked as a visiting nurse, often leaving her daughters to fend for themselves and encouraging them to be self-reliant. She also nurtured their love of literature and music by making sure, despite the family's poverty, that they always had access to books and music lessons.

From her earliest years, Millay excelled at both music (she once thought of becoming a concert pianist) and writing.

Through her mother's influence she was exposed to the work of such well-regarded poets as William Shakespeare (1564–1616), John Milton (1608–1674), and William Wordsworth (1770–1850), as well as novels by nineteenth-century authors Charles Dickens (1812–1870) and George Eliot (1819–1880). In her early teens Millay had some poems published in the *St. Nicholas* children's magazine. In high school, she contributed poems to the school's magazine and also served as its editor.

Millay graduated in 1909, but the struggling family had no money to send her to college. The launching of her literary career came about through her mother, who spotted an advertisement for a poetry contest. The winning works would be published in an anthology to be called *The Lyric Year*. Millay submitted a long poem titled "Renaissance," which was written in traditional couplet form (two-line stanzas, in which the last words in each line rhyme) and infused with a mystical sense of appreciation for the imagination.

One of the contest's judges, Ferdinand Earle, immediately recognized Millay as a major talent and began corresponding with her (it was he who suggested that she change the poem's title to "Renascence"), predicting that she would win first prize. As it turned out, the rest of the judges disagreed and gave Millay the fourth prize. Still, when the poem appeared in *The Lyric Year* in November 1912, Millay attracted a great deal of attention, with critics hailing her as a poet destined for greatness.

One of Millay's new admirers was Caroline B. Dow, director of the YWCA's (Young Women's Christian Association) National Training School. She helped Millay get a scholarship to Vassar College, a prestigious women's school in Poughkeepsie, New York. After spending a semester of preparation at New York City's Barnard College, Millay entered Vassar in the fall of 1913. She studied literature and languages and published poems and plays in the campus publications. She also played the lead in a play she had written, *The Princess Marries the Page* (not published until 1932). During her college years, Millay made several strong friendships with her fellow students and received a solid grounding in literary history that would serve her well, although, as a young woman already in her early twenties, she disliked Vassar's strict rules.

The Bohemian life in New York City

Millay's first poetry volume, *Renascence and Other Poems*, appeared in 1917, soon after Millay's graduation from Vassar. It includes six sonnets (a poem with fourteen lines, often of ten syllables each, and employing a regular rhyme scheme), a poetic form that Millay would use often throughout her career. The book and the poetry readings she gave established Millay's reputation in the literary world but did not bring her much money. She moved to New York City, where she lived in a small apartment with her sister Norma and made a meager living through her work as an actress (and sometimes a playwright and director) with the Provincetown Players, an experimental theater group.

Millay became involved with a community of young artists and writers living in the city's Bohemian (socially unconventional) neighborhood of Greenwich Village. They projected a new, modern perspective with their belief in nonconformity (refusal to go along with society's expectations), equality between men and women, and free love. Millay began a series of love affairs, the first one with journalist and playwright Floyd Dell (1887–1969), who was an editor of the socialist publication (the belief in a political and economic system in which the means of production, distribution, and exchange are owned by the community as a whole, rather than by individuals) *The Masses*.

In 1918 Millay met Arthur Davison Ficke (1883–1945), a poet with whom she had corresponded for several years. Ficke stopped in New York to visit Millay on his way to military service in France (the United States had just entered World War I, a conflict that began in Europe in 1914 when Great Britain, France, and Italy opposed Germany's aggression). The two had an intense, three-day affair that Millay would write about in several of her best-known poems. Although the romance eventually ended, Millay and Ficke remained friends for the rest of their lives.

To support herself, Millay began selling short stories to the popular magazine *Ainslee's*, writing under the name Nancy Boyd. These were tales populated by characters from her own life: young writers and artists who lived unconventional, nonconformist lives in Greenwich Village. In 1920 Millay met

Modernist Poet T.S. Eliot

Unlike Edna St. Vincent Millay, T.S. Eliot wrote in a distinctly modern style, creating poetry that was not easily grasped by a wide audience. Nevertheless, both his poems and his literary criticism had a profound influence on the development of twentieth-century literature.

Thomas Stearns Eliot was born in 1888. Educated at Harvard University and England's Oxford University, Eliot studied literature and philosophy and edited the Harvard literary magazine, the *Advocate*. After earning his PhD at Oxford, he settled in London, where he first worked as a teacher at a boy's school and then took a position at a bank.

It was at this time that Eliot also began to write both poetry and literary criticism, publishing his work in a number of journals and magazines. In 1917 his acclaimed poetry collection *Prufrock and Other Observations* was published. Like most of Eliot's work the poems in this work feature a blend of formal and informal speech, a use of both symbolism and realistic detail, and vivid metaphors.

As the 1920s began Eliot suffered from a nervous breakdown brought on by the combined pressures of a failed marriage and exhausting work and creative demands. While recovering, he wrote the book-length poem for which he is most famous, *The Waste Land* (1922). Highly unconventional and innovative, it is one of the most celebrated and controversial works of twentieth-century literature. Divided into five parts, *The Waste Land* is made up of seemingly random, disconnected images. It is narrated by several very different voices and includes both everyday and lyrical language, including many quotes from other writers. The poem's main theme is the disillusionment and spiritual emptiness of the post-World War I period.

In 1925 Eliot became an editor at the London publishing firm of Faber and Faber. From 1922 until 1939 he also served as editor of the distinguished literary journal *Criterion*, in which appeared the work of such important modern writers as Ezra Pound, William Butler Yeats, Virginia Woolf, and Marcel Proust.

By 1927 Eliot became a British citizen. He also joined the Anglican Church, and his strong commitment to spiritual and religious values is evident in such volumes as *The Journey of the Magi* (1927) and *Ash Wednesday* (1930). During the 1930s he spent periods of varying length in the United States, teaching and lecturing at several universities, and he published several books describing his ideas on literature and critical thought.

Eliot also began writing plays in verse, which were generally well-received by both critics and audiences. The best known of these are probably *Murder in the Cathedral* (1936) and *The Cocktail Party*.

Eliot received the Nobel Prize for Literature in 1948. He died in 1965.

Edmund Wilson (1895–1972), who would one day become a famous literary critic and who was so taken with the vibrant young poet that he asked her to marry him; she declined. Wilson was then serving as editor of the sophisticated magazine *Vanity Fair,* and he began publishing Millay's poems in its pages. This brought her not only more income but also a wider audience.

Millay's second poetry volume, *A Few Figs from Thistles,* appeared in 1920. These poems are marked by a breezy, carefree tone that, despite the disapproval of some critics, accurately reflected the rebellious mood and freedom-seeking lifestyle of a daring, feminist-minded young woman of the 1920s. Perhaps most representative of this perspective is the often-quoted "First Fig," which is probably Millay's most famous poem: "My candle burns at both ends;/It will not last the night;/But ah, my foes, and oh, my friends—/It gives a lovely light."

Despite the unconventional voice and content found in her poetry, Millay differed in one significant way from some of the other significant poets of the period. Unlike modernists T.S. Eliot (1888–1965) and e.e. cummings (1894–1962), Millay usually employed not free verse but traditional forms that incorporated set patterns of rhyme and meter. In fact, she was said to straddle two centuries, in that her poems often looked and sounded like those of the nineteenth century, while their themes and sentiments were drawn from the twentieth.

Hard work, and time in Europe

One of Millay's favorite achievements was a one-act play in verse, *Aria da Capo,* that was produced by the Provincetown Players during their 1919–20 season. Millay's next volume of poetry, *Second April* (1921), contains the same childlike spirit and appreciation for nature found in her previous work, along with a new sense of disenchantment and loss. Particularly moving were the sonnets written in honor of Millay's Vassar classmate and friend Dorothy Coleman, who had died in the influenza epidemic that gripped the world in 1918. Another notable poem in this collection is "The Bean-Stalk," based on the fairy tale of Jack and the beanstalk, for which Millay had earlier won an one-hundred-dollar award from the well-respected *Poetry* magazine.

Overworked and exhausted, Millay was still able to set off on a two-year trip through Europe in early 1921. *Vanity Fair* agreed to pay her a regular salary in exchange for articles, written under the name Nancy Boyd, that she was to send back to the United States. Soon after her arrival in Europe, Millay finished a five-act verse play called *The Lamp and the Bell,* which would be performed at the fiftieth-anniversary celebration of Vassar College's alumnae association. Based loosely on the fairy tale of Snow White and Rose Red, this work highlighted the value of strong friendships between women.

During her time in Europe, Millay traveled to France, England, Albania, Italy, Austria, and Hungary. Her mother joined her in the spring of 1922, thus relieving the loneliness she had been feeling and boosting her spirits. Returning to the United States in the spring of 1923, Millay met Eugen Boissevain, a handsome, vigorous, Dutch-born businessman. By April, the two were married. Soon after the wedding, Boissevain drove Millay to a hospital for intestinal surgery, thus beginning a pattern of devotion that would last until his death more than twenty years later. Boissevain appreciated his wife's talent and took care of all her practical needs and arrangements. He also allowed Millay the sexual freedom she desired.

Later in 1923 Millay's *The Harp-Weaver and Other Poems* was published, earning for Millay that year's Pulitzer Prize for Literature. The title poem tells the story of a woman who weaves a set of princely clothes for her young son and then dies. This tale of motherly affection and sacrifice was seen as a tribute to Millay's own mother, who had given her daughters the gift of culture, despite difficult circumstances. This volume also includes *Sonnets from an Ungrafted Tree,* in which a woman separated from her unloved husband returns to nurse him as he dies. These poems feature many strikingly realistic images of life on a New England farm.

A famous figure

In 1924 Millay went on a poetry-reading tour of the Midwest, where she was enthusiastically received by large audiences. Then she and her husband began a period of travel abroad that took them to Asia, India, and France. After their return, Boissevain bought a 700-acre (280-hectare) farm near Austerlitz, New York. This home, which they named Steepletop, would provide a welcome refuge for Millay until the end of her life.

Poet Edna St. Vincent Millay participated in a demonstration concerning the Sacco and Vanzetti case, like the one pictured here, and was inspired to write a poem about the case titled "Justice Denied in Massachusetts."

(© Bettmann/Corbis. Reproduced by permission.)

Millay's interest in and talent for music and drama as well as poetry came together in her next project: writing the libretto (lyrics) for the opera *The King's Henchman,* with music by Deems Taylor (1885–1966). Performed by the Metropolitan Opera in 1927, this work received mixed reviews from the critics but was a hit with audiences.

Later in 1927 Millay's concern for social issues led to her involvement in protests arranged in support of Nicola Sacco (1891–1927) and Bartolomeo Vanzetti (1888–1927). They were Italian immigrants who had been convicted of murder, on rather flimsy evidence, and sentenced to die in the electric chair. Millay was arrested for picketing a government building in Boston, Massachusetts, and made an unsuccessful plea to the state's governor to halt the execution. The Sacco and Vanzetti case inspired a poem, "Justice Denied in Massachusetts," that appeared in her next poetry collection, *The Buck in the Snow and Other Poems* (1928).

Millay continued to tour, impressing audiences with both her striking appearance—which featured flaming red hair, a slim figure, and elegant clothes—and her effective delivery of her poetry. Her next book, *Fatal Interview* (1931), contained fifty-two sonnets that chronicled a love affair from a distinctly feminine point of view. The poems were inspired by Millay's relationship with George Dillon, a young poet she had met while giving a reading at the University of Chicago. Later, Millay would collaborate with Dillon on a translation of French poet Charles Baudelaire's (1821–1867) *Flowers of Evil*.

Achievements and challenges

The poems collected in *Wine from These Grapes* (1934) show not only Millay's personal grief over her mother's death but also her concerns about global affairs. For example, in the grimly toned "Epitaph for the Race of Man," she claimed it was both a tribute and a challenge to humanity to save itself from destruction.

In 1936 Millay was writing an experimental work called *Conversation at Midnight* when her manuscript was lost in a hotel fire while she was vacationing in Florida. Back home in New York, she painstakingly recreated the book from memory. These poems comprise an after-dinner conversation between seven men from very different economic and ideological backgrounds. Millay used a variety of poetic forms to convey their reflections on contemporary concerns and uncertainties.

It was during this period that, already in poor health, due partly to her heavy drinking and smoking, Millay was injured in a car accident that resulted in chronic pain and a dependence on addictive, painkilling drugs. Her next collection did not appear until 1939. *Huntsman, What Quarry?* included poems on lost love, death, nature, and the contrast between male and female perspectives on the world.

Long a pacifist (someone who believes that conflicts should be resolved through peaceful means, not through violence or war), Millay felt her outlook profoundly changed by the outbreak of World War II (1939–45) and the revelations of Nazi atrocities against Jews. She began writing poetry in support of the Allies' war effort (the nations, including the United States, that fought against Nazi Germany, Italy, and Japan). Most critics, as well as Millay herself, in later years, consider these poems, published in *Make Bright the Arrows: 1940 Notebook,* pure propaganda (written to promote a particular cause) and not worthy of her talent.

In general, the 1940s were difficult for Millay. She was hospitalized in 1944 for a nervous breakdown brought on at least in part by her addiction to alcohol and drugs, and she lost several close friends (including Arthur Ficke) to death. In 1949 Boissevain died after surgery for lung cancer. Devastated, Millay insisted on returning alone to Steepletop. She spent a year there, continuing to write until her death from a heart attack in 1950.

In 1954 a final volume titled *Mine the Harvest* was published. It includes poems that are both sensitive and intellectual, and that affirm life while acknowledging the fact of physical decline. In a tribute to Millay that appears on the *Modern American Poetry* web site, Robert L. Gale summed up her appeal to her own and later generations of readers: "Millay is the poetic voice of eternal youth, feminist revolt and liberation, and potent sensitivity and suggestiveness."

For More Information

Books

Brittin, Norman A. *Edna St. Vincent Millay*. Rev. ed. Boston: Twayne, 1982.

Epstein, Daniel. *What Lips My Lips Have Kissed: The Loves and Love Poems of Edna St. Vincent Millay*. New York: Henry Holt, 2001.

Freedman, Diane P. *Millay at 100: A Critical Reappraisal*. Carbondale: Southern Illinois University Press, 1995.

Gould, Jean. *The Poet and Her Book: The Life of Edna St. Vincent Millay*. New York: Dodd, Mead, 1969.

Gurko, Miriam. *Restless Spirit: The Life of Edna St. Vincent Millay*. New York: Thomas Y. Crowell, 1962.

Milford, Nancy. *Savage Beauty: The Life of Edna St. Vincent Millay*. New York: Random House, 2001.

Nierman, Judith. *Edna St. Vincent Millay: A Reference Guide*. Boston: G.K. Hall, 1977.

Web Sites

"Edna St. Vincent Millay." *The Academy of American Poets*. Available online at http://www.poets.org/poet.php/prmPID/160. Accessed on June 28, 2005.

Gale, Robert L. "Edna St. Vincent Millay's Life." *Modern America Poetry*. Available online at http://www.english.uiuc.edu/maps/poets/m_r/millay/millay_life.htm. Accessed on June 28, 2005.

Georgia O'Keeffe

Born November 15, 1887 (Sun Prairie, Wisconsin)
Died March 6, 1986 (Santa Fe, New Mexico)

Artist

"Where I was born and where and how I lived is unimportant. It is what I have done with where I have been that should be of interest."

The work of Georgia O'Keeffe ranks among the finest art of the twentieth century, but it is also loved by, and accessible to, a wide variety of people. A strong, independent person, O'Keeffe resisted being labeled as a female artist, preferring to be considered simply an artist. Similarly, her strikingly original works refuse to be categorized. It was during the Roaring Twenties that O'Keeffe, with the help of the famous photographer and gallery owner Alfred Stieglitz (1864–1946), first captured the public's attention with some of her most notable paintings. These include the enlarged, sharply focused, and richly colored views of flowers for which she is perhaps best known.

An artist from an early age

Born in the rural community of Sun Prairie, Wisconsin, Georgia O'Keeffe was the second of seven children born to Francis O'Keeffe, a farmer of Irish descent, and Ida O'Keeffe, who had grown up in a rich, cultured European family. O'Keeffe's mother encouraged her children's interest in art and set aside part of the family's rather meager income for art lessons.

The work of Georgia O'Keeffe ranks among the finest art of the twentieth century, but it is also loved by, and accessible to, a wide variety of people.

(AP/Wide World Photos. Reproduced by permission.)

Young Georgia showed her talent for drawing very early, and by the age of ten she had decided that she wanted to become an artist. Her favorite subjects, such as palm trees and beach scenes, were drawn from worlds very different from her own.

While attending the Sacred Heart Convent School in nearby Madison (the state capital), O'Keeffe continued her art education by drawing still-life compositions, an exercise that helped her develop the close attention to detail that would always mark her work. While she was still a student there, her father moved his family to Williamsburg, Virginia. O'Keeffe eventually joined her parents and siblings and spent her high school years at Chatham Episcopal Institute (located about 200 miles [322 kilometers] from Williamsburg). There she enjoyed wandering through the Virginia countryside and drawing the flowers, rocks, and other natural objects she saw on her hikes.

After her 1905 graduation, O'Keeffe moved to Chicago, Illinois, to attend that city's Art Institute. There she learned about the works and artistic techniques of the masters of European art, and she practiced drawing live human models. Although O'Keeffe did not particularly care for the traditional styles that had dominated art in past centuries, she worked hard and became one of the school's top students. She spent only a year at the Art Institute, though, returning to Virginia when she contracted typhoid fever (a serious intestinal disease).

In 1907, when she was twenty years old, O'Keeffe went to New York City to attend classes at the Art Students League. She excelled in her studies but felt that she had not yet discovered her own distinct artistic style or calling. At this time in history, the art world, like most other parts of society, was dominated by men, and women were usually not taken seriously or considered to have equal abilities. Despite O'Keeffe's obvious talent, no one seemed to expect her to pursue art as a serious career.

Becoming a teacher

When O'Keeffe's family began experiencing financial problems, she had to withdraw from the Art Students League. She went to Chicago to live with an aunt and worked as a commercial artist making drawings for advertisements. After contracting the measles, she returned to Virginia, and when she had recovered she began a series of teaching jobs. The first was at her own high school, Chatham Episcopal Institute.

O'Keeffe's family was now living close to Charlottesville, Virginia, and during the summer she enrolled in art classes at the nearby University of Virginia. She studied with Alon Bement, who was on the faculty of New York's Columbia University and who inspired her with his unconventional approach to artistic expression. Along with his colleague Arthur Wesley Dow,

Bement encouraged artists to use line and color freely and to follow their own emotional needs in their work.

From 1912 to 1913 O'Keeffe worked as an art instructor in the public schools of Amarillo, Texas. There she first developed an appreciation for the stark southwestern landscapes that would always fascinate her. She returned in the summer to teach summer school at the University of Virginia. It was during this period that O'Keeffe discovered the modernistic work of Wassily Kandinsky (1866–1944), a Russian artist whose colorful, abstract paintings (done in a style that does not try to represent something realistically) encouraged a break with tradition.

O'Keeffe next spent a year in New York City, working as a graduate assistant to Bement and studying with Dow at Columbia. She was energized by the city's thriving creative life, which was then abuzz with the innovative modern art being produced in both the United States and Europe. Like other art students, O'Keeffe visited the 291 Gallery, which had been founded in 1907 by two pioneering photographers, Alfred Stieglitz and Edward Steichen (1879–1973). The gallery served not only as an exhibit space for such artists as Auguste Rodin (1840–1917), whose drawings were displayed there during this period, but also as a gathering place for the city's avant-garde (new and experimental) artistic community. At this time O'Keeffe had not yet met Stieglitz, who would later play an important role in her life.

A bold, original talent is recognized

In the fall of 1915 a lack of money forced O'Keeffe to leave New York and take a teaching job at Columbia College in South Carolina. Depressed and lonely, she felt very far away from the exciting world of New York City, but she was sustained through a correspondence with her friend Anna Pollitzer. An artist and active feminist (someone who believes that women should have equal rights and opportunities), Pollitzer kept O'Keeffe informed about news from New York's artistic community and sent her books and art supplies.

Around this time, O'Keeffe gave up oil painting to work exclusively in charcoal on paper. The images she began creating were unusual, abstract visions representing her deepest

Photographer and Arts Advocate Alfred Stieglitz

Photographer and art gallery owner Alfred Stieglitz strongly influenced U.S. culture through both his own groundbreaking work and his sponsorship of modern artists. Among these artists was Georgia O'Keeffe, whom he married in 1925.

Stieglitz was born in 1864. His parents were German-Jewish immigrants, and he grew up in New Jersey, New York City, and, later, Germany. Regardless of where his family resided, Stieglitz was raised in an atmosphere appreciative of the arts, and he developed an early interest in photography.

While studying engineering at the University of Berlin, Stieglitz also educated himself about the history of art and the still-young craft of photography. In 1887 he won first prize in a photo contest sponsored by *Amateur Photographer*, a British publication. Several years traveling around Europe allowed Stieglitz the opportunity to absorb its cultural influences and develop his photography skills.

When Stieglitz returned to New York with his family in 1890, at age twenty-six, he was already famous as a photographer. At his father's request, he set up a photoengraving business and married the sister of a friend. Both the business and the marriage would eventually fail. Meanwhile, however, he continued to improve his photography. Stieglitz began roaming the streets of New York with his camera, capturing striking shots of common scenes such as men working, horses pulling streetcars, and snow falling on city streets.

Stieglitz's style differed from the European approach to photography, which tended to imitate paintings. They were softly focused, even blurry, and depicted sentimental subjects. Stieglitz's style was direct, clear, crisp images that contrasted black and white, and shadow and light. He preferred to feature ordinary people, objects, and scenes in his work, and tried to promote a distinctly American form of photography. His efforts were frustrated by resistance from more conservative artists.

In 1902 Stieglitz helped found the Photo-Secession group with several like-minded photographers, including Edward Steichen and Clarence White. The group's mission was to promote photography as a distinct art form rather than as a reflection of paintings. In 1903 he began serving as the editor of a new, lavishly illustrated journal called *Camera Work*.

Stieglitz established himself as a leading advocate of new and experimental art when he opened a gallery known as 291, the address of the building on Fifth Avenue on which it was located. Works of contemporary photographers were showcased, as well as such exciting modern painters as Henri Matisse, Paul Cezanne, Pablo Picasso, and eventually the young Georgia O'Keeffe. To O'Keeffe, Stieglitz produced hundreds of photographs of her. Over the next several decades, Stieglitz promoted O'Keeffe's career and continued his advocacy of other artists.

Following a 1928 heart attack, Stieglitz grew increasingly weak, and by 1937 he could no longer lift a camera. After his 1946 stroke, O'Keeffe selected sixteen hundred of his best images to donate to the National Gallery in Washington, D.C. He died that same year.

emotions. She sent a series of these drawings to Pollitzer, telling her friend not to show them to anyone. Pollitzer ignored O'Keeffe's directions and showed the drawings to Stieglitz, who was extremely impressed. Unusual in his day for his liberal attitude toward women and their abilities as artists, Stieglitz included O'Keeffe's work in a show at his gallery. That summer, when O'Keeffe discovered that he had exhibited her drawings without her permission, she angrily confronted Stieglitz. He was quickly able to persuade her, however, to accept what he had done.

That fall, O'Keeffe began her new teaching job at West Texas Normal College. Meanwhile, she continued to correspond and visit with Stieglitz, who featured her works in a 1917 solo show. The two became lovers, even though Stieglitz was married, and he finally convinced her to return permanently to New York, which she did in 1918. Gradually O'Keeffe gained recognition for her stunningly original, bold, and sensual work. At the same time, she also gained fame as the subject of photographs by Stieglitz. He took more than three hundred photographs that captured O'Keeffe's natural elegance and beauty and that he exhibited in a 1921 show called "Portrait of a Woman."

A period of startling creativity

O'Keeffe and Stieglitz now lived together, dividing their time between a New York apartment and a country home at Lake George, New York. In the city, O'Keeffe worked on paintings portraying the New York skyline, such as *New York Night* (1929); at Lake George, she focused on the natural views and simple architecture around her, creating such paintings as *Lake George Barns* (1926). Her style was becoming less abstract, though was it not clearly representational or realistic. In 1919 she painted the first of the oversized flowers upon which much of her fame would rest.

These paintings emphasized the inner design of the flower, rendering their folds and cavities with vibrant colors and mysterious shadows. Some observers have interpreted the flower paintings as having sexual overtones, but O'Keeffe, who always resisted such limiting views of her work, claimed that her intent had simply been for the viewer to look more closely at a familiar object. Some of the most notable works from this period include *Black Iris* (1926), *Oriental Poppies* (1928), and the *Jack-in-the-Pulpit* series (1930).

In 1924, after Stieglitz had divorced his first wife, he and O'Keeffe were married. They would forge an unconventional relationship, however, as O'Keeffe came to feel somewhat trapped by her older, rather needy husband and by the environments in which he chose to live. An important change came in 1929 when O'Keeffe traveled to Taos, New Mexico, to visit some friends. She had been attracted to the dry landscapes of the Southwest since her time in Texas, but this time she found herself awestruck. O'Keeffe decided to make these dramatic surroundings of sunshine, adobe buildings (made from a kind of clay brick), and cactus a permanent part of her life.

O'Keeffe began spending each summer in New Mexico, creating paintings that were simplified yet startlingly beautiful portrayals of that environment. During a southwestern drought, O'Keeffe came upon some bleached animal bones lying on the ground. She was struck by their beauty and began incorporating them into such paintings as *Cow's Skull: Red, White and Blue* (1931) and *Ram's Head, White Hollyhock* (1935). Like the flowers she had painted earlier, these images would forever be associated with O'Keeffe.

At the end of each summer, O'Keeffe would carry her paintings back to New York and turn them over to Stieglitz. He had complete control over exhibiting them, and he worked hard to promote O'Keeffe's work and to keep her at the forefront of the art world.

O'Keeffe's artistic prominence was confirmed when the Art Institute of Chicago held a retrospective exhibit of her work in January 1943; New York's Museum of Modern Art held a similar show in 1946. Having never completed an academic degree during her younger years, O'Keeffe was pleased to receive honorary degrees from the College of William and Mary in 1938 and from the University of Wisconsin at Madison in 1942.

Continuing a productive career

After Stieglitz died in 1946, O'Keeffe directed the distribution of his personal art collection and papers. Then she returned to live in New Mexico (although she traveled east in 1947 and 1949 to organize retrospective exhibits of Stieglitz's work in both New York and Chicago). She established two permanent homes, one in the village of Abiquiu and one farther north, near the resort area called Ghost Ranch. The southwestern colors of brown, tan, and red and the vast landscapes, geometric shapes, and play of light and shadow that she saw around her continued to dominate her canvases.

During the 1950s O'Keeffe began to travel more extensively, visiting such countries as Peru, Greece, France, Japan, and India. She overcame her initial fear of flying through a newly awakened appreciation for the view through an airplane window. O'Keeffe painted several large works, including *Sky Above Clouds* (1963–1965), that portray not only dazzling cloud formations but also glimpses of the landscape beneath.

In the early 1970s a young sculptor named Juan Hamilton, who initially came looking for work as a handyman, became an important part of O'Keeffe's life. Hamilton served as a companion and assistant to O'Keeffe, who was then in her eighties and suffering from weakened eyesight. The exact nature of their relationship is not clear: some observers suspected a romantic connection between the two, while others speculated that the childless O'Keeffe viewed Hamilton as a kind of son. In any case, Hamilton would inherit most of the artist's estate, including twenty-four paintings that were valued at seventy million dollars.

A dwindling of interest in O'Keeffe's work ended when she was featured in a 1968 cover story in *Life* magazine, followed by a retrospective exhibit in New York in 1970. With the growth of the women's movement in the 1970s, O'Keeffe began to be hailed for her achievements within a male-dominated culture and field. Despite her reluctance to allow her gender to define her art, O'Keeffe seemed to embody the independence, self-reliance, and success valued by the women of the late twentieth century.

Determined, perhaps, to set down in her own words how she felt about her life as an artist, O'Keeffe wrote a self-titled autobiography that appeared in 1976. Accompanied by a number of beautiful illustrations, the book focuses not on biographical details but on her work. In the introduction, she states that "Where I was born and where and how I lived is unimportant. It is what I have done with where I have been that should be of interest." *Georgia O'Keeffe* sold more three hundred thousand copies.

In 1977 O'Keeffe was awarded the Medal of Freedom by President Gerald Ford (1913–; served 1974–77), and in 1983 she became the first recipient of the National Medal of the Arts. Meanwhile, her work had become a common sight on calendars, posters, and other items, highlighting the vast popularity of the images she created. O'Keeffe died in Santa Fe, New Mexico, at the age of ninety-nine. Her ashes were scattered across her beloved New Mexico hills. In 1997 the Georgia O'Keeffe Museum opened in Santa Fe. It houses more of her work than any other institution.

For More Information

Books

Berry, Michael. *Georgia O'Keeffe*. New York: Chelsea House, 1988.

Gherman, Beverly. *Georgia O'Keeffe*. New York: Atheneum, 1986.

Lisle, Laurie. *Portrait of an Artist: A Biography of Georgia O'Keeffe*. New York: Seaview Books, 1980.

O'Keeffe, Georgia. *Georgia O'Keeffe*. New York: Viking Press, 1976.

Stieglitz, Alfred. *Georgia O'Keeffe: A Portrait*. New York: Metropolitan Museum of Art, 1978.

Web Sites

Georgia O'Keeffe Museum. Available online at http://www.okeeffemuseum. org/background/. Accessed on June 29, 2005.

"Georgia O'Keeffe." *American Masters*. Available online at http://www. pbs.org/wnet/americanmasters/database/okeeffe_g.html. Accessed on June 29, 2005.

Satchel Paige

Born July 7, 1906 (Mobile, Alabama)
Died June 5, 1982 (Kansas City, Missouri)

Baseball player

During the prosperous Roaring Twenties, more U.S. citizens than ever before had extra income to spend on entertainment. Many were purchasing tickets to sporting events, and athletes like baseball's **Babe Ruth** (1895–1948; see entry) and boxing's **Jack Dempsey** (1895–1983; see entry) were becoming major celebrities. Meanwhile, the segregation (separation of white and black people) of U.S. society, which applied to professional sports as well as other areas, meant that African Americans had to find their own heroes. Fortunately, the Negro baseball leagues that were formed at the beginning of the 1920s provided plenty of stars to thrill black fans. Perhaps the brightest of these was pitcher Satchel Paige. Although many of his major accomplishments occurred in later decades (and Paige lived long enough to play in the Major Leagues after they were integrated), it was during the 1920s that his career got off to its brilliant start.

> "I practiced all the time. . . . Anything you practice, you begin to come good at, regardless of what it is."

Young, tall, and talented

The son of a gardener named John Paige and his wife Lula, Leroy Paige was born into a family of eight children that lived in poverty in the coastal city of Mobile, Alabama. When he was

215

Pitcher Satchel Paige was one of the brightest stars of the Negro baseball leagues, which were formed during the 1920s.

seven, Paige went to work at the local railroad station, contributing to the family income by carrying passengers' luggage for tips. He earned the nickname "Satchel" (a satchel is similar to a duffel bag) after he invented a special sling that allowed him to carry more bags at once; his friends said that he looked like a "satchel tree."

As an elementary school student, Paige was not particularly interested in either perfect attendance or studying, but he did enjoy playing on his school's baseball team. He started as an outfielder and first baseman but eventually became a pitcher, practicing his aim by throwing stones at tin cans. Throughout his life, Paige would stress the value of practice, telling a *Sports Illustrated* reporter, "I practiced all the time.... Anything you practice you begin to come good at, regardless of what it is."

When he was twelve, Paige was arrested for pocketing some toy rings from a glittering store display. He was sentenced to attend the Industrial School for Negro Children in Fort Meigs, Alabama. The school's strict discipline and the stable life it provided proved to be just what the unruly young boy needed. He also had a chance to play baseball and soon became a star of the school's team. Paige stayed at the school for five-and-a-half years, growing into a tall, lanky young man who was determined to make baseball his livelihood.

In 1924 Paige started to pitch for an all-black, semiprofessional team called the Mobile Tigers, on which his older brother Warren had already been playing. Earning one dollar a game, he began to develop both his crowd-pleasing style—featuring a deceptively slow, leisurely stroll up to the mound followed by blisteringly fast throws—and his battery of pitches. In addition to his awesome fastball, Paige perfected such pitches as the screwball, the wobbly ball, and the looper. He began attracting large crowds, winning thirty games and losing only one in the two years he played with the Tigers.

Hopping from team to team

Throughout Paige's career, he would be known as a player who always had one eye out for a better opportunity. He began his pattern of team-hopping with his 1926 move to the Black Lookouts, a professional team based in Chattanooga, Tennessee. It was here that Paige developed his trademark hesitation pitch, which involved an unexpected, momentary delay in throwing the ball that tended to confuse batters. He was initially paid fifty dollars a month, but his salary soon doubled, then doubled again. Nevertheless, Paige kept moving, playing with the Birmingham Black Barons, the Chicago American Giants, the Cleveland Cubs, the Kansas City Monarchs, and the Baltimore Black Sox over the next few years.

The segregated system of U.S. baseball meant not only that black and white players played on separate teams but also that their playing and living conditions were different. In addition

The Negro Leagues

In the early twentieth century, African Americans were either strongly discouraged or actually prohibited from playing sports with whites. There were a few exceptions, especially in boxing: Joe Gans held the lightweight title from 1901 to 1908, Jack Johnson won the heavyweight crown from Tommy Burns in 1908, and Tiger Flowers was the middleweight champion in 1926. In horse racing, the black jockeys who had dominated the sport in the nineteenth century were banned from participating at the beginning of the twentieth century, when white jockeys formed their own unions and established that rule.

Although they could not play on white professional teams, African Americans began playing baseball on their own teams and leagues in the 1890s. These were loosely structured, though, and it was not until the 1920s that a more organized system came into existence with the founding of the National Negro Baseball League (NNLB) in 1920 and the Eastern Colored League (ECL) in 1923. Although both of these leagues disbanded in the early 1930s, African Americans continued to play on black teams until 1947, when Major League baseball was integrated.

The founder and president of the NNLB was Andrew "Rube" Foster, a savvy businessman whose leadership helped the organization draw more than four hundred thousand spectators and earn two hundred thousand dollars in ticket sales in 1923. Expenses were considerable, because black teams often had to pay high rents to play in white-owned ballparks. The salaries of black ballplayers varied greatly, but some of the stars made as much as one thousand dollars a month.

Teams came and went quickly, moving from city to city or disbanding altogether. Performance statistics were not well maintained, which made it difficult to establish solid proof of the reputed excellence of particular players. Still, in the 1970s, major efforts were made to track down records on the ballplayers of the Negro Leagues. As a result, such outstanding athletes as pitcher Satchel Paige, catcher Josh Gibson, shortstop and second baseman John Henry "Pop" Lloyd, and outfielders John "Cool Papa" Bell and Oscar Charleston were all inducted into the Major League Baseball Hall of Fame in Cooperstown, New York.

to earning less money than white professional players, African Americans often played in run-down, poorly lit stadiums; traveled in rickety buses; and either stayed in dingy hotels or slept in their own buses or cars. Even worse was the fact that black players did not receive sufficient credit for their prowess and achievements in the sport. The Negro Leagues did not keep good or consistent records, so it was difficult to authenticate performance. Nevertheless, black fans and some white baseball lovers flocked to the games and took pride in the skills of these African American athletes.

In addition to regular team play during the summer seasons, Paige often participated in barnstorming, which meant playing in exhibition games, often against Major League teams. This was the one venue in which black players could test their abilities against those of white players. Paige also spent many winters playing in various countries in Latin America and the Caribbean, where baseball was very popular and African American players were welcomed.

From 1931 to 1934 Paige played for the Pittsburgh Crawfords, and this is when his career took a steep upward turn toward greatness. In 1933 he pitched forty-two games and won thirty-one; one winning streak included twenty-one consecutive games and sixty-two innings in a row in which he prevented batters from getting hits. The Crawfords were considered one of the best teams in baseball at this time, for the lineup included not just Paige but also the great catcher Josh Gibson (1911–1947), James "Cool Papa" Bell (1903–1991), Judy Johnson (1899–1989), and Oscar Charleston (1896–1954).

It was Paige, however, who drew the most fans to every ballpark in which the team played. While recognizing his talent, his fellow players considered him a loner who was always looking out for his own interests first, and he had few close friends. In 1934 Paige spent a year playing with an all-white, semiprofessional team in Bismarck, North Dakota, during which time he lost only 1 of 104 games. In October of that year, he married a nineteen-year-old waitress named Janet Howard; their nine-year marriage would produce one son.

Baseball is integrated

Paige spent the 1937 season in the Dominican Republic after that Latin American nation's president, Rafael Trujillo (1891–1961), invited him to join a winter-league, all-black team that he had organized. Returning to the United States, Paige joined the Kansas City Monarchs again. Between 1930 and 1942 he led the team to victory in every Negro American League championship. He was the winning pitcher in the 1942 Negro World Series against the Homestead Greys. By that point in his career, Paige was believed to have pitched in 2,500 games, including 45 no-hitters.

The Kansas City Monarchs Satchel Paige winds up for a pitch during a practice session. Paige was the winning pitcher in the 1942 Negro World Series against the Homestead Greys. (© *Bettmann/Corbis. Reproduced by permission.*)

Paige continued barnstorming during the off-seasons. Having pitched against many white players, he knew that he was good enough to play in the Major Leagues. Although he rarely expressed any bitterness about what was known as the "color bar," Paige did resent it and nurtured a hope of one day jumping over it. By the late 1940s, however, his famous fastball was starting to slow down. His personal life was looking up, though, for in 1947 he married Lahoma Brown, with whom he would go on to have six children (in addition to the two that he and his new wife brought to the marriage).

In 1947 the integration of U.S. baseball that so many fans and players had eagerly anticipated finally occurred. Branch Rickey (1881–1965), the president and general manager of the Brooklyn Dodgers, signed stellar Negro League player Jackie Robinson (1919–1972) to a team contract, making him the first black player in the Major Leagues. The following year, Paige became the seventh black player, and first black pitcher, to be signed by a Major League team. In his first game with the Cleveland Indians, owned by Bill Veeck (1914–1986), Paige led the club to victory over the Chicago White Sox with a score of five to zero, allowing only nine hits.

At the age of forty-two, and already past his prime as an athlete, Paige was the oldest rookie (beginning player) in the Major Leagues. Nevertheless, in his first season with the Indians, Paige won six games and lost only one, and in the 1938 World Series, he pitched a hitless inning in front of eighty-seven thousand fans. By the next season, however, Paige was suffering from a nagging stomach ailment. In addition, he was skipping games, missing trains, and generally not playing well. The Indians released him after his second season.

A return to play

After recovering from his stomach problems, Paige returned to the Negro Leagues. By 1950 he was playing for the Monarchs again, pitching sixty-two games and showing off the fastball he had somehow recovered. The following year, Veeck bought the St. Louis Browns and again signed Paige to a Major League contract. Paige played for three seasons, retiring in 1953. During the next decade, he spent his time making public appearances, barnstorming, and playing some minor league baseball. While playing for the Miami Marlins, he made fun of his advanced age by sitting in a rocking chair in the bullpen.

In 1965, when Paige was fifty-nine, he became the oldest player in baseball when he pitched three innings with the Kansas City Athletics, which many commentators said was purely a publicity stunt. After an unsuccessful bid for election to the Missouri state legislature in 1968; Paige found himself in trouble both financially and physically, he suffered from heart disease and emphysema (a lung ailment). In sympathy with his plight, the owner of the Atlanta Braves allowed Paige to pitch several innings for the team at the end of the 1969 season so that he could qualify for a pension (a regular payment made to retired people).

In 1971 Paige became the first African American player to be elected to the Baseball Hall of Fame in Cooperstown, New York. He was soon joined by others, but a controversy erupted when the black players' plaques were placed in a separate area. Some called this another form of segregation, but Paige claimed that it did not bother him. On June 5, 1982, the city of Kansas City dedicated its new youth baseball field to Paige, and he threw out the first ball at a Kansas City Royals game. Three days later, he died of a heart attack.

For More Information

Books

Ashe, Arthur R. Jr. *A Hard Road to Glory.* New York: Amistad Press, 1988.

Holway, John B. *Josh and Satch: The Life and Times of Josh Gibson and Satchel Paige.* Westport, CT: Meckler, 1991.

Humphrey, Kathryn Long. *Satchel Paige.* New York: Franklin Watts, 1988.

LaBlanc, Michael L. *Hotdogs, Heroes & Hooligans: The Story of Baseball's Major League Teams.* Detroit, MI: Visible Ink Press, 1994.

Paige, Leroy "Satchel", and David Lipman. *Maybe I'll Pitch Forever.* Garden City, NY: Doubleday, 1962.

Ribowsky, Mark. *Don't Look Back: Satchel Paige in the Shadows of Baseball.* New York: Simon & Schuster, 1994.

Riley, James. *A Biographical Encyclopedia of the Negro Baseball Leagues.* New York: Carroll and Graf Publishers, 1994.

Rubin, Robert. *Satchel Paige: All-Time Baseball Great.* New York: G.P. Putnam's Sons, 1974.

Shirley, David. *Satchel Paige.* New York: Chelsea House, 1993.

Smith, Robert. *Pioneers of Baseball.* Boston: Little, Brown, 1978.

Periodicals

Sports Illustrated. (June 21, 1982): p. 9.

Web Sites

"Satchel Paige." *National Baseball Hall of Fame.* Available online at http://www.baseballhalloffame.org/hofers_and_honorees/hofer_bios/paige_satchel,htm. Accessed on June 29, 2005.

Satchel Paige: The Official Web Site. Available online at http://www.cmgww.com/baseball/paige/. Accessed on June 29, 2005.

Dorothy Parker

Born August 22, 1893 (West End, New Jersey)
Died June 7, 1967 (New York, New York)

Short-story writer, poet, dramatist, and critic

D orothy Parker's sharply witty voice was one of the most memorable of the Roaring Twenties. She was a member of the talented circle of writers and critics who gathered every week at New York City's Algonquin Hotel to trade gossip and humorous comments. Parker would later prefer, however, to be known as the author of insightful criticism, moving short stories, and deceptively light verse. As someone who did not express herself in the polite, gracious manner expected of women, Parker embodied the shift in attitudes about female behavior that began in the 1920s. She would become a role model for younger women seeking success in the male-dominated realms of literature and journalism.

> "Guns aren't lawful,/ Nooses give;/Gas smells awful;/You might as well live."

A sharp tongue and a talent for writing

Dorothy Parker was born Dorothy Rothschild in West End, New Jersey, a suburb of New York City. Her father was a wealthy Jewish businessman and her mother a Protestant of Scottish heritage who died when Parker was four. In the years to come, Parker would describe her mixed ethnic background in negative terms. Her father subsequently married a highly

Dorothy Parker's witty voice was one of the most memorable of the Roaring Twenties. *(AP/Wide World Photos. Reproduced by permission.)*

religious Catholic woman who attempted to force Parker into the same mold by enrolling her in a Catholic school. Parker attended the Blessed Sacrament Convent School from the age of seven until she was fourteen. She was finally expelled for acting disrespectful, and she would later joke that all she learned at this school was that pencil erasers would erase ink when dampened.

In 1907 Parker entered Miss Dana's School in Morristown, New Jersey. She was not much happier at this exclusive private academy for girls, but she did acquire a good education there. She graduated in 1911 and moved into a New York City boardinghouse, writing during the day while supporting herself by playing piano in a dancing school. She began selling her poems to various magazines and was finally hired by *Vogue* as a copywriter, assigned to write captions for fashion illustrations.

Parker's witty style soon caught the attention of Frank Crowninshield, the editor of a sophisticated magazine called *Vanity Fair* that was owned by the same publisher as *Vogue*. He hired Parker, and her critical essays, satirical writing, and poetry began appearing in the magazine. She began to gain a reputation for her devastating wit, which both delighted and shocked readers.

In June 1917 Parker married businessman Edwin Pond Parker II, who soon enlisted in the army and was sent overseas to serve in World War I (a global conflict fought between 1914 and 1918, which the United States entered in 1917). Parker's career continued to develop. She became *Vanity Fair*'s drama critic in 1918, and the next year she became friends with Robert Benchley (1889–1945) and Robert E. Sherwood (1896–1955), who had joined the magazine as staff writers.

The Algonquin Round Table

Parker, Benchley, and Sherwood began having weekly lunches together at the Algonquin Hotel. Soon they were joined by critic Alexander Woolcott (1887–1943), newspaper columnist Franklin P. Adams (1881–1960), and Harold Ross (1892–1951), who would found the *New Yorker* magazine in 1925. Other notable writers, such as humorists Ring Lardner (1885–1933) and James Thurber (1894–1961), would show up occasionally at what came to be called the Algonquin Round Table. Parker was usually the only woman present.

Adams publicized the group's gatherings, which became famous for their witty exchanges and lively conversation. Parker's role was particularly noteworthy for its radical departure from tradition. Whereas women were expected to be mild-mannered and gentle, she delighted in being tough and sarcastic, even to the point of nastiness. But Parker's sharp tongue got her into trouble in 1920. She was fired from her job at *Vanity Fair* for reportedly poking fun at the wife of one of the magazine's financial backers.

Ring Lardner: Satire and Sports

The popularity of witty writers like Dorothy Parker and James Thurber during the Roaring Twenties highlights the appreciation that the people of this period had for humor writing and satire. One of the best known writers in this category was Ring Lardner.

Ringgold "Ring" Lardner was born into a wealthy family in Niles, Michigan, in 1885. After he finished high school, his father insisted that he enter engineering school. He soon flunked out. In 1905 he got a job as a reporter for a South Bend, Indiana newspaper, the *Times.* Two years later Lardner moved to Chicago, Illinois, where he worked as a sports columnist for several of the city's newspapers, including the *Tribune.* As time went by he became known for the humorous, informal, engaging style that would characterize his fiction and that would be imitated by other sportswriters for generations to come.

In 1915 Lardner wrote a story in the form of a letter from a dimwitted, obnoxious baseball pitcher named Jack Keefe to a friend back home. Originally published in the *Saturday Evening Post* magazine, the story was so popular that Lardner wrote a whole series of letters, which appeared in 1916 as a book called *You Know Me, Al.* Lardner was much admired for his cynical humor and skillful rendering of slang, and the book became a classic of U.S. sports fiction. In 1917 Lardner served briefly as a World War I correspondent for *Colliers* magazine, but he soon returned to his stateside writing career. He started writing a weekly newspaper column in 1919.

Some of Lardner's best short stories were published during the Roaring Twenties. Such tales as "Champion," "Some Like Them Cold," "Haircut," and "Golden Honeymoon" were collected in *How to Write Short Stories* (1924) and *The Love Nest and Other Stories* (1926). Toward the end of the decade, Lardner collaborated with producer George M. Cohan on a Broadway show called *Elmer the Great* (1928) and with playwright George S. Kaufman on *June Moon* (1929). Lardner died of a heart attack in 1933.

Parker was quickly hired to write a monthly theater column for *Ainslee's* magazine, and she continued to publish humorous pieces, essays, character sketches, and her own brand of funny, epigrammatic (short and witty) verse in such publications as *Saturday Evening Post, Ladies Home Journal,* and *Everybody's.* Already her work demonstrated the qualities for which she would long be praised, including her ability to invoke laughter in the face of tragedy and to expose the contradictions of human behavior.

Productivity and depression

Parker and her husband separated in 1928, and Parker had a love affair that ended badly. This led to a period of depression and the first of her two suicide attempts. For the rest of her life, Parker would alternate between periods of productivity and bouts of depression and heavy drinking.

Her first published short story, "Such a Pretty Little Picture," which featured a theme of failed marriage, appeared in *Smart Set* at the end of 1922. Her first poetry collection, *Enough Rope* (1926) included the famous and much-quoted poem "Resume," which treats the subject of suicide in a humorous way, concluding "Guns aren't lawful,/Nooses give;/Gas smells awful;/You might as well live." Many of the poems in this best-selling collection document the costs of false promises and broken romance. Later poems were collected in *Sunset Gun* (1927) and the even more pessimistic *Death and Taxes* (1931).

From time to time Parker had contributed pieces to the *New Yorker*, and in October 1927 she began writing a weekly book review column, which she signed "Constant Reader," for that magazine. Her reviews now began to include more in-depth analysis, and she was recognized as a reliable, insightful judge of literary merit.

The writing skill and understanding of human weakness that Parker showed in her short stories were confirmed in 1929 when she won the O. Henry Memorial Award for "Big Blonde." At the center of this sad story is Hazel Morse, an attractive and pleasant-natured woman with a pathetic dependence on men for both emotional and financial support. In her alcoholism, frequent affairs, and suicide attempt, Hazel bore some resemblance to Parker, who was praised for creating a truly tragic figure who, despite her weaknesses, does not deserve her grim fate.

Despite the success she had achieved in her professional life and her growing reputation as an important figure in the U.S. literary scene, Parker continued to lead a messy personal life. She was divorced from Edwin Parker in 1928 and lost several good friends due to her sharp tongue. She was also drinking too much, which sometimes interfered with her ability to meet deadlines.

From New York to Hollywood and back

In 1934 Parker married a young actor named Alan Campbell, and the pair moved to Hollywood to become screenwriters. Over the next sixteen years, they would collaborate on twenty-two film scripts, including one for the Academy Award-winning film *A Star Is Born*. Along with dramatist Lillian Hellman (1906–1984) and fiction writer Dashiell Hammett (1894–1961), Parker and her husband helped to organize the Screen Actors Guild, an organization designed to protect the interests of actors involved in the movie industry.

As the 1930s progressed, Parker became increasingly involved in liberal political causes. As early as 1927 she had marched in a protest against the execution of Nicola Sacco (1891–1927) and Bartolomeo Vanzetti (1888–1927), Italian immigrants convicted of murder in a trial that many felt had been unfair. She helped to set up the Anti-Nazi League in 1936 and traveled to Spain to report on that nation's

Dorothy Parker and her husband Alan Campbell collaborated on twenty-two film scripts, including the Academy Award-winning *A Star Is Born,* and helped to organize the Screen Actors Guild. *(© Bettmann/Corbis. Reproduced by permission.)*

civil war for the radical leftist publication *New Masses*. She was not writing as much poetry and short fiction now, but collections of her work in both of these genres appeared in the last half of the 1930s.

Parker divorced Campbell in 1947. The two would remarry in 1950, but would soon divorce again. Despite her distaste for the superficiality of Hollywood's movie industry, Parker returned to screenwriting. Two years later she collaborated with Ross Evans on a play called *The Coast of Illyria*, which was based on the lives of the English essayist Charles Lamb and his sister Mary. Her best play, however, and the accomplishment of which she claimed to be most proud, was *Ladies of the Corridor* (1953), which she wrote with Arnaud D'Usseau. This drama centers on the lives of two lonely elderly ladies who live in shabby New York hotel rooms.

Amid the anti-Communist hysteria that prevailed in the United States during the late 1940s and early 1950s, Parker was targeted by Senator Joseph McCarthy (1908–1957) and the House Un-American Activities Committee for her leftist politics and supposed Communist sympathies. In her final decade she continued to write, contributing pieces to the *New Yorker,* adapting her short stories for television, and writing a monthly book review column for *Esquire* magazine from 1957 to 1963; she was also a visiting professor at California State College in Los Angeles. She sometimes expressed regret that the reputation for sarcastic wit she had attracted during the Algonquin days had overshadowed her attempts at serious writing.

Parker died of a heart attack in 1967, alone in her room at the Volny Hotel in New York. She left most of her estate to civil rights leader Martin Luther King Jr. (1929–1968) and the National Association for the Advancement of Colored People.

For More Information

Books

Calhoun, Randall. *Dorothy Parker: A Bio-Bibliography.* Westport, CT: Greenwood Press, 1992.

Frewin, Leslie. *The Late Mrs. Dorothy Parker.* New York: Macmillan, 1986.

Kinney, Arthur. *Dorothy Parker.* Boston: Twayne, 1978.

Meade, Marion. *Dorothy Parker: What Fresh Hell Is This?* New York: Penguin, 1989.

Parker, Dorothy. *Enough Rope.* New York: Boni & Liveright, 1926.

Web Sites

Dorothy Parker (1893–1967). Available online at http://www.levity.com/corduroy/parker.htm. Accessed on June 29, 2005.

"Dorothy Parker (1893–1967)." *American Poems.* Available online at http://www.americanpoems.com/poets/parker/. Accessed on June 29, 2005.

"Dorothy Parker (1893–1967)—original surname Rothschild." *Books and Writers.* Available online at http://www.kirjasto.sci.fi/dparker.htm. Accessed on June 29, 2005.

George Herman "Babe" Ruth Jr.

Born February 6, 1895 (Baltimore, Maryland)
Died August 17, 1948 (New York, New York)

Baseball player

"I swing big, with everything I've got. I hit big or I miss big. I like to live as big as I can."

The Roaring Twenties was a decade of heroes. In search of proof that human effort still mattered in a time of great change and technological advances, the U.S. public was eager for celebrities. Aviator **Charles Lindbergh** (1902–1974; see entry) earned the public's admiration for flying solo over the Atlantic Ocean, and movie stars like Douglas Fairbanks (1883–1939) and Rudolph Valentino (1895–1926) caused women to swoon. But in a decade that many called the "Golden Age of Sports," it was George Herman "Babe" Ruth who captured the imagination of sports fans. He is credited with having transformed baseball from a game of bunts, pitching, and base running to a more exciting realm of long balls and spectacular home runs. An athlete of dazzling talent and a man with very human weaknesses, Ruth won the hearts of people all over the nation and the world.

A "bad kid" makes good

George Herman Ruth Jr. was born in Baltimore, Maryland, to George Herman Ruth Sr. and Katherine Schamberger Ruth, who were both of German ancestry. His father was

In a decade that many called the "Golden Age of Sports," it was Babe Ruth who captured the imagination of sports fans. *(Hulton Archive/Getty Images. Reproduced by permission.)*

sporadically employed as a bartender and slaughterhouse worker and could barely support his family. Of the eight children born to the family, only young George and his sister Mamie survived past infancy. According to *The Babe Ruth Story as Told to Bob Considine,* from a very young age, Ruth was a self-described "bad kid" who cursed, chewed tobacco, and ran wild through the streets, hanging out in saloons and pool halls.

Unable to control the boy, Ruth's parents signed over custody, when he was seven years old, to St. Mary's Industrial School for Boys. He would remain a ward of this Catholic reform school until he was nineteen and would very rarely see his family members again. The program at St. Mary's featured hard work—with the boys learning to make shirts, cabinets, and cigars—and strict discipline. Ruth had a difficult adjustment but found a friend and father figure in one of the monks who ran the school, Brother Mathias.

Brother Mathias encouraged Ruth to channel his energies into sports. Baseball was then the most popular sport at St. Mary's, and it quickly became obvious that Ruth had exceptional skills. He soon became the star player on the school's team. At first he played the position of catcher, but eventually he became a pitcher. It was also at this time that he began to imitate Brother Mathias's unusual style of walking with his toes turned slightly inward, which would become a Ruth trademark in the years to come.

When Ruth was in his late teens, his remarkable abilities came to the attention of Jack Dunn, the owner of the Baltimore Orioles baseball team (then part of the International League, and a minor-league team of the Boston Red Sox). In February 1914 Dunn agreed to become Ruth's legal guardian so that he could leave St. Mary's and become a pitcher for the Orioles. When Ruth joined the team, someone noted that he was Dunn's latest "babe" (the term for the young, up-and-coming players that Dunn recruited), and the nickname stuck. From then on, he would be known as Babe Ruth.

Becoming a legend

That same year, Dunn sold Ruth to the Red Sox for $2,900. Playing under manager Bill Carrigan (who was Ruth's favorite among all his managers), Ruth won his first two games. But since it was clear that the Red Sox did not have a chance to win the pennant (awarded to the top finisher in each league; in this case, the American League), Ruth was sent down to Providence, Rhode Island, to assist the Red Sox minor-league team there. He performed brilliantly and helped the team win the International League pennant.

Over the next three years, Ruth's pitching helped the Red Sox win three American League pennants and three World Series titles. A left-hander with terrific speed and a good curveball, he pitched a shutout (a game in which the opposing team scores no runs) in the 1918 World Series, the first in a long string of scoreless World Series innings in Ruth's career.

Ruth's ability as a pitcher was matched by his skill and power as a hitter. Describing his attitude to hitting (and life), as quoted in a biography by Robert Creamer, Ruth explained that "I swing big, with everything I've got. I hit big or I miss big. I like to live as big as I can." The fact that Ruth was also an excellent fielder and, despite the skinny legs attached to his bulky body, a good base runner is often overlooked. This wide range of talents, in fact, ended Ruth's pitching career. In 1918 manager Ed Barrow decided to put him in the outfield so that he would be able to play in more games than he would have if he had continued to pitch.

That same year, Ruth had a .300 batting average and hit eleven home runs while also winning thirteen games (and losing seven) that he pitched. During spring training in 1919, he hit a baseball nearly 600 feet (183 meters), which was farther than anyone had ever hit a ball before. That season, Ruth's average was .322, and he hit an amazing twenty-nine homers. Ruth was rapidly becoming a superstar, and in their enthusiasm for him the public seemed to forget all about the scandal, when several Chicago White Sox players were banished from the game for intentionally losing the World Series, that had rocked baseball only a few years earlier.

Yankee fans rejoice

A major turning point in Ruth's life came at the end of the 1919 season, when Red Sox owner Harry Frazee, who needed money to finance a Broadway show, sold Ruth to the New York Yankees for $125,000 and a $350,000 loan. Red Sox fans were enraged, but New York's fans and press corps were ecstatic. During the 1920 season, Ruth hit fifty-four home runs (the runner-up in the American League hit nineteen, and the National League contender hit only fifteen); the next year, he hit fifty-nine home runs. It was now clear to everybody that he had taken over the spot once occupied by Ty Cobb

(1886–1961) as the nation's leading baseball hero. His hard-hitting, so-called "Big Bang" style of play was being imitated by other players. Many legends would be told about him over the years. The most famous was that, during the 1932 World Series, he had pointed toward the fence and then hit a home run that landed in that same spot.

Ruth would dominate baseball from 1920 to 1935, leading the Yankees to seven pennants and five World Series championships. His rising salary figures reflected his success: in 1917 he made five thousand dollars per year, in 1919 that figure had doubled, and in 1920 he made twenty thousand. By the time Ruth's salary peaked in 1930, he was making eighty thousand a year, which was then a higher salary than that of the president of the United States. Altogether he earned a career total of about one million dollars in salary, and another million in endorsements and public appearances.

To the Yankees, Ruth was worth the expense. His fame reached to every corner of the United States, as he proved when he took a trip to the far West and was greeted by huge crowds. At home, Ruth brought in record numbers of fans, so that the Yankees were able to build a new stadium with room for sixty thousand. Yankee Stadium, fondly referred to as "the House That Ruth Built," opened in 1923, the same year that Ruth was named the American League's most valuable player.

Private life attracts attention

Throughout his career, Ruth's private life attracted a lot of attention. He was known for his excessive eating, drinking, womanizing, and spending. But all these weaknesses were forgiven by the public, especially in view of his frequent appearances at the bedsides of sick, baseball-loving, Ruth-idolizing boys. He usually arrived wearing a big overcoat and a hat, along with a wide grin and a cigar hanging out of his mouth.

In October 1914 Ruth married Helen Woodford, a Boston waitress. The two would have no children but would adopt daughter Dorothy in 1920. In the mid-1920s they would separate, and Helen would be killed in a fire in early 1929. That same year Ruth married Claire Merritt Hodgson, a former actress and model, and adopted her daughter, Julia.

Babe Ruth follows through on his sixtieth home run of the 1927 baseball season. Most people feel that this was the best season of his career. *(© Bettmann/Corbis. Reproduced by permission.)*

In addition to his big appetites, Ruth was famous for his frequent disputes with managers and baseball officials and for his brawls with other players, resulting in numerous fines, curfews, and suspensions. He missed two months of playing time when he was hospitalized and operated on for an intestinal abscess. Upon his return, Ruth got more serious about disciplining himself, even hiring a trainer to help him lose weight. He came back stronger than ever.

Best season ever

Ruth had what most agree was his best season in 1927, when he played on a team that has been labeled the finest ever assembled. Opposing players had to face the famous

Grand Slam Golfer Bobby Jones

Prominent among the athletes who became celebrities and heroes during the Roaring Twenties was Bobby Jones, a golfer with remarkable natural ability who won many prestigious tournaments in the United States and Great Britain.

Born to a wealthy family in Atlanta, Georgia, in 1902, Jones was often ill as a child. His family lived at the edge of a golf course in the resort community of East Lake, and he began playing the game at a very early age. In fact, Jones won his first children's tournament at the age of six. He continued to win tournaments, and when he was only fourteen he reached the third round of the U.S. Amateur Tournament.

Between 1923 and 1930, Jones won thirteen of the twenty-one major championships he entered. Because he had a violent temper and a strong desire for perfection, he decided to avoid the pressure of professional play by remaining an amateur. This meant that he earned no money from any tournament in which he played. Jones also hated to practice and often went for fairly long periods without playing golf at all. Nevertheless, he managed to capture five U.S. Amateur titles, four U.S.

Opens, three British Opens, and one British Amateur.

In 1930 Jones won a series of tournaments called the Grand Slam: the British Amateur, the British Open, the U.S. Amateur, and the U.S. Open. Having accomplished this feat, the twenty-eight-year-old decided to retire from competitive golf. During his playing years, he had somehow been able to earn an engineering degree from Georgia Technical University and a degree in English literature from Harvard University. Jones started work on a law degree at Emory University but passed the bar examination early and joined his father's law firm.

Jones remained active in the golf world, designing golf clubs, overseeing the construction of the Augusta National course in Augusta, Georgia, in 1933 and helping to establish the Masters Tournament, which is still held every year at Augusta. He also wrote about golf and appeared in a series of films in which he gave movie stars golf lessons.

In the late 1940s, Jones began to suffer from symptoms that were later diagnosed as syringomyelia, a serious disease of the nervous systems that causes muscle deterioration and pain. By the end of his life in 1971, Jones was confined to a wheelchair.

"Murderers' Row" of stellar players, led by Ruth, of course, as well as his fellow slugger Lou Gehrig (1903–1941). Ruth hit sixty home runs that year, plus two more in the World Series against the Pittsburgh Pirates, which the Yankees swept in four games.

Ruth set many records in his fifteen years with the Yankees, some of which have since been broken. The best known was his home run tally of 714, which stayed intact until 1974, when Atlanta Braves slugger Henry "Hank" Aaron (1934–) hit 715. Ruth's lifetime batting average of .342 ranked ninth, and he came in third in strikeouts, with 1,330.

By the middle of the 1930s, Ruth's abilities were waning. The Yankees released him to the Boston Braves in 1935. He soon realized that this had just been a ploy to increase ticket sales, and he quit midseason, but not before hitting three home runs in his last Major League game. Ruth had hoped to become a team manager when his career as a player was over, but this is one dream that never came true for him. Although he was hired as a coach by the Brooklyn Dodgers in 1938, he left before the end of the season for the same reason he had quit the Braves.

Ruth continued to be a beloved public figure. He was elected to the Baseball Hall of Fame in 1936, and he appeared in movies. He sold war bonds during World War II (1939–45), and he served as director of the Ford Motor Company's junior baseball program.

In 1946 Ruth was diagnosed with throat cancer. Surgery and radiation therapy failed to halt the progress of the disease. In June 1948, two months before his death, he appeared at Yankee Stadium to bid farewell to his fans. He died in August at the age of fifty-three. In the days before his funeral, Ruth's casket was placed outside Yankee Stadium, and an estimated one hundred thousand fans filed by to pay their respects.

For More Information

Books

Bains, Rae. *Babe Ruth*. Mahwah, NJ: Troll Associates, 1985.

Berke, Art. *Babe Ruth*. New York: Franklin Watts, 1988.

Creamer, Robert. *Home Run: The Story of Babe Ruth*. New York: Simon & Schuster, 1974.

Gilbert, Thomas. *The Soaring Twenties: Babe Ruth and the Home Run Decade*. New York: Franklin Watts, 1996.

Macht, Norman. *Babe Ruth*. New York: Chelsea House, 1991.

Ruth, George Herman. *The Babe Ruth Story as Told to Bob Considine.* New York: E.P. Dutton, 1948.

Wagenheim, Kal. *Babe Ruth: His Life and Legend.* New York: Henry Holt, 1992.

Web Sites

"About Babe Ruth." *The Official Web Site of the Sultan of Swat.* Available online at http://www.baberuth.com/flash/about/biograph.html. Accessed on June 29, 2005.

Margaret Sanger

Born September 14, 1879 (Corning, New York)
Died September 6, 1966 (Tucson, Arizona)

Advocate

Outspoken in her defense of women's rights to control their reproductive lives, Margaret Sanger was a leading founder of the U.S. movement to make birth control widely available. It was during the Roaring Twenties—a time of great social change, when sexual matters were starting to be more openly discussed, and women began demanding the same sexual freedoms that men had always enjoyed—that Sanger opened the first physician-directed birth control clinic in the United States. Although Sanger was not the first or only advocate of family planning, she was certainly among the most energetic and dedicated. Fighting opposition from government and church leaders, as well as public opinion, she helped to change attitudes about birth control.

"By word and deed, [Sanger] pioneered the most radical, humane, and transforming political movement of the century."

Gloria Steinem, journalist and feminist

Influenced by mother's life and death

Sanger was born Margaret Louisa Higgins into a large Irish American family in Corning, New York. Her father, Michael Hennessey Higgins, was a stonecutter with unconventional, liberal views who was more interested in political arguments than in making a steady income for his family. Her mother,

Fighting opposition from government and church leaders, as well as public opinion, Margaret Sanger helped to change attitudes about birth control beginning in the 1920s. *(AP/Wide World Photos. Reproduced by permission.)*

Annie Higgins, was a devout member of the Roman Catholic religion, which forbids the use of birth control. Consequently Annie endured eighteen pregnancies and eleven live births (Margaret was the sixth), while at the same time suffering from tuberculosis, a serious lung disease that was usually fatal.

Sanger would watch as her mother, worn out from many difficult births, from her illness, and from the pure exhaustion of looking after eleven children, died before she reached fifty. This tragedy would strongly influence Sanger's views about the effects of unwanted, unplanned pregnancies. The unequal relationship between her strong-willed father and meek, obedient mother also shaped her ideas about men and women.

After a negative encounter with an eighth-grade teacher, Sanger's older sisters paid for her to attend Claverack College, a private academy. She had to work in the school's kitchen to help pay for her room and board, but she much preferred life at school to being at home. After three years, however, she had to return to her family to help nurse her mother through her final days. Mounting tensions between Sanger and her father, and her mother's death, propelled Sanger into her next step. Lacking the money to pursue her dream of becoming a doctor, she enrolled in nursing school at White Plains State Hospital, where she spent much of her training time in the maternity ward.

A young nurse, wife, and mother

Having completed two years of training, Sanger was ready to begin work on a three-year nursing degree program. Meanwhile, however, she had met an architect and artist named William Sanger, who was eight years her elder. He persuaded her to marry him, which she did rather reluctantly. Soon she was pregnant. During her pregnancy, Sanger began showing signs of tuberculosis infection, and after the birth of son Stuart in 1903, the young family moved to Westchester County, a suburb of New York City.

Sanger had two more children: son Grant was born in 1908, and daughter Peggy in 1910. She was restless in the life of a suburban homemaker, however, and eventually she and her husband moved with their children to an apartment in Manhattan, a neighborhood of New York City. There they became involved in a radical political group, many of whose members believed in Socialism, a political and social system in which the means of production, distribution, and exchange of goods are owned by the community as a whole, rather than by individuals. Some of the most famous members of this group included activist Emma Goldman (1869–1940) and revolutionary poet and journalist John Reed (1887–1920).

Emma Goldman: Anarchist Crusader

While living in New York City in the decade before the Roaring Twenties, Margaret Sanger met an older woman activist who encouraged her work in promoting the use of birth control. Emma Goldman was strongly committed to social change, and she paid a high price for her beliefs.

Goldman was born in 1869 in the eastern European country of Lithuania, which was then part of Russia. A rebellious young woman, she became interested in radical causes even before her arrival in the United States. She moved to Rochester, New York, in 1885 to live with a married sister. After twice marrying and divorcing, Goldman moved alone to New York City. Goldman's opposition to capitalism, the system in which a country's trade and industry are controlled by private owners for profit, led to her involvement with the anarchist movement, made up of people who believe that all forms of government are undesirable.

Goldman became a passionate political activist, even taking part in a failed assassination attempt against an industrial tycoon. Arrested in 1893 for her role in a protest demonstration in New York City, she spent a year in prison. After her release, she went to Europe to obtain training and certification as a nurse and midwife who assists women in childbirth.

Returning to New York, Goldman began working among the poor while speaking out on such issues as international peace and free love (by which she meant not casual sex but a committed love and sexual relationship outside of marriage, which she considered too restrictive to women's freedom). In 1906 Goldman founded the publication *Mother Earth* as a forum for all the causes in which she believed, including anarchism and free speech. Between 1906 and 1916 she wrote and delivered hundreds of lectures, particularly advocating access to birth control as an essential right that women should have.

Goldman's outspoken opposition to World War I and her previous political activity made her an obvious target of the government's actions against radicals just before the Roaring Twenties began. She was one of more than two hundred individuals who were tried and deported for holding beliefs considered anti-American. Forced to live in Russia, Goldman traveled frequently around Europe and Canada. She was able to return to the United States only briefly, for a 1934 speaking tour. She died in Toronto, Canada, in 1940.

Witnessing women's suffering

Sanger became a union activist (someone who fights for the right of workers to organize into unions, which give them more power to bargain for better wages and working conditions). She also started working as a visiting nurse and midwife among the poor people living in New York's Lower East Side.

She witnessed firsthand the poverty, misery, and desperation endured by women who were forced to go through repeated, unwanted pregnancies. It was clear to Sanger that the inability to control their reproductive lives robbed these women of their health, their economic stability, and in some cases even their lives.

The first few decades of the twentieth century were like the hundreds of years preceding them, in that sexual matters were not open to public discussion, and doctors were not even taught about contraception (devices and methods for avoiding pregnancy) in medical school. Many people believed that it was wrong or even sinful to interfere with the natural process of reproduction. They thought that women should submit to intercourse whenever their husbands desired it, and that families should be as large or small as the resulting pregnancies made them. There were strict laws to enforce this view, and the Roman Catholic Church was especially active in promoting it.

Sanger's work made her aware of what she increasingly viewed as needless suffering and waste of life. She was especially shocked by the death of an immigrant woman named Sadie Sachs, who had repeatedly begged her doctor to advise her on how to avoid another pregnancy. The doctor's only suggestion was that Sadie's husband not sleep with her. A few months later, Sachs died from blood poisoning after a self-induced abortion. Indeed, Sanger knew that this was only one of many deaths resulting from a woman's strong desire to terminate a pregnancy, often performing abortions under unsanitary, extremely dangerous conditions.

This tragedy spurred Sanger to set herself the goal of one day establishing centers where women could come for information and guidance on how to take charge of their reproductive lives. At the same time, she noticed that despite all their talk about building a better world, many of her radical friends failed to take the special needs of women into account. Her belief that the ability to limit family size was an even more important reform than achieving higher pay or improved working conditions caused friction between Sanger and other labor activists, including her own husband. Sanger was particularly outraged by the fact that birth control, though illegal, was already available and widely used by people with the knowledge and money to obtain it, but not by the poor and uneducated.

Devoted to the cause

In 1912 Sanger quit her nursing work to devote herself to the cause of reproductive freedom. That November she began writing articles on women's health and sexuality for *The Call,* a weekly socialist newspaper that published Sanger's writing in a column titled "What Every Girl Should Know." Soon, however, Sanger found herself in trouble with the law. In 1873, at the urging of postal official Anthony Comstock (1844–1915), a federal law had been passed that made it illegal to send obscene or pornographic materials through the mail. Printed material about birth control was included in this category because of the widespread belief that birth control was evil. In addition to the federal Comstock Law, many similar state laws were in effect. In early 1913, after the appearance of Sanger's article on syphilis (a serious sexually transmitted disease), the U.S. Post Office placed a ban on *The Call.*

During the summer of 1914, Sanger traveled to Europe for the first time, where she investigated the birth control practices used in countries like France, where family planning was accepted and common. Returning to the United States, Sanger started a publication called *The Woman Rebel,* through which she intended to inform people about what she had learned. Soon, however, Sanger was charged under the Comstock Act with sending obscene material through the mail. If convicted, she might face as many as forty-five years in jail. Sanger fled to Europe, but not before publishing a sixteen-page pamphlet called *Family Limitation,* which provided direct instructions, including diagrams, on ways to avoid pregnancy.

In Europe Sanger met with a number of activists, physicians, and other birth control advocates. One of these was the famous psychologist Havelock Ellis (1859–1939), who had studied and written extensively about human sexuality. It was partly through her contact with Ellis, with whom she had a love affair, that Sanger began to develop the view that women were capable of enjoying sex and had as much right to such enjoyment as men. Ellis advised Sanger that if she softened her approach to the birth control cause, she would be more likely to attract support from rich, powerful people.

While in Europe, Sanger visited clinics in the Netherlands, where she learned about a new, spring-loaded device called the diaphragm that was proving very successful in preventing pregnancy. Sanger became convinced that the diaphragm was the best birth control method available.

The birth control movement gains support

Meanwhile, troubling events were occurring at home. Sanger's husband was arrested and jailed for thirty days for giving a copy of *Family Limitation* to an undercover agent. Even more heartbreaking was the death of Sanger's five-year-old daughter Peggy from pneumonia. Sanger returned to the United States. Soon it appeared that her well-publicized troubles had gained her sympathy among the general public. The charges against her were dropped, and some speculated that this was because the government did not want to create any more support for Sanger by prosecuting her. In any case, Sanger went on a tour of the nation to promote the use of birth control.

In the fall of 1916 Sanger, along with her sister Ethel Byrne, opened a birth control clinic in a poor neighborhood in Brooklyn (a part of New York City). The clinic had been open for only ten days, during which time almost five hundred women came for birth control literature and advice and to obtain contraceptive devices, before it was raided by the police and shut down. Both sisters were arrested and tried for "maintaining a public nuisance." Although Sanger spent a month in jail, the whole sequence of events had attracted national and mostly positive attention.

When Sanger's case was appealed, the judge ruled that doctors could offer patients contraceptive devices if their purpose was the prevention of disease and not to avoid pregnancy. This was a small step in the right direction. From now on, Sanger began to take a very practical approach that sometimes brought her into conflict with other birth control advocates, who felt she was trying too hard to appeal to conservatives. In an effort to gain the support of doctors, since she considered their participation crucial and envisioned physician-run clinics in the future, she focused on lobbying for their right to give out birth control information. She also sought the backing of wealthy philanthropists (those who donate money to help others).

Margaret Sanger's sister Ethel Byrne counsels a patient at the birth control clinic that they opened in Brooklyn, New York. The clinic was open for only ten days before it was raided by police and shut down.

(© Bettmann/Corbis. Reproduced by permission.)

Controversy and progress

What was even more controversial, however, was Sanger's apparent support for some of the views of the eugenics movement. A pseudoscience that gained popularity during the 1920s, eugenics involved a belief in the inferiority of anyone who was not of northern European descent, as well as those with mental or physical defects. Eugenicists warned of the dangers of what they called "mongrelization," or the mixing of superior white blood with that of people deemed inferior. (Their focus, however, was more on promoting a higher birth rate among healthy whites than on urging the use of birth control.) Although Sanger never supported racist views, she did express the idea that uncontrolled pregnancies led to increased rates of babies with mental and physical disabilities, and at various times she approved of the sterilization (depriving of the ability to reproduce by removing or blocking sexual organs) of mentally ill and physically disabled people.

In 1920 Sanger divorced her husband, and two years later she married millionaire J. Noah Slee, who supported both her independent spirit and her cause. With Slee's financial support, Sanger was able to begin smuggling diaphragms into the United States. She established the American Birth Control League in 1921 (it would become the Planned Parenthood Federation of America in 1942) and continued to fight not only for easy access to birth control but also for more attention to the issues of global overpopulation, dwindling food supplies, and international peace.

In 1923 Sanger opened the Birth Control Research Bureau in New York City, with Dr. Hannah Stone (1893–1941) as director. This was the first physician-run birth control clinic in the United States, and it was a model for what would eventually be a nationwide network of similar facilities. In addition to offering contraceptive devices and information for patients, the clinic kept detailed records to document how well different methods of birth control worked, and it offered training for doctors. Over the next fifteen years, more than three hundred such clinics would be established across the country.

The loosening of restrictions on birth control came about gradually. A major milestone was reached in 1936, when a court decision made it legal to mail contraceptive materials to physicians. Another step forward occurred a year later, when the American Medical Association, a powerful lobbying group for doctors' interests, officially recognized the dispensing of contraceptives as a legitimate medical service that physicians should learn about in medical school. Meanwhile, Sanger continued to expand the scope of the birth control movement by organizing national and international conferences, achieving worldwide fame as she traveled as far away as Japan, China, and India to talk about family planning.

By the early 1940s Sanger had slowed down her efforts, moving with her husband to a retirement home in Arizona. During the late 1940s and early 1950s, however, concerns about the dangers of world overpopulation brought Sanger into the spotlight again. She was one of the founders, and the first president, of the International Planned Parenthood Federation, which was established in 1952. It was around this time that she also helped to find funding for the work of biologist Gregory Pincus (1903–1967), which would lead to the development of the birth control pill. This highly effective contraceptive would become available to women in the early 1960s.

Sanger died in a Tucson nursing home in 1966. After her death, feminists (those who believe in equal rights for women) credited Sanger with influencing the women's movement immeasurably through her insistence on a woman's right to control her own body and destiny. In 1973 the Supreme Court ruled that the constitutional right to privacy extended to a woman's choice to end a pregnancy, making abortion legal. Many considered this a major victory that would save the lives of the many women who would otherwise have sought illegal abortions; others, however, continued to believe that abortion is wrong. According to feminist leader Gloria Steinem (1934–) in an article written for *Time* magazine, "By word and deed, [Sanger] pioneered the most radical, humane, and transforming political movement of the century."

For More Information

Books

Bachrach, Deborah. *The Importance of Margaret Sanger*. San Diego, CA: Lucent Books, 1993.

Chesler, Ellen. *Woman of Valor: Margaret Sanger and the Birth Control Movement*. New York: Simon & Schuster, 1992.

Cigney, Virginia. *Margaret Sanger: Rebel with a Cause*. Garden City, NY: Doubleday, 1969.

Douglas, Emily Taft. *Margaret Sanger: Pioneer of the Future*. New York: Holt, Rinehart and Winston, 1970.

Kennedy, David M. *Birth Control in America: The Career of Margaret Sanger*. New Haven, CT: Yale University Press, 1970.

Moore, Gloria. *Margaret Sanger and the Birth Control Movement: A Bibliography, 1911–1984*. Metuchen, NJ: Scarecrow Press, 1986.

Sanger, Margaret. *An Autobiography*. New York: W.W. Norton & Company, 1938.

Web Sites

"Biographical Sketch." *The Margaret Sanger Papers Project.* Available online at http://www.nyu.edu/projects/sanger/msbio.htm. Accessed on June 29, 2005.

"Margaret Sanger." *Planned Parenthood Federation of America, Inc.* Available online at http://www.plannedparenthood.org/pp2/portal/files/portal/ medicalinfo/birthcontrol/bio-margaret-sanger.xml. Accessed on June 29, 2005.

Steinem, Gloria. "Margaret Sanger: Her Crusade to Legalize Birth Control Spurred the Movement for Women's Liberation." *The Time 100.* Available online at http://www.time.com/time/time100/leaders/ profile/sanger.html. Accessed on June 29, 2005.

Where to Learn More

The following list focuses on works written for readers of middle school or high school age. Books aimed at adult readers have been included when they are especially important in providing information or analysis that would otherwise be unavailable.

Books

Abels, Jules. *In the Time of Silent Cal*. New York: Putnam, 1989.

Allsop, Kenneth. *The Bootleggers: The Story of Chicago's Prohibition Era*. New Rochelle, NY: Arlington House, 1968.

Bacho, Peter. *Boxing in Black and White*. New York: Henry Holt, 1999.

Bachrach, Deborah. *The Importance of Margaret Sanger*. San Diego, CA: Lucent Books, 1993.

Bains, Rae. *Babe Ruth*. Mahwah, NJ: Troll Associates, 1985.

Bateson, Mary Catherine. *With a Daughter's Eye: A Memoir of Margaret Mead and Gregory Bateson*. New York: William Morrow, 1984.

Bergreen, Laurence. *Capone: The Man and the Era*. New York: Simon & Schuster, 1992.

Bergreen, Laurence. *Louis Armstrong: An Extravagant Life*. New York: Broadway Books, 1997.

Berg, Scott. *Lindbergh*. New York: Putnam, 1998.

Berke, Art. *Babe Ruth*. New York: Franklin Watts, 1988.

Berry, Michael. *Georgia O'Keeffe*. New York: Chelsea House, 1988.

Bloom, Harold, ed. *Zora Neale Hurston*. Broomall, PA: Chelsea House, 1986.

Blumhofer, Edith. *Aimee Semple McPherson: Everybody's Sister*. Grand Rapids, MI: Erdmans, 1993.

Bode, Carl. *Mencken*. Carbondale: Southern Illinois University Press, 1969.

Brittin, Norman A. *Edna St. Vincent Millay*. Boston: Twayne, 1967. Rev. ed. 1982.

Burby, Lisa. N. *Margaret Mead*. New York: Rosen, 1996.

Burlingame, Roger. *Henry Ford: A Great Life in Brief*. New York: Knopf, 1969.

Brown, Sandford. *Louis Armstrong*. New York: Franklin Watts, 1993.

Burner, David. *Herbert Hoover: A Public Life*. New York: Knopf, 1978.

Cairns, Huntington. *H.L. Mencken: The American Scene*. New York: Vintage Books, 1982.

Calhoun, Randall. *Dorothy Parker: A Bio-Bibliography*. Westport, CT: Greenwood Press, 1992.

Cheney, Robert W. *A Righteous Cause: The Life of William Jennings Bryan*. Boston: Little, Brown, 1985.

Chesler, Ellen. *Woman of Valor: Margaret Sanger and the Birth Control Movement*. New York: Simon & Schuster, 1992.

Cigney, Virginia. *Margaret Sanger: Rebel with a Cause*. Garden City, NY: Doubleday, 1969.

Clinton, Susan. *Herbert Hoover: Thirty-First President of the United States*. Chicago: Children's Press, 1988.

Coletta, Paolo E. *William Jennings Bryan—Political Evangelist, 1860–1908*. Lincoln: University of Nebraska Press, 1964.

Collier, Peter, and David Horowitz. *The Fords: An American Epic*. New York: Simon & Schuster, 1987.

Creamer, Robert. *Home Run: The Story of Babe Ruth*. New York: Simon & Schuster, 1974.

Crouch, Tom D., ed. *Charles A. Lindbergh: An American Life*. Washington, DC: Smithsonian, 1977.

Dardis, Thomas. *Keaton: The Man Who Wouldn't Lie Down*. Minneapolis: University of Minnesota Press, 2002.

D'Augustino, Annette M. *Harold Lloyd.* Westport, CT: Greenwood Press, 1994.

De Camp, L. Sprague. *The Great Monkey Trial.* Garden City, NY: Doubleday, 1968.

Dempsey, Jack. *Dempsey.* With Barbara Piatelli Dempsey. New York: Harper & Row, 1977.

Donenberg, Barry. *An American Hero: The True Story of Charles A. Lindbergh.* New York: Putnam, 1998.

Dooley, D.J. *The Art of Sinclair Lewis.* Lincoln: The University of Nebraska Press, 1967.

Douglas, Emily Taft. *Margaret Sanger: Pioneer of the Future.* New York: Holt, Rinehart and Winston, 1970.

Downes, Randolph C. *The Rise of Warren Gamaliel Harding: 1865–1920.* Columbus: Ohio State University Press, 1970.

Driemen, John E. *Clarence Darrow.* New York: Chelsea House, 1992.

Dumenil, Lyn. *The Modern Temper: American Culture and Society in the 1920s.* New York: Hill and Wang, 1995.

Epstein, Daniel M. *Sister Aimee: The Life of Aimee Semple McPherson.* New York: Harcourt, 1993.

Epstein, Daniel. *What Lips My Lips Have Kissed: The Loves and Love Poems of Edna St. Vincent Millay.* New York: Henry Holt, 2001.

Evensen, Robert J. *When Dempsey Fought Tunney: Heroes, Hokum, and Storytelling in the Jazz Age.* Knoxville: University of Tennessee Press, 1996.

Fausold, Martin. *The Presidency of Herbert C. Hoover.* Lawrence: University Press of Kansas, 1985.

Ferrell, Robert H. *The Presidency of Calvin Coolidge.* Lawrence: University Press of Kansas, 1998.

Fisher, Jim. *The Lindbergh Case.* New Brunswick, NJ: Rutgers University Press, 1994.

Freedman, Diane P. *Millay at 100: A Critical Reappraisal.* Carbondale: Southern Illinois University, 1995.

Frewin, Leslie. *The Late Mrs. Dorothy Parker.* New York: Macmillan, 1986.

Gherman, Beverly. *Georgia O'Keeffe.* New York: Atheneum, 1986.

Gilbert, Thomas. *The Soaring Twenties: Babe Ruth and the Home Run Decade.* New York: Franklin Watts, 1996.

Gould, Jean. *The Poet and Her Book: The Life of Edna St. Vincent Millay.* New York: Dodd, Mead, 1969.

Gurko, Miriam. *Restless Spirit: The Life of Edna St. Vincent Millay*. New York: Crowell, 1962.

Hardy, P. Steven, and Sheila Jackson Hardy. *Extraordinary People of the Harlem Renaissance*. New York: Children's Press, 2000.

Hanson, Erica. *The 1920s*. San Diego, CA: Lucent Books, 1999.

Haynes, John Earl. *Calvin Coolidge and the Coolidge Era: Essays on the History of the 1920s*. Washington, DC: Library of Congress, 1998.

Heckscher, August. *Woodrow Wilson: A Biography*. New York: Scribner, 1991.

Hemenway, Robert. *Zora Neale Hurston: A Literary Biography*. Chicago: University of Illinois Press, 1977.

Higdon, Hal. *Crime of the Century: The Leopold & Loeb Case*. New York: Putnam, 1975.

Hoffman, Frederick J. *The 1920s: American Writing in the Postwar Decade*. New York: Free Press, 1965.

Hoff-Wilson, Joan. *Herbert Hoover: A Public Life*. Boston: Beacon, 1984.

Hoff-Wilson, Joan. *Herbert Hoover, Forgotten Progressive*. Boston: Little, Brown, 1975.

Holway, John B. *Josh and Satch: The Life and Times of Josh Gibson and Satchel Paige*. Meckler, 1991.

Howard, Jane. *Margaret Mead: A Life*. New York: Simon & Schuster, 1984.

Howard, Lillie P. Zora Neale Hurston. Boston: Twayne, 1980.

Hutchisson, James M. *The Rise of Sinclair Lewis, 1920–1930*. University Park: Pennsylvania State University Press, 1996.

Jacques, Geoffrey. *Free Within Ourselves: The Harlem Renaissance*. New York: Franklin Watts, 1996.

Jablonsky, Edward, and Lawrence D. Stewart. *The Gershwin Years*. Garden City, New York: Doubleday and Co., 1973.

Jones, Max and John Chilton. *Louis: The Louis Armstrong Story*. Boston: Little, Brown, 1971.

Kahn, Roger. *A Flame of Pure Fire: Jack Dempsey and the Roaring 20s*. New York: Harcourt Brace, 1999.

Katz, Ephraim. *The Film Encyclopedia,* 4th ed. New York: HarperResource, 2001.

Kavanaugh, Jack. *Shoeless Joe Jackson*. New York: Chelsea House, 1995.

Kennedy, David M. *Birth Control in American: The Career of Margaret Sanger*. New Haven: Yale University Press, 1970.

Kerr, Walter. *The Silent Clowns.* New York: Knopf, 1975.

Kent, Zachary. *Charles Lindbergh and the Spirit of St. Louis in American History.* Berkeley Heights, NJ: Enslow Publishers, Inc., 2001.

Kimball, Robert, and Alfred Simon. *The Gershwins.* New York: Atheneum Publishers, 1972.

Kinney, Arthur. *Dorothy Parker.* Boston: Twayne, 1978.

Kobler, John. *Capone: The Life and World of Al Capone.* New York: Putnam, 1971.

LaBlanc, Michael L. *Hotdogs, Heroes & Hooligans: The Story of Baseball's Major League Teams.* Detroit, MI: Visible Ink Press, 1994.

Lacy, Robert. *Ford: The Men and the Machine.* Boston, MA: Little, Brown, 1986.

Leavell, J. Perry, Jr. *Woodrow Wilson.* New Haven, CT: Chelsea House, 1987.

Leinwald, Gerald. *1927: High Tide of the 1920s.* New York: Four Walls Eight Windows, 2001.

Levine, Lawrence W. *Defender of the Faith.* Cambridge, MA: Harvard University Press, 1965.

Levin, Phyllis Lee. *Edith and Woodrow: The Wilson White House.* New York: Scribner, 2001.

Lichtman, Allan J. *Prejudice and the Old Politics: The Presidential Election of 1928.* Chapel Hill: University of North Carolina Press, 1979.

Lisle, Laurie. *Portrait of an Artist: A Biography of Georgia O'Keeffe.* New York: Seaview Books, 1980.

Ludel, Jacqueline. *Margaret Mead.* New York: Franklin Watts, 1983.

Lynn, Kenneth C. *Charlie Chaplin and His Times.* New York: Simon & Schuster, 1997.

Lyons, Mary E. *Sorrow's Kitchen: The Life and Folklore of Zora Neale Hurston.* New York: Scribner, 1990.

MacCann, Richard Dyer. *The Silent Comedians.* Metuchen, NJ: Scarecrow Press, 1993.

Macht, Norman. *Babe Ruth.* New York: Chelsea House, 1991.

Manchester, William. *Disturber of the Peace: The Life of H.L. Mencken.* New York: Harper, 1951.

Marable, Manning. *W.E.B. Du Bois: Black Radical Democrat.* Boston, MA: Twayne, 1986.

McCaffrey, Donald W. *Great Comedians: Chaplin, Lloyd, Keaton, and Langdon.* New York: A.S. Barnes, 1968.

McCoy, Donald R. *Calvin Coolidge: The Quiet President.* Lawrence: University Press of Kansas, 1988.

McKissack, Patricia and Frederick McKissack, Jr. *Black Diamond: The Story of the Negro Baseball Leagues.* New York: Scholastic Trade, 1994.

McPherson, Edward. *Buster Keaton: Tempest in a Flat Hat.* New York: Newmarket Press, 2005.

Meade, Marion. *Dorothy Parker: What Fresh Hell Is This?* New York: Penguin, 1989.

Meltzer, Milton. *Langston Hughes.* Brookfield, CT: Millbrook Press, 1997.

Milford, Nancy. *Savage Beauty: The Life of Edna St. Vincent Millay.* New York: Random House, 2001.

Miller, Nathan. *New World Coming: The 1920s and the Making of Modern America.* New York: Scribner, 2003.

Milton, Joyce. *Loss of Eden: A Biography of Charles and Anne Morrow Lindbergh.* New York: HarperCollins, 1993.

Moore, Edward A. *A Catholic Runs for President: The Campaign of 1928.* New York: Ronald Press, 1956.

Moore, Gloria. *Margaret Sanger and the Birth Control Movement: A Bibliography, 1911–1984.* Metuchen, NJ: Scarecrow Press, 1986.

Nash, George H. *The Life of Herbert Hoover, Vol. I.* New York: Norton, 1983.

Ness, Eliot. *The Untouchables.* New York: Messner, 1957; 1987 reprint.

Nevins, Allan, and F.E. Hill. *Ford: The Times, the Man, the Company.* New York: Scribner, 1954.

Nierman, Judith. *Edna St. Vincent Millay: A Reference Guide.* Boston: G.K. Hall, 1977.

Nye, Frank T., Jr. *Door of Opportunity: The Life and Legacy of Herbert Hoover.* West Branch, IA: The Herbert Hoover Presidential Library Association, 1988.

Ogren, Kathy J. *The Jazz Revolution: Twenties America and the Meaning of Jazz.* New York: Oxford University Press, 1989.

O'Keeffe, Georgia. *Georgia O'Keeffe.* New York: Viking Press, 1976.

Orgill, Roxanne. *If I Only Had a Horn: Young Louis Armstrong.* Boston: Houghton Mifflin, 1997.

Orgill, Roxanne. *Shout, Sister, Shout! Ten Girl Singers Who Shaped a Century.* New York: Margaret McElderry, 2001.

Paige, Leroy "Satchel", and David Lipman. *Maybe I'll Pitch Forever.* Garden City, NY: Doubleday, 1962.

Parker, Dorothy. *Enough Rope.* New York: Boni & Liveright, 1928.

Perret, Geoffrey. *America in the Twenties.* New York: Touchstone, 1982.

Polikoff, Barbara G. *Herbert C. Hoover: 31st President of the United States.* Ada, OK: Garrett Educational Corporation, 1990.

Randolph, Blythe. *Charles Lindbergh.* New York: Franklin Watts, 1990.

Reef, Catherine. *George Gershwin: American Composer.* Greensboro, NC: Morgan Reynolds, 2000.

Ribowsky, Mark. *Don't Look Back: Satchel Paige in the Shadows of Baseball.* New York: Simon & Schuster, 1994.

Roberts, Randy. *Jack Dempsey: The Manassa Mauler.* Baton Rouge: Louisiana State University Press, 1979.

Robinson, David. *Chaplin: His Life and Art.* New York: McGraw-Hill, 1985.

Russo, Guy. *The Outfit: The Role of Chicago's Underworld in the Shaping of Modern America.* New York: Bloomsbury, 2001.

Ruth, George Herman. *The Babe Ruth Story as Told to Bob Considine.* New York: E. P. Dutton, 1948.

Sanger, Margaret. *An Autobiography.* New York: W.W. Norton & Company, 1938.

Schoenberg, Robert. *Mr. Capone: The Real—and Complete—Story of Al Capone.* New York: Morrow, 1992.

Schorer, Mark. *Sinclair Lewis: An American Life.* New York: McGraw-Hill, 1961.

Schroeder, Alan. *Charlie Chaplin: The Beauty of Silence.* New York: Franklin Watts, 1997.

Schwartz, Charles. *Gershwin: His Life and Music.* Indianapolis: Bobbs-Merrill Co., 1973.

Seymour, Harold. *Baseball: The Golden Age.* New York: Oxford University Press, 1971.

Sharman, Margaret. *1920s.* Austin, TX: Raintree Steck-Vaughn Publishers, 1992.

Shirley, David. *Satchel Paige.* New York: Chelsea House, 1993.

Smith, Robert. *Pioneers of Baseball.* Boston: Little, Brown, 1978.

Smith, Toby. *Kid Blackie: Jack Dempsey's Colorado Days.* Ouray, CO: Wayfinder Press, 1987.

Sobel, Robert. *Coolidge: An American Enigma.* Washington, DC: Regnery, 1998.

Stenerson, Douglas C. *H.L. Mencken: Iconoclast from Baltimore.* Chicago: University of Chicago Press, 1971.

Stieglitz, Alfred. *Georgia O'Keeffe: A Portrait.* New York: Metropolitan Museum of Art, 1978.

Teachout, Terry. *A Life of H.L. Mencken.* New York: HarperCollins, 2002.

Thomas, Lately. *Storming Heaven: The Lives and Turmoils of Minnie Kennedy and Aimee Semple McPherson.* New York: Ballantine Books, 1973.

Tierney, Kevin. *Darrow: A Biography.* New York: Crowell, 1979.

Tessitore, John. *F. Scott Fitzgerald: The American Dreamer.* New York: Franklin Watts, 2001.

Trani, Eugene P., and David L. Wilson. *The Presidency of Warren G. Harding.* Lawrence: Regents Press of Kansas, 1977.

Turnbull, Andrew. *Scott Fitzgerald.* New York: Scribner, 1962.

Wagenheim, Karl. *Babe Ruth: His Life and Legend.* Chicago: Olmstead Press, 2001.

Ward, Geoffrey, and Ken Burns. *Jazz: A History of America's Music.* New York: Knopf, 2000.

Weinberg, Arthur, and Lila Weinberg. *Clarence Darrow: A Sentimental Rebel.* New York: Putnam, 1980.

Woog, Adam. *Louis Armstrong.* San Diego: Lucent Books, 1995.

Yanuzzi, Della A. *Ernest Hemingway: Writer and Adventurer.* Springfield, NJ: Enslow Publishers, 1998.

Yanuzzi, Della A. *Zora Neale Hurston: Southern Story Teller.* Springfield, NJ: Enslow Publishers, 1996.

Ziesk, Edna. *Margaret Mead.* New York: Chelsea House, 1990.

Web Sites

"About Babe Ruth." *The Official Web Site of the Sultan of Swat.* Available online at http://www.baberuth.com/flash/about/biograph.html. Accessed on August 14, 2005.

"American Cultural History, Decade 1920–1929." *Kingwood College Library.* Available online at http://kclibrary.nhmccd.edu/decade20.html. Accessed on August 14, 2005.

Best of History Websites. Available online at http://www.besthistorysites.net/USHistory_Roaring20s.shtml. Accessed on August 14, 2005.

"Biographical Sketch." *The Margaret Sanger Papers Project.* Available online at http://www.nyu.edu/projects/sanger/msbio.htm. Accessed on August 14, 2005.

"Calvin Coolidge: 30th President of the United States." *The Calvin Coolidge Memorial Foundation.* Available online at http://www.calvin-coolidge.org/index.html. Accessed on August 14, 2005.

"Charles Lindbergh Biography." *Charles Lindbergh: An American Aviator.* Available online at http://www.charleslindbergh.com/history/index.asp. Accessed on August 14, 2005.

"Charlie Chaplin." *American Masters (PBS)*. Available online at http://www.pbs.org/wnet/americanmasters/database/keaton_b.html. Accessed on August 14, 2005.

"Clarence Darrow (1857–1938)." *Eastland Memorial Society*. Available online at http://www.inficad.com/~ksup/darrow.html. Accessed on August 14, 2005.

Clash of Cultures in the 1910s and 1920s. Available online at http://history.osu.edu/Projects/Clash/default.htm. Accessed on August 14, 2005.

"Coolidge and Foreign Affairs: Kellogg-Briand Pact, August 27, 1928." *U-S-History.com*. Available online at http://www.u-s-history.com/pages/h1485.html. Accessed on August 14, 2005.

"Dorothy Parker (1893–1967)." *American Poems*. Available online at http://www.americanpoems.com/poets/parker/. Accessed on August 14, 2005.

"Edna St. Vincent Millay." *The Academy of American Poets*. Available online at http://www.poets.org/poet.php/prmPID/160. Accessed on August 14, 2005.

Flaherty, Tarraugh. "Margaret Mead: 1901–1978." *Women's Intellectual Contributions to the Study of Mind and Society*. Available online at http://www.webster.edu/~woolflm/margaretmead.html. Accessed on August 14, 2005.

The F. Scott Fitzgerald Society. Available online at http://www.fitzgeraldsociety.org/. Accessed on August 14, 2005.

George Gershwin. Available online at http://www.gershwinfan.com/biogeorge.html. Accessed on August 14, 2005.

Harlem: Mecca of the New Negro. Available online at http://etext.lib.virginia.edu/harlem/. Accessed on August 14, 2005.

"Henry Ford, 1863–1947." *A Science Odyssey: People and Discoveries*. Available online at http:www.pbs.org/wgbh/aso/databank/entries/btford.html. Accessed on August 14, 2005.

Burke, Gibbons. "Henry Louis Mencken (1880–1956)." *The H.L. Mencken Page*. Available online at http://www.io.com/gibbonsb/mencken/. Accessed on August 14, 2005.

"Herbert Clark Hoover (1929–1933)." *American President*. Available online at http://www.americanpresident.org/history/herberthoover/. Accessed on August 14, 2005.

Interpreting Primary Sources. Digital History. Available online at http://www.digitalhistory.uh.edu/historyonline/us16.cfm. Accessed on August 14, 2005.

Jazz Age Culture. Available online at http://faculty.pittstate.edu/~knichols/jazzage.html. Accessed on August 14, 2005.

Library of Congress. *America from the Great Depression to World War II: Photos from the FSA-OWI, 1935–1945*. Available online at http://memory.loc.gov/ammem/fsowhome.html. Accessed on August 14, 2005.

Library of Congress. "Prosperity and Thrift: The Coolidge Era and the Consumer Economy." Available online at http://lcweb2.loc.gov/ammem/coolhtml/coolhome.html. Accessed on August 14, 2005.

Linder, Douglas. "Tennessee vs. John Scopes, The Monkey Trial, 1925." *Famous Trials in American History*. Available online at http://www.law.umkc.edu/faculty/projects/ftrials/scopes/scopes.htm. Accessed on August 14, 2005.

Reuben, Paul R. "Chapter 9: Harlem Renaissance—A Brief Introduction." *PAL: Perspectives in American Literature*. Available online at http://www.csustan.edu/english/reuben/pal/chap9/9intro.html. Accessed on August 14, 2005.

Satchel Paige: The Official Web Site. Available online at http://www.cmgww.com/baseball/paige/. Accessed on August 14, 2005.

"Sinclair Lewis and His Life." *The Sinclair Lewis Society Web Page*. Available online at http://www.english.ilstu.edu/separry/sinclairlewis/. Accessed on August 14, 2005.

The 1920s Experience. Available online at http://www.angelfire.com/co/pscst/index.html. Accessed on August 14, 2005.

Warren G. Harding. Available online at http://www.whitehouse.gov/history/presidents/wh29.html. Accessed on August 14, 2005.

"Who Is Louis Armstrong?" *Satchmo.net: The Official Site of the Louis Armstrong House & Archives*. Available Online at http://satchmo.net/bio/. Accessed on August 14, 2005.

"Woodrow Wilson." *The White House*. Available online at http://www.whitehouse.gov/history/presidents/ww28.html. Accessed on August 14, 2005.

"Zora Neale Hurston." Women in History. Available online at http://www.lkwdpl.org/wihohio/hurs-zor.htm. Accessed on August 14, 2005.

Index